Green Travel Guide to
Southern Wisconsin

T0163458

GREEN TRAVEL GUIDE TO
Southern Wisconsin

Environmentally and
Socially Responsible Travel

Pat Dillon *and* Lynne Diebel

THE UNIVERSITY OF WISCONSIN PRESS

The University of Wisconsin Press
1930 Monroe Street, 3rd Floor
Madison, Wisconsin 53711-2059

uwpress.wisc.edu

3 Henrietta Street
London WC2E 8LU, England
eurospanbookstore.com

5   4   3   2   1

Printed in the United States of America

Library of Congress Cataloging-in-Publication Data
Dillon, Pat (Patricia J.), 1956–
Green travel guide to southern Wisconsin : environmentally and
socially responsible travel /
Pat Dillon and Lynne Diebel.
p. cm.
Includes index.
ISBN 978-0-299-23544-4 (pbk. : alk. paper) — ISBN 978-0-299-23543-7 (e-book)
1. Wisconsin—Guidebooks. I. Diebel, Lynne Smith. II. Title.
F579.3.D55   2010
917.75´0444—dc22   2009040637

In loving memory of Mom and Dad,
children of the Great Depression who brought me up
green by default

—LSD

To my Mom, and in loving memory of my Dad,
who sent me outside so often I finally loved
being there

—PJD

CONTENTS

FOREWORD

In all my travels as tourism secretary, nothing touches my soul in quite the same way as our pristine natural resources. I believe the land, sky, lakes, and rivers define us as a people, inspire us to think differently, and rejuvenate our bodies and spirits. By preserving these precious resources, we make an offering to our children and grandchildren and all others whose path may lead them here someday, ensuring they too will experience the wonders found only in Wisconsin.

As a young girl growing up in Wisconsin Dells, I explored the fragrant pine forests, the Wisconsin River with its towering honey-hued bluffs, the community's naturally cool canyons, and great expanses of farmers' fields, often at the heels of my photographer father. That secured in me a sentiment that stewardship is the responsibility of each one of us.

At the Department of Tourism, we created our own stewardship program, Travel Green Wisconsin, recognizing tourism businesses that are doing their part, in both big ways and small, to be gentle to the environment. When you consider this state's proud farming heritage, breathtakingly beautiful vistas, and passionate people who have made stewardship their legacy, like Gaylord Nelson, John Muir, and Aldo Leopold, Travel Green Wisconsin was not just a good thing to do, it was the right thing to do.

You can imagine my delight, then, when I learned that two books were to be written about green travel in our state. Authors Pat Dillon and Lynne Diebel have combed Wisconsin, unearthing an incredibly wide range of sustainable businesses, destinations, and attractions, from well-known hotels, restaurants, and natural attractions to little-known lodges, markets, and land preserves. I've often professed that Wisconsin embraced sustainability long before being "green" became the popular thing to be, and Pat and Lynne have proved that to be true with these wonderful journals of theirs.

Now, with gratitude to the authors of these books, I invite you to get to know the people who grow the food you eat, to complete the cycle of sustainability by buying local, and to tread gently on the earth wherever your travels may take you. That, my friends, is the certain path to protecting all the things we hold dear here in our corner of the world.

Travel well. Travel green. Travel Wisconsin.

KELLI A. TRUMBLE
Secretary, Wisconsin Department of Tourism

ACKNOWLEDGMENTS

Thank you, Pat, for having the wonderful idea of writing these books and for being such an outstanding coauthor. And thank you Eva Šolcová, Mark Knickelbine, Melissa Faliveno of Trails Books, and Raphael Kadushin and Adam Mehring at the University of Wisconsin Press for believing in the idea and patiently guiding us through the editing process.

To all the farmers, innkeepers, and restaurant owners I visited, thank you for all you do as loyal stewards of this lovely corner of our green earth. Penny Vodak and Margaret Jackson, our trip around Grant County was inspiring; Penny and Greg Vodak, thank you for your test-travel enthusiasm. I thank Rink DaVee for showing me the green face of Mineral Point and Jane Varda of Mazomanie for her invaluable help. Thank you, Lisa Kivirist and John Ivanko of Inn Serendipity, for sharing your vision; and Frank Goodman and Nancy Langston, for all that you do to make Green County even greener. Thank you, Camille Zanoni of the Natural Resources Foundation of Wisconsin, for showing me that our State Natural Areas are indeed a living library of the Wisconsin's original landscape.

I thank my son Matt for answering all my questions about bicycles, rivers, and fish; his partner, Rebecca Gass, for her enthusiastic encouragement; my son Greg for patiently showing me how to decipher the mysteries of technology; and my son James and daughter, Anne, for their long-distance cheerleading.

Most of all, I thank my husband, Bob, for his sense of humor, his great photos, and his unfailing support of yet another book project.

LSD

Thank you, Lynne. Without your patient and guiding hand, this never would have been written. To Kelli Trumble for her generous contribution to these books. To Eva Šolcová, Mark Knickelbine, Melissa Faliveno of Trails Books, and Raphael Kadushin and the people at University of Wisconsin Press, for sharing our vision for responsible travel. To the naturalists, foresters, great land stewards, and all the welcoming people throughout Wisconsin who take as good care of me while I travel as they do this beautiful state.

To my wonderful daughters, Maura and Nina, who have lovingly accompanied me up and down the Mississippi River, followed me down countless Wisconsin roads, but who have led me down just as many. To Mark Salisbury, who was born on the Mississippi River and shared his love and knowledge of the river with me. To my siblings Michael Dillon, Mary K McCanna, Peggy Johnston, and Ann Moran, who have each taken turns as my navigator while making me laugh, sometimes right off the road. To my dear, sweet mother, Mary Dillon, the reason I keep writing. To Jennifer Buxton, my endlessly patient friend and travel companion. To Dennis Appleton, my dear friend who helped me edit these books. To my friend Ann Rutecki, who introduced me to back-breaking CSA work, and who brings me kohlrabi from the farm. To my dear friend and fellow writer Peg Masterson Edquist, a great travel companion, who helped me research this book. To Kate Galantha, who beautifully captured the Baraboo Hills and the streets of Madison. To my friend and editor Brennan Nardi, who published my first green travel story. To my friend Joanne Riley, who helped me see the forest for the trees. To Arthur Ross at the City of Madison, who helped me make sense out of the Madison bike routes. To Kari Zambon and Chris Zambon, who took me in and made me family. To Carla Minsky, my endlessly optimistic colleague. To Fran DiGraff, who lovingly held my hand through the tall grass. Thank you.

PJD

Green Travel Guide to
Southern Wisconsin

Introduction

What is green travel? That's the question we explored as we researched the southern and northern halves of Wisconsin for our two books. Here is what "green" means to us.

Green travel is *locally owned lodging* where the innkeepers are committed to continuously improving their operations in ways that reduce their environmental impact. Some are certified by Travel Green Wisconsin (travelgreenwisconsin.com). Some are what we call green-thinking, by which we mean that they strive to reduce their environmental impact but have not sought certification. Being green wasn't enough to get in the book—these places are also comfortable and charming.

Green travel is *locally owned eateries* that serve local, sustainably grown food as much as possible, food that is even more delicious because it is so fresh.

Green travel is *local foraging* at farmers' markets and co-ops that sell the truly fresh food that's grown right in their area. We especially like these places. If your lodging has a kitchen, you can cook your own fresh feasts.

Green travel is *farm tours* to see all the exciting, innovative things folks are doing to treat the earth with respect and still earn their livings as small farmers, fruit growers, and artisan cheesemakers.

Green travel is *getting around by bicycle, on foot, or by public transit* once you've reached your destination. We found lots of places where you can do just that.

Green travel is the great *natural beauty* of Wisconsin that we found in places like State Natural Areas, conservancy land, national and state parks, and quiet little county parks—the state's natural attractions.

Green travel is finding places where *silent sports*—low-impact outdoor stuff like hiking, biking, canoeing, kayaking, angling, cross-country skiing, snowshoeing, rock climbing, and disc golf—take us into those beautiful places in fun ways.

Green travel is taking home a *new skill* instead of something you bought—we found classes in cooking, gardening, art, kayaking, yoga, solar energy, pottery, weaving, and more.

Green travel is shopping for *local products*, especially arts and crafts.

Green travel is attending fun *low-impact annual events*.

Green travel is choosing Wisconsin businesses that take care of their own communities and of the incredible natural beauty that fills every corner of Wisconsin, so that our kids and grandkids will be able to know and love it too.

Green travel is small-footprint fun. And we found lots of it!

A Note from Pat

While Lynne and I researched our Green Travel Guides there were skeptics. Some said the world isn't green enough to support two whole books on eco-travel in the state. We disagreed. So we picked our destinations as a testament to our faith in people who have loved Wisconsin long before they were told to. We found many great lodges and restaurants and businesses that care just as much about the land around them as they do about making a buck. People who paddle the water the way some of us ride in our cars.

Farmers who know that raising a happy cow makes a healthy earth—and great steak. We rode in farmers' trucks and listened to their stories and were convinced. We ate their heirloom tomatoes and were even more convinced.

We ate in restaurants whose owners know that whether they buy their food from local farmers or grow it themselves, they not only feed their customers, they feed the neighboring environment and keep the cash in the community, which in turn creates jobs.

And then there are the renewable energy people. Once thought of as freaks, they're now forging the way for the rest of us to look differently at how we use up our natural resources in the name of our creature comforts—more heat, more cool air, more water to play in all year-round. We found them, their lodges, and listened in awe.

Those are the places we wrote about. People and businesses that have been grooming trails for guests for generations, taking care of their waterways, promoting local goods and services, taking good care of their animals, and being every bit the land steward yesterday when the rest of us weren't caring so much as they are today and will be tomorrow.

The natural attractions speak for themselves. Wisconsin is green without a movement. We went into heavily traveled tourist areas and found the places that people hold sacred. Forests and preserves where we could go to hear the swish of prairie grass, the discussion of wetland birds, the movement of wind coming up across an open plain, the colliding of branches in towering pine trees, the trickle of water cascading over the end of a paddle.

The kind of sports Wisconsin supported long before European settlers arrived with their fancy gear.

And we rooted out the people who smiled when we stated our purpose and said, "Come in and let me show you how I used my grandfather's barn in this new wing of my lodge." And even better, those who said, "We can't wait to read your books!" We know you have to travel in a car to experience all these great offerings, so bring your bike and break in those hiking shoes, so once you get there, you'll leave less of you behind when you leave.

Happy Trails!

A Note from Lynne

For the last fifteen years, this quote from E. B. White has been taped to my refrigerator: "I arise in the morning torn between a desire to improve the world and a desire to enjoy the world. This makes it hard to plan the day."

We travel to enjoy our beautiful world but we also long to tread more lightly as we go. We want to know the farmer who grows our food, stay in lodging that conserves our earth's precious resources, support local businesses, explore the beauty of the natural world at a nonmotorized pace. We want green travel. That's what these books are about.

And unlike E. B. White, you can leave the planning problems to us.

When we began this project, I didn't presume to know what "green" means to the world at large. I still don't know what it means but I do know how it feels to me. Green is the instinct that stops me from throwing out stuff that still has use in it and stops me from buying stuff I don't need (usually). It's the respect for the earth that keeps me from using chemicals on my ratty-looking lawn. Green makes me remember to turn down the thermostat and ride my bike or walk so I don't guzzle too much petroleum. Green is the primitive desire to grow my own food, to plant a vegetable garden every year of my adult life, even when I lived in an apartment. And it's the connection to nature that I'm after when I float a river or listen to the sandhill cranes croaking overhead on their way to work. It's simple and it's close to home.

So when I looked for places that I could honestly call green, I looked for places that my instincts told me would offer those things I crave. I listened to what people said when I told them about the project. After they talked awhile, I knew where they stood.

I had so much fun exploring green Wisconsin that I know you will too.

Southeast Wisconsin

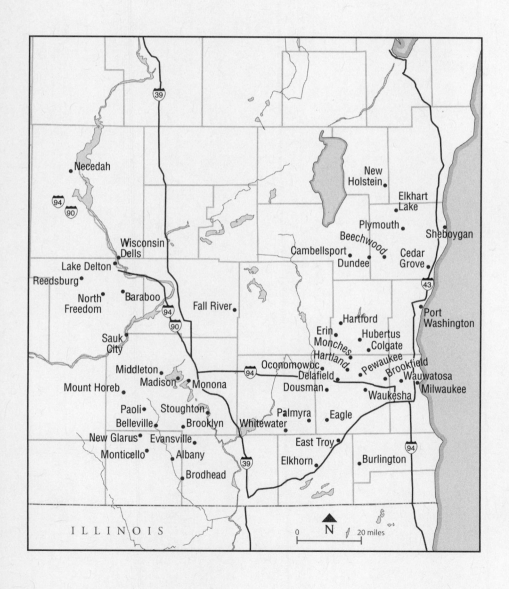

Necedah

New Holstein

Elkhart Lake

Plymouth

Beechwood

Cambellsport

Dundee

Cedar Grove

Sheboygan

Wisconsin Dells

Lake Delton

Reedsburg

North Freedom

Baraboo

Fall River

Sauk City

Hartford

Erin

Monches

Hubertus

Colgate

Hartland

Port Washington

Middleton

Madison

Monona

Oconomowoc

Delafield

Dousman

Pewaukee

Brookfield

Wauwatosa

Milwaukee

Waukesha

Mount Horeb

Paoli

Stoughton

Belleville

Brooklyn

Palmyra

Eagle

Whitewater

New Glarus

Evansville

Monticello

Albany

East Troy

Elkhorn

Burlington

Brodhead

ILLINOIS

0   N   20 miles

Bicycling Green

Sugar River Area

The bicycle is the most civilized conveyance known to man. Other forms of transport grow daily more nightmarish. Only the bicycle remains pure in heart.

—IRIS MURDOCH, *The Red and the Green*

Cycling enthusiasts, Green and Rock counties are laced with quiet country byways perfect for bicycle rambles. Explore a fascinating variety of farmsteads: a sheep farm, a goat farm, or an emu farm. Discover little surprises like a church museum, a cheese co-op dating from the nineteenth century, or an artisans' gallery housed in a renovated creamery. On the Sugar River State Trail, prairie flowers bloom in summer and fall brings spectacular color. The Badger State Trail extends the biking to Madison. The network of trails makes this a great destination for biking families.

The Sugar River valley, rolling off the soft eastern edge of the hilly Driftless Area, is a sweet land indeed. Softly rolling hills—patchwork quilts of meadow, woodlot, pasture, and crop field—are laced with little streams and wetlands. Sheep, llamas, horses, bison, and cows graze the pastures. Organic, sustainable agriculture is expanding rapidly to feed farmers' markets in Madison, Stoughton, Janesville, and Chicago.

A growing community of artists and artisans' studios has sunk roots in small towns like Evansville and in the area countryside. And a concentration of galleries has sprung up in Paoli, nine miles south of Madison, making the tiny township a popular destination. Most are housed in elegantly renovated historic buildings, beautiful to behold.

Bicycling and eating make a good combo. Snack on pie at an Amish country bakery east of Brodhead. Pedal to Evansville for weekend brunch, then shop for pottery at a local studio while you digest. Ride the Sugar River Trail to Monticello to dine at a delightful restaurant featuring local fiber arts on its walls. Or pedal this lovely route all the way to New Glarus to visit an artisan brewery, stopping in Monticello for homemade ice cream. Or hook up with the Badger State Trail in Monticello and ride to Paoli to shop for local artisans' work and lunch on local foods.

Chicagoland visitors have the green option of taking the bus to Janesville (bikes ride in the luggage compartment—no need to disassemble) and biking the scenic twenty-five miles to Brodhead and the trailhead of the Sugar River Trail. From there, it's twelve miles on the trail to a cozy rural guest house near the town of Albany.

Where to Stay

Just upstream from the confluence of the Sugar River and the Little Sugar River, and just a quarter mile from the Sugar River Trail, lies the eponymous *Little Sugar River Farm*. Here, Frank Goodman and Nancy Langston's guest house—open year-round—offers a rich, bucolic respite from our busy world.

Farm life is quiet. Only one group (up to two adults) at a time stays in the comfortable, casually appointed vacation rental. The owners' house is separate, Schneeberger Road is a seldom-traveled country byway, and the farm backs up to part of the Albany State Wildlife Refuge. In the morning, the loudest sounds you hear outside are the clucks of the hens as they strut from their house to greet the day.

Gather eggs from that henhouse for breakfast, pick berries and asparagus and dig potatoes in Frank's organic garden, hike in the refuge, canoe the gentle Sugar River, and bike the quiet country roads or the Sugar River State Trail, accessible near the farm. It's easy to spend a car-free weekend, or even a week, exploring the nuances and details of this rural landscape. If you don't bring your own bikes, you can borrow Frank's two hybrid bicycles. Be sure to ask Frank for the best back road bicycle routes.

And yet the award-winning American vernacular homestead—designed by Doug Kozel and Mike Zuehlke of KEE Architecture in Madison—makes one want to stay indoors. What to do? Stay longer, and definitely plan to cook.

At Frank and Nancy's farm, the guest house has a well-fitted kitchen and a gas grill outside. In season, the farm's bounty—fresh vegetables, berries, apples, eggs, honey, herbs, and flowers—is there for you to harvest and use. A bike ride to Silver Lewis Cheese Co-op or Decatur Dairy (see Local Foraging) will score you some nice local cheeses.

In winter, if you can pull yourself away from the wood burning stove and the extensive book collection, Frank's prairie and the wildlife refuge are lovely to explore on snowshoes. You can go ice skating on the farm's skating pond or cross-country skiing on nearby groomed trails.

Where to Eat

Guests at the Little Sugar River Farm may want to cook their own dinners, savoring all the home grown goodies. And when dining out is called for, no car is needed. The Sugar River Trail leads to Monticello and dinner at *The Dining Room at 209 Main*, which is housed in a renovated 1910 brick storefront. Chef David "Wave" Kasprzak and his wife, Jane Sybers, showcase regional foods, including Hook's seven-year cheddar, made in Mineral Point. Breads are baked locally. A local woman provides salad greens, fresh herbs, and edible flowers in season. Elk and bison are raised near Monroe. The menu focuses on international dishes and all-around great eating. The elegantly simple interior is graced with displays of local knitting and textile art and international ethnic textile collections. Reason enough to visit the restaurant, the textile art makes dining here a truly memorable experience.

Frank Goodman's organic gardens are right outside the door of the guest house, ready for harvesting. (photo by Robert Diebel)

Weekend riders cruising through Monticello in the heat of the day will definitely want to stop for homemade ice cream at *The Crossover*. Frank Goodman's food cart is parked between the Sugar River Trail and Badger State Trail on the east side of town near where the two trails intersect. Frank's ice cream is laced with berries grown on the Little Sugar River Farm, his nearby organic farm and guest house (see Where to Stay). In the fall, the menu includes heartier fare, such as tomato-tarragon soup (see the sidebar) also made from ingredients grown on the farm. Look for the signs along the trail. You'll find a shady spot to rest, picnic tables, free ice water, a bathroom, a view of the nearby wetlands, and fabulous food prepared fresh daily. Also on Frank's land is the old Monticello power plant, later used as a mink-processing facility and now renovated into a workshop and storage facility for the cart.

Another Monticello goodie is the *M & M Cafe* for tasty homemade soup and pie (the Amish Cream is a winner). Former owner Mary Davis still makes her famous pies and other bakery and desserts. New owner Jim Schubert uses local foods, including corned beef, cheeses, and seasonal vegetables, in his diner-style cooking.

Tomato Soup with Caramelized Onions and Tarragon

NOTE: This is yummy stuff

10 minutes chopping; 20 minutes cooking
Makes 4 appetizer servings, or 2 bowls

1 medium red onion, chopped
1 tablespoon butter
1 clove crushed garlic
15 ounces peeled, diced tomatoes with juice (canned or fresh)
2 teaspoons honey
salt (about ½ teaspoon) and freshly ground pepper to taste
1½ cups organic broth: chicken is best, beef is fine
2 teaspoons dried tarragon or 1 tablespoon fresh tarragon, chopped
½ cup heavy cream

Sauté the onions in butter on medium-high heat until they're slightly caramelized—about 10 minutes. Stir in the garlic, tomatoes, honey, and salt and pepper, and cook 5 minutes over high heat. Add the broth and tarragon. Cover and simmer on medium-low for 15 minutes. Just before serving, blend with immersion blender (leave little chunks; don't overblend). Stir in cream, heat gently for a moment, check for salt and pepper, and serve.

—Frank Goodman, Little Sugar River Farm and The Crossover

In New Glarus, at the end of the Sugar River Trail, an unchanging fixture is historic *Puempel's Olde Tavern*, where you can get a nice limburger and onion on rye sandwich to fuel your return ride (see the Monroe chapter for more information on local limburger).

In Paoli, another excellent biking destination, the *Creamery Cafe* will serve you lunch on its riverside terraces or inside. Chef Ben Konkel uses locally raised ingredients such as chicken, eggs, and bacon. Go to *Paoli Local Foods* for homemade-from-scratch, totally local lunches and dinners to eat in or carry out, an organic juice bar and coffee, and a wide range of locally and sustainably raised foods.

On Saturdays and Sundays, *Real Coffee and Food* in Evansville is our brunch destination. It's thirty scenic miles round trip from the Little Sugar River Farm if you take the back roads, so you can justify filling up on its fabulous food offerings. There's an espresso bar, in case you need an immediate buzz. Before owners Susan Finque and Maria Martinez came to town in 2006, Evansville didn't have a coffeehouse. The two renovated the building that was the original post office, and Real Coffee became a town gathering spot. They serve breakfast and lunch and hold wine and food nights. And then there's the fabulous weekend brunch. . . . After Eggs Benezola made from local eggs; Belgian french toast with bananas, walnuts, and real maple syrup; Abuelita's hot chocolate; and Alterra fair trade coffee, you may want to take a nap. Instead, browse the displays of eclectic local arts and used books for sale in the coffeehouse. Another bonus: Real Coffee hosts lives musical performances and art openings.

Local Foraging

Head east from Albany to visit three Amish businesses. *Detweiler's Bulk Foods* has a nutrition center as well as bulk foods of all kinds. Check out *Detweiler's Bent & Dent* for potential bargains in health and beauty products. Or browse for hand-crafted oak and cherry furniture at *Detweiler and Kauffman.*

Another intriguing destination is seven miles south of Brodhead. Ride to the *Sugar Maple Emu Farm* to visit some of the strangest birds in Wisconsin. Joylene and Michael Reavis raise these natives of the Australian Outback for their meat, eggs, leather, and oils, and sell their products, including jewelry made from eggshells, in the farm store. Call ahead, May through September.

At the *Silver Lewis Cheese Co-op* northwest of Albany on County Road EE, Josh and Carla Erickson make cheese in a plant built in 1897. The Ericksons are new owners but the milk still comes from the Silver family farm. Buy their fresh cheese curds, farmer's cheese, brick cheese (a Wisconsin invention), and muenster cheese at a counter inside the plant.

To stock up on more great local cheeses, ride south on County Road F to the *Decatur Dairy* factory and store. Wisconsin master cheesemaker Steve Stettler crafts these excellent award-winning cheeses, including a European-style havarti that swept the 2007 U.S. Championship Cheese Contest and a muenster that took first place in the 2008 World Championship Cheese Contest.

Another tasty expedition is to Paul and Louise Maki's *Blue Skies Berry Farm* northwest of Evansville to pick your own sustainably grown raspberries. They also raise heirloom vegetables, herbs, and edible flowers. In 2007, after reading Michael Pollan's *Omnivore's Dilemma*, the couple decided to forgo organic certification by the USDA; although they still use traditional organic methods, they don't support government certification. Blue Skies, along with the Madison Finnish-American Society, holds a Finnish Midsummer Celebration called Juhannus on their farm. Think live music and dancing, homemade food and drink, bonfires, and, of course, sauna time. They're Finns, after all.

And a visit to the *Paoli Cheese Shop*, home of all cheeses local, is a must if you ride to that artisans' village.

What to Do

Hit the byways on two wheels to explore the countryside east of Brodhead. First stop is *Morningstar Farm*. Vickie and Brett Condon sell their fresh asparagus in May, strawberries in June, and red raspberries in September. Open from 8 a.m. to 8 p.m. during those months, they welcome visitors. During July and August, call ahead.

If it's a Friday or Saturday, your next stop is the *Amish Country Lane Bakery*, just 8.5 miles from town. Try a tasty piece of pie or buy a jar of homemade jam. The Brodhead area is home to many Amish families.

Then tour local farms where visitors are welcome—by appointment. *Scotch Hill Farm*—home to adorable goats, chickens, and dogs—is also where Dela and Tony Ends make and sell their farmstead goat milk soap and raise over a hundred different veggies for their CSA. Please call ahead.

Around the bend is *Kinkoona Farm*, owned by Australian transplant Suellen Thompson-Link and her three children. If you guessed that an Australian would raise sheep, you're right on. With their fleece, she creates chemical-free mattress toppers and comforters as well as animal beds. She also sells washed

Dela Ends of Scotch Hill Farm displays her handmade farmstead goat milk soap.
(photo by Robert Diebel)

fleeces to fiber artists. And Thompson-Link has never met a challenge she didn't like. The amazing variety of farm projects—an aquaponic system for raising perch and watercress, a three-thousand-gallon rain barrel, and a calendula garden watered by the rain barrel, to name a few—are evidence.

Thompson-Link's home-schooled kids are involved in every aspect of the farm and often design and execute their own projects. The family hosts a series of three-day summer *Kinkoona Farm Day Camps* for elementary school children. Kids meet the multitude of animals (including a darling potbellied pig named Daisy Mae and a chicken named Mrs. Robinson), learn all about making compost, or learn to skirt, wash, and felt wool. The theme changes every week. Kinkoona means laughter in an Aboriginal Australian language, so there's always fun on this farm.

The *Sugar River State Trail*, a twenty-three-mile-long recreation trail open to bicyclists and hikers, connects four small towns: Brodhead, Albany, Monticello, and New Glarus. Once the bed of the Chicago, Milwaukee & St. Paul Railroad, the crushed limestone trail is practically flat, with a grade of 3 percent. Think of this trail as a twenty-three-mile band of bird habitat, home to most avian species that live in Wisconsin and lots of ground-dwelling critters as well. North of Brodhead, you ride through the Clarence Covered Bridge, a replica of a historic bridge originally located south of town.

The Sugar connects with the *Badger State Trail*, which will be a forty-mile recreational trail when it's complete. And the Badger runs from Illinois's Jane Addams Trail to the southwest edge of Madison. By June 2010, it will finally connect with Madison's Southwest Path, gateway to downtown Madison. The Badger, built on an abandoned Illinois Central Gulf Railroad right-of-way, includes thirty-nine bridges and a 930-foot-long tunnel built in 1887. A trail pass is required for bicyclists who are sixteen and older to ride on all state trails—you can get one online from *Friends of Wisconsin State Parks*.

A ride to New Glarus on the Sugar River Trail can include a visit to Deb and Dan Carey's *New Glarus Brewing Company*. It's the home of Fat Squirrel, one of the tastiest brews we know, and Organic Revolution, a pale ale. You can tour their nearby brand-new facility, but please call first. Because the Careys are big on sustainability, they use many Wisconsin ingredients. Their malt comes from Chilton, and a farmer near Argyle grows the barley for Spotted Cow, their biggest seller. And there's more. When hiring, they give preference to those who live nearby. They sell their beer only in Wisconsin. A new high tech heat exchanger from Germany that recycles condensed steam as hot water resulted in huge savings on natural gas. Their new Japanese-designed wastewater system dramatically improved the effluent clarity. "We have a moral imperative to be responsible to the environment," said Dan Carey.

Across the road from the brewery are the prairie and oak forest hiking trails of *New Glarus Woods State Park*. Take a break from the pedaling to explore eight miles of hiking trails through woods and prairies. Hikers are allowed to gather edible fruits, nuts, asparagus, and wild mushrooms. Families may borrow one of the park's Discovery Backpacks to learn more about trees, raptors, insects, and birds of Wisconsin. Or check out the amphitheater's schedule of interpretive programs.

An off-trail rural ramble around Green County can lead to some interesting spots, like Muralt Bluff Prairie Natural Area on County Road F between Monticello and Albany. Located on a long ridge midway between the glaciated lands to the east and Driftless Area to the west, this dry prairie is home to rare plants like Hill's thistle, kittentails, and One-flowered Broomrape. The Bell's vireo, a species on Wisconsin's threatened list, nests here.

Riding the back roads can reveal bits of local history as well. In little Attica at the intersection of county roads X and C, you'll spot a handsome old limestone building with the door boarded up. Heading west on County Road EE, the 1863 Norwegian Settlement Church Museum sounds the same quiet historic tones. Also on EE, a limestone rock outcrop stained with blue-green mineral streaks evokes both the ancient sea that once covered the area and the building material back in Attica.

Free range nester in Green County.

Speaking of history, south of Brodhead stands an old bur oak called the Half-Way Tree. Even though it's in a private pasture and thus must be viewed from the road, it's worth a visit. Ride south on First Center Avenue (Highway 11), turn left on Airport Road, and turn right at the stop sign—the marker is on the left side of the road. The back story: Native Americans knew it was the halfway mark between Lake Michigan and the Mississippi River—they determined the distance by counting how many moons it took to walk between the lake and the river. When government surveyors measured the distance in the 1830s, they found that the Native Americans' calculation was off by only 2.5 miles. In 1867, a tribal elder told landowner Charles Warner not to cut down the tree, and this stipulation was added to the title papers.

Tired of riding? Paddle the Sugar River, a lovely peaceful stream that flows through wooded stretches, pastureland, and bird-filled marshes, with well-maintained landings. If you stay at the Little Sugar River Farm, Frank will let you use his canoe or kayaks. Our green tip is to shuttle by leaving a bike at your takeout and pedaling back to the put-in point. Within a half-hour drive, paddlers will also find entertaining riffles to paddle on Badfish Creek, the Yahara River, and the Pecatonica River. For more information on area paddling, see Mike Svob's excellent guide *Paddling Southern Wisconsin*.

If you'd rather wade than paddle, the best trout fishing for brookies and brown trout in the area is on Story Creek, east of Belleville (a town on the Badger State Trail). The Natural Heritage Land Trust holds a forty-nine-acre conservation easement protecting the headwaters of Story Creek (also known as Tipperary Creek), which flows through Tipperary Marsh and the Brooklyn State Wildlife Area. Story is the preferred common name from the mouth up to a point about halfway between Highway 92 and Bell Brook Road; Tipperary is the preferred common name from that point up to the headwaters. One access for anglers is at the Highway 92 bridge. The online *Dane County Recreation Map* is a good resource for the upper creek.

Local Arts

After brunching at Real Coffee in Evansville (see Where to Eat), stroll down Main Street to the *Allen Creek Gallery*, new home of Matthias James Pottery. Be sure you have your bike bags; you won't want to leave town without at least one piece of Matthias James pottery. The gallery, which also features the work of more than a dozen Midwest artists, is housed in a historic building which Matthias renovated himself. Hours vary, so please call ahead or check the Web site. Matthias's other studio and outdoor hard-brick, high-fire kiln are next to the Evansville home he shares with his wife, Lisa James, a recycling specialist; their two children, both budding potters; and Clay, the studio cat. An award-winning potter, Matthias most recently won the 2007 Best of Ceramics award at Madison's Art Fair Off the Square for his beautiful pottery. His work—known for his use of copper red, very volatile in the kiln—is displayed in galleries and at art shows throughout the Midwest. Over the years, Matthias has donated several thousand of his hand-thrown stoneware bowls for Evansville's annual spring "The Heat Is On" chili cook-off.

A good time to see Matthias's pottery is during one of the regional 14 South Artists events (see Annual Events). In addition, Matthias's fall studio sale in November draws a number of customers from Chicago to watch the kiln opening and the throwing demonstrations.

Evansville is home to more than 170 buildings and houses of historic significance, a pretty high score for a town of less than five thousand. And the town is committed to preserving its storybook Victorian homes. While in Real Coffee, pick up a copy of *Historic Evansville: A Walker's Guide* and head out to admire the town's many handsome old houses. The *Historic Walking Tour* guide is also available online at the city's Web site. Be sure to visit the recently renovated Eager/Economy building at 7 East Main Street, with several interesting galleries and a restored two-story windmill inside. In Brodhead, *The Willow Tree* carries restored furniture, antiques, and folk art.

The Sugar River Trail connects to the Badger State Trail in Monticello. Near the northern end of the Badger State Trail is the little town of Paoli. And in Paoli is the *Artisan Gallery*, the cornerstone business in what has become Art Gallery Central. The Upper Sugar River flows right by the Gallery, housed in a renovated 1910 creamery which still looks like a creamery. That is, until you walk inside, where the space is filled with regional fine art and fine crafts. The *Paoli House Gallery* (in a restored 1890 hotel) and *Paoli Schoolhouse Shops* (in an 1854 schoolhouse) are similar. Paoli is heavily into both art and historic restoration.

Annual Events

On *Tour the Farms Day* in 2009, five farms, including the four listed above, offered tours and activities on a Saturday in May, and you can visit all of the farms by bicycle. Check the Brodhead Chamber of Commerce Web site for information on the next tour.

14 South Artists holds a fall studio tour in September and a spring art show in April. Discover local art in seven historic towns: Stoughton (also home to the historic *Stoughton Opera House* and the *Yahara Grocery Co-op*, which has a great lunch bar and lots of local foods), Oregon, Evansville, Brooklyn, Fitchburg, Verona, and Paoli.

In September, the *Sugar River Bike Tour* is a fully supported loop ride, with routes of fifteen, thirty, fifty, and one hundred miles. The ride begins and ends in Brodhead with an after-ride party, and food and drink are included in the entry fee. The Brodhead Optimists sponsor the ride, and proceeds go to fighting childhood cancer.

The *Clearview School Amish Auction*, held the last Saturday in July, draws huge crowds. Bid on handmade quilts, handmade furniture, and antiques, or just mingle with the crowds. Enjoy some Amish baked goods and homemade ice cream. Clearview School is at the corner of Highway 104 and Atkinson Road, about five miles north of Brodhead.

A Little Town with Heart

Elkhart Lake Area

Say "Elkhart Lake" and chances are someone within ear shot will actually hear "Road America." Tell them that this lake town has a boatload of holistic tourist options and they just might tell you it seems unlikely. But it does. Given that Elkhart Lake's main tourist attraction is about no-holds-barred carbon emissions, it stands to reason one might not be sold. But believe it. Elkhart Lake, named by the Potawatomi Indians who saw an elk heart–like shape to the lake that stands central to its town, may be home to the longest natural (*not* as in "green" natural) race track in America, but on nonracing weekends it is a charming, slow-paced village with forward-thinking merchants and artists.

Its downtown shops are delightful and unassuming, with many that promote recycling, reusing, and restoring. Its small community grocer sells local and organic products and the local spa is simple and beautiful, with an organic and elegant architectural design that incorporates the area's long gone Potawatomi earth-driven traditions with the proven serenity of Eastern ones. And the Elkhart Lake people claim this clear, spring-fed lake is pristine. Maintaining pristine water is a feat that alone makes Elkhart Lake a serious green contender.

Where to Stay

The *Osthoff Resort* is mammoth, so bring your tennies. Getting from one end to the other might be the best (and cleanest) energy you expend all day. As you drive into Elkhart Lake, you might initially perceive the resort to be a landscape hog with its expansive five-hundred-foot shoreline. This stands out in stark contrast to the town's small, quaint downtown. But once you settle into the area, the dominant architecture quickly becomes a natural part of the landscape. The Osthoff Resort was built in 1989 when consumption was popular and more was more. The rooms are spacious: one-, two-, and three-bedroom suites with a full kitchen and either a lake or woodland view. Walking from one end to the other requires great navigational skills. The layout is mapped and posted, but you might find yourself asking for directions as you work your way from the Aspira Spa to the front desk. Yet, as a twenty-first-century resort, it is run by a general manager, Lola Roeh, who has a "less is more" sensibility and sustainability is woven into new policy decisions. From recycling to the resort's organic garden and local farms that supply its two restaurants and culinary school, to Lola's policy that employees and guests use reusable products rather than disposable ones, there is a sense that minimal packaging and consumption dominate the thinking here despite its palatial layout. At the lake, the resort is well stocked with sports equipment of a very silent nature. You can rent a kayak, canoe, hydrobike, sailboat, or paddleboat, so your options are plentiful. There is even a footpath that circles the lake, but it traverses private property so be courteous if you prefer to hoof it rather than boat it. An educational Pleasures Activity Program engages the kids in craft-making, such as creation of memory stones using handprints and the kids' own designs.

The Osthoff Resort sits on Elkhart Lake, named by the Potawatomi Indians for its shape being that of an elk's heart. (photo supplied by Osthoff Resort)

The organic thread running through the resort's Aspira Spa is no small green issue, either. Aspira Spa brings the natural outdoor setting indoors with a floor plan that embraces feng shui design, with rounded corners and the presence of the five Chinese element symbols: wood, fire, earth, water, and metal. A host of indigenous sacred traditions is evidenced in the tiles that evoke an ancient Indian medicine wheel, in the Tibetan prayer bells, or in the Chinese lotus blossom soapstone sculpture near the treatment rooms. You can begin an array of services in a large whirlpool set indoors next to expansive windows, and end them in a smaller meditation sanctuary with a copper-lined gazing pool at its center. The trickling sound of water over rock that drops in the pool is a truly soothing transition back to reality.

Aspira Spa, which means "infused with spirit," offers a range of services that are holistic and organic. Some of the treatments include chroma facials, crystal chakra balancing massage, and a violet clay body-silking. Having painstakingly designed the spa to reflect the powers of Elkhart Lake's "sacred waters," which are thought to be blessed through its Native American influence, and to evoke her belief in the principles of feng shui, Lola has received international recognition for the spa's design. She created this space and its treatments to offer guests a sense of spiritual and physical well-being . . . you be the judge.

The recreation here is all about family. You can opt to sit and admire the surroundings inside or beachside, or pick a resort activity, like pedaling the lake on a hydrobike or paddling it in a canoe. A real bonus is that many Elkhart Lake destinations are walkable—unless you're heading out to the nearby Kettle Moraine Forest.

Where to Eat

The Osthoff Resort's two restaurants are working hard to incorporate more and more local and sustainably grown foods into the menu. *Lola's on the Lake* offers fresh regional dishes, including produce from the resort's own organic garden as well as organic chicken, and an assortment of desserts that originate as recipes out of L'ecole de la Maison, the resort's culinary school. The more casual *Otto's Restaurant* has a menu that features steel-cut oatmeal and dishes from local meat purveyors as well as a constant supply of organic eggs. Of all the restaurants in Elkhart Lake, these two are the "greenest."

And then there's the Osthoff's house culinary school. *L'ecole de la Maison* features chef Scott Baker, CIA graduate whose specialty is pastries (as his name would indicate!), and offers a wide range of classes and sessions for individuals and small groups. Many of the courses are faithful to traditional recipes, yet adaptable in your own kitchen. The school uses produce grown from the resort's organic garden when it's available; Lola plans to expand the garden to ensure that all ingredients at the school and the restaurants are organic. Participants in a farmers' market class shop at the Elkhart Lake Farmers Market and later convert locally grown selections into a culinary feast.

Local Foraging

A short walk north from the Osthoff Resort will take you to the downtown area of Elkhart Lake where a number of shops and restaurants have sprouted in recent years. Because of its history as a vacation and racing destination, there is no shortage of food and shopping, and you can find both in the *Feed Mill Shops.* What was once a shipping point for cattle and grain in two buildings dating back to 1895 is now three distinct businesses owned by Julie and Steve Sutcliffe. The couple purchased the building in 2000 and renovated it over the course of one year, using reclaimed boards around new windows, retaining original wood floors, and leaving the exposed walls with graffiti markings from the 1940s intact. Along the front of the building is *Thyme Savours,* a deli/cafe with homemade soups, wraps, and coffee purchased from nearby Cedarburg Roastery. Owner Jim Giese uses locally made cheeses and meats when possible. Just behind the store is the *Feed Mill Market,* where a bounty of locally made items are sold, including Schwaller's Meats from Plymouth, Beechwood cheese from Adel, and fresh baked goods from West Side Bakery in Plymouth. Fresh herbs from the Sutcliffes' home just down the road are packaged in small plastic bags and brought in daily.

Flea and farmers' marketers will like the Farmers and Artisan Market at the corner of Rhine and Lake streets every Saturday morning from June through September. Local vendors sell fresh produce, handmade craft items, original works of art, antiques, and more.

You aren't going to find too much green cuisine in Elkhart Lake that you're not making yourself, but one of the most interesting and healthful eateries is one that was carved out of an old blacksmith shop now known as the *Brown Baer* restaurant and bar at 181 Rhine Street. This is a testament to reclaiming one man's junk and turning it into your own idea of beauty, and it's a winner. Owner Mike Baer demolished the interior but left the soot-covered ceilings intact to offer patrons one of the more eclectic interiors in town. Reclaimed bars, stools, doors, couches, and tables are all unmatched but give the space a charm all its own. You'll find no "bar food" at the Brown

Baer, as the vegetarian chef cooks specials each day. Regular menu items include homemade cornbread, falafels with original tahini sauce, and a rib night that sells out even before the doors open on Mondays. Baer brings in national talent for Sunday evening entertainment during the warmer months.

Grassway Organics Farm Store on Plymouth Trail just outside of New Holstein sells products, such as raw milk under a farm share program, from Grassway Organic Farm. Owners Kay and Wayne Craig started slowly in 1993, producing a few breeding Jersey beef steers for their own consumption. Soon they were sharing their beef with friends and stocking chickens for eggs and later to sell as free-range poultry. The couple was certified organic in 2004 and opened their store in 2005. It includes everything from organic sorghum to grains, nuts, oils, produce such as shiitake mushrooms, and their own grass-fed organic meats. With only a one-time ten-dollar farm share membership, customers can line up to order fresh chickens twice a year and purchase raw milk with their own jars. Kay and Wayne have tried to stay with all whole foods and say many of their customers come from as far as Illinois and Michigan's Upper Peninsula to purchase their products. Kay likes to remind visitors that the black bones in commercially grown chicken signify that arsenic was used in their handling to kill the thyroid and plump the bird, "and God knows what that is doing to us," she warns.

You can forage for food and collectibles every Saturday from June to October at the open-air *Farmer/Artisan Market* held in downtown Elkhart Lake. Fresh produce and baked goods, many from certified organic producers, sell alongside collectibles and artistic creations. Bring an umbrella; this farmers' market goes on regardless of the weather.

What to Do

Shop for consignment items at *Three Gables Consignment Shop*, a renovated, sunny clapboard house that now serves as a fresh backdrop for home accessories, furniture, and unusual art reminiscent of grandma and great-grandma's era.

Across the street and west a bit, *Mix and Mingle* has one of those names that doesn't let you in on what you'll find inside. So here's the inside scoop—a wonderful assortment of vintage and antique merchandise, from birdhouses to nautical details to grandma's linens. Both places will have you poring over pieces nostalgically if not just longingly.

Two Fish Gallery is the spot for original pieces by local artists and artisans. Owner Pat Robison is a gifted ceramicist and fills his gallery with his own clay

bird feeders and functional pottery, and the yard with paths and native plantings. But he also represents scores of area artists, like Plymouth *plein air*
painters Paula Swaydan Grebel and Lori Beringer. This place is packed with
functional and decorative pieces from fun to fabulous, but call ahead to find
out the summer and winter hours if you want to be sure someone is there
working the shop.

Silent Water Tours by *Ecology Outfitters* in Sheboygan will bring you
kayaks, life jackets, splash skirts, and pumps; teach you the ropes (like how
to save yourself if you tip and roll); and then send you out onto the water for
a couple of hours. Or they'll guide for the same price. And if you're ambitious, they'll give you private lessons. In the winter months, they'll rent you
cross-country skis and snowshoes so you can tackle the paths around the lake
or inside Broughton Sheboygan Marsh Park just two miles outside of Elkhart
Lake. At this thirty-acre nature park, you can walk trails or rent rowboats and
canoes to use on Sheboygan Marsh.

Greenbush Kettle at the north end of the Northern Unit of the Kettle
Moraine Forest, just six miles southwest of Elkhart Lake, is one of the most
symmetrical deep kettles in the area. The Greenbush Trail is a hilly trail system through the Kettle Moraine Forest that can be used for hiking and
mountain biking. In winter, cross-country skiers come here from all over the
Midwest to train for the annual American Birkebeiner, a 51K race from Cable
to Hayward. Other larger, more irregularly shaped kettles within the Northern Unit include the area between the Ice Age Trail and Long Lake, which is
said to contain one of the most striking groups of kames (ground deposits
left by retreating glaciers that form a hill or mound) to be found anywhere in
the world. Some of the best known hills—Dundee, Johnson, and McMullen—
can be viewed from atop the *Parnell Observation Tower*, which stands 300 to
450 feet overlooking the surrounding countryside. The tower can be accessed
at Parnell Trail, just southeast of Greenbush Trail. You can also link up to the
Old Plank Road Trail and ride clear over to Lake Michigan at Sheboygan (see
the Port Washington and Sheboygan chapter).

Bike the 6.5-mile route of the 1951–52 Elkhart Lake Open Road Race.
The course circumvents the lake and is on the National Register of Historic
Places. Markers highlight historic points along the way. To follow the route
beginning in Elkhart Lake, turn west on Rhine Street and go to the Village
Square. The Web site of *Historic Race Circuits of Elkhart Lake* provides a map
and details.

Sustain in Dane

Madison Area

When one tugs at a single thing in nature, he finds it attached to the rest of the world.

—JOHN MUIR

Cross over the Dane County line and you are basically on eco-travel auto-pilot. The people of Madison have plans for the environment on their mind the way some of us are planning our next meal—and sustainably raised food is no small part of it. The city is an eco-municipality. It has adopted The Natural Step, a thriving Swedish framework for sustainability. It is a Department of Energy Solar America City, a League of American Bicyclists gold level bike city working its way to platinum, and it gets 24 percent of its energy from renewable resources. Even the State Capitol is about to be fitted for solar panels.

This is where Sierra Club founder John Muir was bitten by the botany bug. It's where Wisconsin's beloved environmentalist Aldo Leopold taught wildlife management and introduced his land ethic. It's where U.S. Senator and environmental activist Gaylord Nelson called Earth Day into action. Their legacy reaches from the Capitol Square clear out to each U.S. coastline. It has leached into the thinking of businesses all over the country, from green builders to sustainable farmers to renewable energy supporters.

The people who live here understand the land ethic. They take care of their green spaces, they know their farmers, and they think of alternative energy as the current wave rather than the next one. The area is loaded with restaurants that have been setting a sustainable table since before anyone knew what a sustainable table was. These restaurants are supplied by more than twenty area organic farms that have put Wisconsin on the map as a leader in community-supported agriculture. And Madison is a city that is forever tweaking its own sustainability plan.

Madison's nationally recognized Dane County Farmers' Market on the Capitol Square (which moves indoors to Monona Terrace in cold months) is first-class agri-tourism on Saturday mornings (a modified version is held on Wednesdays). It's open to travelers looking to take from the environment in ways that also give back. And silent sports opportunities abound. With more than a hundred miles of bike and hike paths that lead to every corner of the city and around the lakes, Madison is all about getting there without leaving oil stains. It boasts a high bike-car ratio, once making it *Bicycling* magazine's top city for biking. You can also get on paths that will take you out of the city and into the patchwork of farmland that surrounds it.

Madison is home to one of the greenest lodges in the state, located directly across the street from an Aldo Leopold legacy. You can stay on a family farm with a commitment to humane animal practices to learn why many Madison chefs opt for local, grass-fed beef and choose to know the people by whom it was raised. Or you can ride your bike out to a pastoral country inn dedicated to land stewardship that's just a seven-mile trek from the Capitol.

Hikers will be delighted with the University of Wisconsin's trails that get you from its famous lakeside Memorial Union Terrace (where you can relax with a locally brewed beer on the return trip) clear out to Madison's west side peninsulas that have spectacular wooded and lake views and support prairie and native plant life. This walk or run is as much about the landscape as it is about the Lake Mendota shoreline that it borders—one of two central lakes accessible by a free-energy, go-anywhere vehicle: your own legs.

Would you rather find serenity offshore? Drop your canoe or kayak into one of three easily accessed waterways leading to many downstream options. Each lake, stream, or river has its own unique watershed that contributes to a diverse urban ecology. Get paddling or experience the fine line between fishing and just sitting in the boat.

And the city of Madison has cornered the market in guiltless consumption. There are scores of great restaurants here that understand that having a relationship with their growers and serving home-spun food creates a healthy local economy, not to mention the people who partake. The food is truly fresh when it has traveled from within or just over the Dane County line. With one of the largest populations of sustainable nondairy farms in the nation right in their backyard, these local restaurateurs have nailed the farm-to-fork philosophy, not as a trend but as a best business practice—theirs and the farmers.

Where to Stay

You know you're green when Aldo Leopold's grandson is an occasional guest at your inn and it has never occurred to you to put him in the Aldo Leopold Room overlooking one of his grandfather's legacies, the University of Wisconsin Arboretum. Getting him a comfortable room is just part of the drill. That was a casual observation, one of many Cathie Imes makes about *Arbor House*, a wildly successful sustainable lodge in the historic Monroe Street neighborhood. She and her husband, John, established this eco-hotel in 1994, and it has grown greener every year. Part historic (that's the original 1853 structure with five rooms so charming you might want to move the rest of your stuff into them permanently) and part new (that's the Annex, the building the Imeses quickly erected right next door to house their staff and raise their brood of four kids), it has an impressive track record for sustainability.

And it's a sustainable smorgasbord, constructed with environmentally sound structural details as well as decorative ones, like the striking blue bathroom tiles made from postconsumer glass (recycled light bulbs and windshields). The wood plank floors are reclaimed lumber from a former Sears building in Chicago. All paint and plaster are nontoxic, which makes moving guests into a newly renovated room a transition accomplished within a day of finishing the job—no toxic odor. The sheets are bamboo. Arbor House has won numerous awards, and people aren't scratching their heads over why. All of this green construction dovetails into the work of John Imes, the executive director and founder of the Wisconsin Environmental Initiative, which has advanced the "doing well by doing good" concept. He's the guy who thought that certifying businesses in Wisconsin for adopting green practices would be a great idea. Out of this came the Travel Green Wisconsin certification. Check their Web site—you might be surprised to see who's on board.

Arbor House followed a mission to create a blend of top-notch hospitality and environmentally responsible urban ecology. Over the years it has received national attention for its simple beauty and sustainability policy, allowing vacationers to maintain both respect for the world around them and high expectations for high-end travel. And they have accomplished it. Cathie says their goal was to have six inns and four kids in ten years. She has the quartet of kids but the Imeses have their hands full with just this one inn. National magazines are coming out of the reclaimed woodwork to get an interview and a room.

Arbor House's Plough Building relays its history through twelve-inch stone walls, airy windows, tile work, and wood floors. The antique furniture décor is what they call the "ultimate recycling program." Their policy for use of earth-sustainable materials is strict: nontoxic products and recycled materials; organic and natural unbleached cotton linens, fabrics, and mattresses; bio degradable cleaners; energy-efficient water appliances; native plant–emphasized landscape; reduction of electromagnetic field exposure; environmental resource center; wind power sponsors; and award-winning architecture and interior design.

Rooms in a range of moderate prices feature different levels of sustainability exhibited in various ways. The Ecovista maintains the highest order of environmental emphasis, from organic linens to natural tiles to energy-saving fixtures. Appropriately, it faces the Arboretum, bringing the inn's namesake into full view. The seven other rooms feature cozy, natural, and historic aspects, making any selection invariably a good one. And the complimentary

The Arbor House is Madison's most ecologically responsible hotel, but it doesn't skimp on charm or luxury. Located across the street from the Arboretum, it's a great location to find a bike path and traverse this bike-friendly city. (photo by Kate Galantha)

Arbor House Baked Pears

Remove the rind from a wheel of soft brie and chop the cheese into cubes. Add 2 tablespoons honey and 1 tablespoon currants. Blend this into a pastry dough consistency. Cut fresh, ripe pears lengthwise and remove the core. Put cheese mixture in center of hollowed pear. Set in baking dish. Add ½ cup apple juice or cider. Bake 40 minutes at 375 degrees.

Saturday and Sunday breakfasts don't drop the "think globally, act locally" ball. Seasonal and local ingredients are used, some of which are grown in Arbor House gardens. The daily popovers, muffins, breads, and croissants come out of the Arbor House's own ovens. Cathie uses rhubarb from her yard, and by fall the pear tree is picked clean.

Set on an open plain near Columbus, in Fall River, *Fountain Prairie Inn and Farms* just might be a perfect agri-tourism model. First of all, John and Dorothy Priske are passionate about what they do. John will happily sit and discuss Aldo Leopold—his land ethic, his vision as reflected in John's farming practices—until the cows come home. At least until he shifts gears to the 280 acres and his herd of Highland cattle that roam freely within cordoned-off parcels, a system they use to organize the herd by age and temperament. They like their cattle . . . a lot! And the ones that give them trouble end up sooner than later on the menus of restaurants in the Madison area, from premier sustainable tables like L'Etoile and the Madison Club to more casual settings like Bradbury Coffee's off Capitol Square and Lazy Jane's on Williamson Street.

The Priskes have the land ethic down pat. They have forged paths throughout their fields that lead to a sixty-acre prairie restoration that they're as proud to show off as they are their cattle. Restoring and protecting the land are just as important to them.

Dorothy runs the bed-and-breakfast in her large fountain-blue Victorian home, offering five very private rooms in a rambling second story. They are welcoming hosts and offer ample space for groups to experience the kind of life on the plain that would make Aldo Leopold proud. If you're lucky, John might insist you return home with a copy of *The Sand County Almanac*. You can buy their beef on-site, too.

Just seven miles northeast of downtown Madison is *The Speckled Hen Inn*, a sweet little rural spot on what owner Patricia Fischbeck calls "the edge of civilization." A night or two here will show off Wisconsin's agriculture in

a gentlemanly (and womanly) farmer sense. The Speckled Hen is a stately
bed-and-breakfast that can be accessed by bike beginning at the Starkweather
Creek Path in the Atwood neighborhood and ending at Reindahl Park at East
Washington and Portage Road. For off- and on-road routes, consult a City of
Madison bike path map. From Reindahl Park, it's a straight two-mile ride up
Portage Road. At the inn, you'll find four spacious rooms, each with a private
bath. Its large gathering room has a piano and wood-burning stove, a home
theater, and a library. The inviting dining room is often candlelit. But the real
treat is its fifty acres of wetlands and pastures that are home to grazing horses,
sheep, and llama. Along the trail and gardens that traverse this setting, you'll
find wildlife, such as nesting sandhill cranes, that live along Starkweather
Creek and within the inn's pine and spruce plantations, apple orchards, and
grape vineyard (used for grape sorbet rather than wine).

Patricia and Robert Fischbeck are committed to sustaining not only their
land but also the local economy by using products from regional farms for
the breakfasts they'll serve at your convenience. They also grow produce and
use herbs from their own gardens.

Where to Eat

L'Etoile Restaurant is a nationally recognized leader in sustainable gourmet
cuisine that's been around for decades. The list of local farms that supply its
kitchen with ingredients is extensive and impressive and can be accessed on
the restaurant's Web site. It's on the Square with a view of the Capitol and is
one of Madison's first and proudest forays into the slow food movement. Its
downstairs sister cafe, *Café Soleil*, is as green as it gets; it is one of the most
environmentally conscientious cafes in town, with strict compost, recycle,
reuse, and don't-use policies. The food, as you can imagine, lives up to the
same quality promise.

Harvest is next door and shares the same Capitol view. It's been written
up in scores of national cuisine-focused magazines, such as *Gourmet*, *Bon
Appétit*, and *New York Times Magazine*. On another side of the Capitol just off
the Square is *Marigold Kitchen*, a downtown breakfast and lunch favorite with
a cooked-from-scratch, seasonal menu chock full of locally grown ingredients.
Sometimes the line stretches out the door, so pick your arrival time carefully.
It's also another venue for local art. On Hamilton Street is *Bradbury's Coffee*,
which serves fair trade coffee and espresso (its specialty item) and crêpes made
with ingredients from local, sustainable farms, such as beef from Fountain
Prairie Farm and spinach from Snug Haven Farm.

Restaurant Magnus, on West Wilson Street just east of Monona Terrace Community and Convention Center, is a happening, jazz-club, fine dining scene with a dedication to sourcing local farms for its meat and produce. Tuesday nights its jazz bar is reserved for neighborhood musicians. Lucky for Magnus customers, world famous jazz great Ben Sidran, a Madison resident, is frequently among the lineup. Currently the chef draws on Wisconsin's Scandinavian heritage in an inventive New Scandinavian seasonal menu that features flavors characteristic to the region.

The *Weary Traveler Freehouse* on Williamson Street is a great spot for lunch or dinner in a laid-back atmosphere of hodgepodge vintage tables, shelving with games, and a big oak back bar that was repurposed from a Chicago speakeasy. The owners advocate buying local and stocking their menu with plenty of ingredients purchased within Dane County. You might want to try Bob's Bad Breath Burger, but the walleye sandwich is a definite contender.

Stop at *Lazy Jane's Cafe and Bakery* one block up for sought-after scones or a healthful sandwich. But the real treat is to sit among the eclectic atmosphere of mismatched furniture and local outsider art.

If you want to see east side Madison in action, have lunch or dinner at the *Harmony Bar and Grill* or *Monty's Blue Plate Diner*. The Harmony packs in locals as a great music venue and serves vegetarian and vegan bar food—the Trempealeau walnut burger is excellent. Monty's is another locally owned (part of Food Fight Restaurant Group), local yokel hangout with many vegetarian options and signature pies and desserts. Head up Atwood Avenue to get fair trade coffee and view local and outsider art at *Cafe Zoma*, a neighborhood coffee and art house.

La Brioche True Food on University Avenue is known for its pastry and is true to its commitment to using local farms and purveyors. If you're at all familiar with Madison's food roots, you know that the restaurant Ovens of Brittany put Madison on the culinary map back in the 1970s. Its demise is history, but La Brioche, owned by David Yankovich, an Ovens founder, has been thriving since 1988, first as a bakery on Midvale Boulevard and now with its recent expansion and relocation to University Avenue. La Brioche True Food combines his passion for slow food with the expertise in chi and feng shui design of his wife, Jackie Patricia. Their entrees use ingredients from local sustainable farms and the sources are called out right on the menu—a true field-to-fork concept. The interior, a blend of upholstered Victorian patterns and contrasting stone pizza oven, is meant to bring you back into a simpler time—Grandma's house. Well, the food is good and local, that much should be everyone's experience.

You'll need reservations, but *Lombardino's*, just off Campus Drive on Old University Avenue, has contemporary Italian fare thought by many to be the best in Madison. Chef-owner Patrick O'Halloran understands the quality found in local ingredients, which is why his menu is seasonal and his dishes are consistently good. Don't let the kitschy Italian interior fool you; this food is first rate. The Lombardino's pizza is worth whatever route it takes you to get there.

If you'd prefer Italian on a smaller, more casual scale, go to *Pizza Brutta* near the corner of Monroe and Grant, where the pizza is thin and delicious and the sustainable practices make it almost irresistible. They will tell you that eating is an "agricultural act and largely determines how the world is used." Their interior woods are from sustainable foresters and their ingredients are local and organic, like greens from Shooting Star Farms in Mineral Point and free-range pork (think prosciutto) from La Quercia in Iowa. Their milk is from Organic Valley and most of their cheeses hail from small Wisconsin family farms.

At *Barrique's Wine Cave* you can sample wines, drink Milwaukee-roasted Alterra coffee, and eat fair trade chocolate and fresh bakery. *Ancora* coffee-house serves organic, fair trade, artisan—all the right kinds of locally roasted coffee—and features work of local artists. Besides their Monroe Street locations, Barrique's and Ancora also have several other Madison locations.

Look for area beers at many Madison restaurants and bars: Capital Brewery of Middleton, New Glarus of New Glarus, Lake Louie of Arena, Asylum Ale of Madison.

Beyond Local and Fair Trade

Just Coffee, a Bike the Barns coffee supplier (see Annual Events), is a local roaster with a global conscience. Located just off of Williamson Street on East Wilson—right next door to *RP's Pasta*, a local source for home-made pasta and sauce—these guys take fair trade very seriously. The company is run as a co-op with what they call a "true democratic process." They use other local co-ops such as growers' co-ops, import through Cooperative Coffees that support equitable and sustainable trade relationships, and sell to and barter with housing co-ops, food co-ops, and other worker co-ops. You can find their coffee around Madison in shops and cafes, but you can also accompany them to the countries from which they source their coffee through Just Coffee Delegations, a "voluntourism" travel experience that focuses on "the production of coffee from the tree to the cup."

Local Foraging

Community Pharmacy on State Street is an alternative co-op-run store that's been around Madison for more than thirty years. The place has a calming energy that comes from its natural and holistic products, everything from bulk laundry detergent to books on homeopathy to very good smelling soaps. You can also get Four Element herbal products from Baraboo. Plus, if you bring in your hotel toiletries, they donate them to Madison's Porchlight Drop-In Shelter, which provides support and job counseling to the homeless.

For second-hand and vintage consignment, there's a wealth of options around Madison that range from St. Vincent de Paul Thrift Store to high-end merchandise coming around for a second or third time. Two favorites are *Atomic Interiors* on Park Street and *Iconi Interiors* on West Washington Avenue. Atomic Interiors owners Dave Vogel and Rebecca Rodriguez specialize in reclaimed, high-end, mid-century furniture but also deal in Herman Miller furniture, a company devoted to environmental advocacy through sustainable building and furniture design. Dave and Rebecca also walk the local-use talk by living blocks from their store, patronizing neighborhood businesses, and buying produce from Harmony Valley CSA. Iconi is a shop of largely reclaimed goods that at first glance appears to be a showroom of merchandise hot off the assembly line. Owner Connie Moratz has a great eye for salvaging pieces, some of which she resurfaces herself, and her store reflects that. Her new items are midwestern manufactured or locally made—repurposing is her goal.

Explore the east side and Lake Monona for a tremendous itinerary of natural attractions and great vintage and one-of-a-kind shops and galleries. From the Capitol Square follow King Street south to East Wilson Street to South Blair Street (be in left lane on Blair) to the Capital City Bike Path; or go to Monona Terrace and take the elevator on the east side of the building down to pick up the path. Head east to Williamson Street, where old and new Madison coalesce. *Hempen Goods* at Paterson and Williamson streets used to be considered on the fringe, but now it's on the cutting edge. Here you can buy clothes that are woven out of an assortment of eco-friendly, sustainable alternatives. Some are made from hemp, some are a blend of hemp and organic cotton, and others are dyed with clay dyes. They also sell products made from recycled rubber and plastic. East on Williamson Street is the *Willy Street Co-op*, a wildly successful model for a cooperative neighborhood grocer that supports Dane County local farmers and socially responsible organizations throughout Madison. Here you can get produce brought in from across the county rather than across the country, get a latté and bagel, do a shot of wheat grass, select deli choices from vegan to meat dishes, or find a holistic herbal remedy. It also holds classes and sessions on wellness and nutrition. It's truly a slice of Madison at its grass roots.

Head east from the co-op for less than a block to the *Green Parasol*, a shop with unique, handmade, one-of-a kind fashions more likely to be found on a street in SoHo. Owners Laurie Rossback and Susan Otterson make wearable art that ranges from redesigned ready-to-wear and vintage pieces to hand-knit styles. They also have original work from local and Chicago dressmakers and vintage accessories, such as a vase full of floral cloth umbrellas unlike any you'll find at a chain department store. Across the street you can pick up a jacket for peanuts at the original and largest *St. Vincent de Paul Thrift Store* in Madison. The clothes racks are neatly arranged by color and style. Need a tool to fix your bike? *Ace Hardware* in the next block east is shopping for lug nuts the old-fashioned way—small narrow aisles of stuff you need sold by guys who know their customers by their first names. Farther down Williamson

Bike to a Bookstore

Madison has no shortage of independent bookstores. Here are the ones that are easily accessed by bike:

State Street Area: *A Room of One's Own Feminist Bookstore* on West Johnson specializes in women's literature and children's books. *Avol's Bookstore* on West Gorham sells general use, rare and out-of-print books, and specializes in academic and scholarly books. *Paul's Book Store* on State Street has that musty used bookstore quality but has well organized general use titles. *JTaylor's Galleries* on Carroll Street is jammed with some of Madison's most interesting (and maybe most valuable) antiques, notable books, and rare maps. The store hours vary, but if you show up and the door is locked, knock. Owner John Taylor is often inside and generally willing to share his knowledge about his amazing collection—well worth the walk, bike, or ride to find out if you can get in. *Rainbow Bookstore Cooperative* on Gilman Street sells progressive literature and holds events with a social conscience. It's for radicals, activists, and book lovers.

East Side: *Saint Vincent de Paul* on Williamson Street has a great selection of used general use and children's books. *Quintessence* on Lakeside Street sells alternative and homeopathic health products and has a selection of books to back up its holistic methods.

is *Gayfeather Fabrics*, a specialty store that's basically two small rooms filled with fabrics of natural fibers and sewing accessories.

Sugar Shack Records, a one-of-a-kind secondhand record shop on Atwood Avenue, makes Santana's *Supernatural* somehow sound like new music. More outsider art fills *Absolutely Art* farther up on Atwood Avenue, a gallery shop devoted to promoting area artists. This place is filled with as much variety as color, and it's connected to a neighborhood that's high energy and, without a doubt, a true Madison scene.

In the Hilldale Shopping Center on the West Side is *Fair Indigo*, a locally owned shop that offers fair trade fashions that pay "a good wage to the good people who make their clothes." It is part of the Cotton from Blue to Green denim drive, which collects used blue jeans for conversion to UltraTouch natural cotton fiber insulation—an eco-friendly home insulation product manufactured by Bonded Logic. The insulation is then donated to communities in need to assist in their building efforts. Locally, five hundred pairs of jeans will insulate one Habitat for Humanity–built home. Next door, *Anaala Salon and Spa* sells and uses the eco-friendly Aveda products—not local, but based in the Midwest—with plant-based, fair trade products sourced from traditional communities around the world.

What to Do

If you didn't pull into town with a kayak strapped to your roof, you can rent a canoe or kayak and paddle the Yahara River. This Dane County waterway flows from Madison's Lake Mendota to Rock County's Rock River. Expert paddlers say Lake Monona to Lake Kegonsa is a best-bet stretch. If you brought a boat, you can access the river at *Tenney Park* on Lake Mendota, or you can rent a sailboat or kayak at *Wingra Boats* on Lake Wingra. You can also rent a canoe or kayak at *Rutabaga, the Paddlesport Shop* in Monona and launch it at their site on the Yahara River. From there you can paddle downstream to Mud Lake or Lake Waubesa or upstream to Lake Monona, where you can see the Monona Terrace and the Capitol from every corner of the lake. And if you're interested in more structure or guidance, the guys at Rutabaga are passionate about paddling and hold weekly water excursions (June through August) and paddling workshops, some just for women. They also have an adaptive paddling program for people with disabilities. Plus they host the annual Canoecopia, the world's largest paddle sport exposition, and one with a conscience. The event donates a portion of its proceeds to local charitable organizations, and then Rutabaga matches that donation.

Foraging for Food

Dane County farmers benefit from the plethora of *Farmers' Markets* set up around the city. Even the central city residents have access to fresh produce farmed right in their neighborhood. Here's a list but check the City of Madison Web site for updated market information.

East Side: Tuesday, 4 to 7 p.m., May to October, 201 Ingersoll Street.

Downtown: Saturday, 6 a.m. to 2 p.m., April to November, Capitol Square; 7:30 a.m. to noon, November and December, Monona Terrace; Saturday, 8 a.m. to noon, January to April, 330 West Mifflin Street (Madison Senior Center); Wednesday, 8:30 a.m. to 2 p.m., April to November, 200 block of Martin Luther King Jr. Blvd (in front of City-County Building).

North Side: Sunday, 8:30 a.m. to 12:30 p.m., May to October, corner of Sherman Avenue and Northport Drive (Northside Town Center).

South Side: Tuesday, 2 to 6 p.m., and Saturday, 9 a.m. to 2 p.m., April to October, 1602 South Park Street (Labor Temple Market); Thursday, 2 to 6 p.m., April to October, 2300 South Park Street (Villager Mall); Monday, 2 to 6 p.m., April to October, 2500 Rimrock Road.

West Side: Wednesday and Saturday, 7 a.m. to 2 p.m., May to October, 702 North Midvale Boulevard (Hilldale Mall west parking lot); Saturday, 7 a.m. to 1 p.m., April to November, 4802 Sheboygan Avenue (Hill Farms Department of Transportation parking lot).

There are scads of places to rent a bike in Madison, like *Budget Bicycle Center* on Regent Street. It has a new and used store and rents bikes for a range of performances—road bikes, hybrid city bikes, mountain bikes—at daily and weekly rates. If you decide you want to own a trailer bike or a trailer for the kids, the rental cost goes toward the purchase price. These guys are good Madison business neighbors—they donate bikes to local charitable auctions and they're a drop-off site for *Wheels for Winners*, a local nonprofit that teaches at-risk kids to fix up their bikes and ride.

While the *Revolution Cycles* shop doesn't rent bikes, it helps save the environment by promoting the use of old bikes through bicycle renovation. It's all about getting you from A to B without being fancy but still being functional. See the Friends page of its Web site for a list of other like-minded Madison businesses. You can go online and get a "Global Cooling Machine" T-shirt like the guys at Revolution Cycles wear, made by *Planet Bike*, an environmentally responsible maker of bike products "for a better world," located in Madison. *Trek Bicycle* is a Wisconsin-based business with shops in Madison that sell and rent bicycles. *Williamson Bikes and Fitness* also rents hybrids and road bikes at its West Washington Avenue location from April to November.

Aldo Leopold is one of Wisconsin's most celebrated environmental conservationists (the Wisconsin State Trail System was recently named the Aldo Leopold Legacy Trail System) and in the Madison area there's no shortage of appreciation for his teachings. The *Aldo Leopold Nature Center* located in Monona carries on his vision through programming that connects kids and families with nature. Award-winning interactive trails lead through ninety-four acres of prairies, wetlands, and woodlands. The center offers several group programs for kids and families, seasonal events, summer nature camps, plus the trails are open for drop-in use "from sun-up to sun-down" provided classes are not in session. You can find a directory of Wisconsin nature centers and download an interactive trail map at the center's Web site.

Monroe Street Area

Arbor House is aptly named for the *University of Wisconsin Arboretum*, home to the world's oldest restored prairie—1,260 acres of four-season, motor-free activity. If observing prairies, savannahs, pine and boreal forests, effigy mounds, bird life, and historic artifacts isn't what you had in mind, then there's a twenty-mile trail system for walking, hiking, snowshoeing, or just sitting still to paint or draw the indigenous Wisconsin plants and wildlife. Give Arboretum naturalists a two-week lead time and they'll put together a tour that covers the Arb's ecosystem, its different prairies, its woodland culture and thousand-year-old effigy mounds, and other aspects of land restoration. Tours can be tailored to cover special themes according to your educational needs. You can also jump on the surrounding bike path that connects to more recreation down the road.

Lake Wingra is a beloved Madison lake surrounded by an aggressive urban environment. The *Friends of Lake Wingra* cherish its contribution to the city with its urban ecology–rich assets—forests, prairies, and wetlands that support a diverse population of plants and wildlife—and encourage visitors to take its Watershed Bike Tour. This carefully detailed map calls out wetland diversity and the watershed that protects it, such as the rain gardens that soak up and recharge rain runoff. In summer months you can rent a variety of boats at *Wingra Boats* located at Lake Wingra's shoreline off Monroe Street. In winter months, the *Vilas Park* warming house rents skates and sells hot chocolate. In either season, it's a lovely spot that offers the serenity of a small-town park.

University of Wisconsin Campus

The *University of Wisconsin Memorial Union Terrace* is where you can access paths to the *Lakeshore Nature Preserve*, three hundred acres that run along Lake Mendota. These trails follow the curve of the lake but wend off onto intersecting trails, like Picnic Point and Frautschi Point. They are paradise for hikers, bikers, birders, snowshoers, and cross-country skiers. Maintained by *Friends of the Lakeshore Nature Preserve* volunteers, these nine distinct footpaths have been a work in progress for decades, and workers can be seen clearing invasive species to make way for indigenous ones to expand and native plants to prosper. Interactive maps available on the university's Web site clearly define each path, Indian habitat sites and effigy mounds, vanished historic features, surviving historic features, and the ecology specific to each area. There are as many ways to roam this land as there are reasons why you should. Here's one—this area is a veritable classroom of past American cultures. The University of Wisconsin campus has more distinct archaeological sites than any campus in the country. For instance, paths at the western edge of campus lead to Eagle Heights Woods, a twenty-eight-acre woodland parcel overlooking Lake Mendota that is home to three effigy mounds built during the Late Woodland Stage between 700 and 1200 AD. These sacred burial grounds are respectfully maintained with the help of Ho Chunk tribal members and are clearly marked.

The autumn views throughout the entire area are awe inspiring, with the violets and blues of Lake Mendota against the bold golden oaks, shocking red sumac, and bright orange maples. You can access Frautschi Point from Lake Mendota Drive just off the University Bay bike path. If you enter here, take the Old Oak path to see what happens when an oak tree has nothing but room to breathe. Although the winter trails are ungroomed, they are well trekked by year-round naturalists, making trail blazing a cinch. Volunteers work to "preserve, protect, and nurture" these woodlands, wetlands, prairies, and shoreline and ask that others do, too. Leashed dogs are welcome.

The *Wisconsin Union Theater* connects the university to the outside community as an innovative performing arts center. You can attend performances that range from world-class jazz vocalists to student concerts to local and national theater groups to independent films. Some performances are free.

The Capitol Square and State Street

Bike around the Capitol Square and you can eat, shop, muse. You can tour the *Wisconsin Capitol* during weekdays. On Saturdays from spring to late fall, the Square fills up with people who come from all over the state to the *Dane County Farmers' Market*, the largest of its kind in the country. Here you can meet area merchants who sell everything from humanely farmed meat to sustainably grown vegetables to pesticide-free apples, flowers, honey, bakery, you name it. And all items are sold by the people who produce them. Local artists also sell their work around the market.

Directly across the street from the Capitol on Pinckney Street, you can visit the *Madison Environmental Group*, an innovative consulting firm focused on sustainable building and operations. These are the guys who have helped to put Madison on the map as a leader in green building and renovation. This team does great things for the health of the world by helping businesses downsize their ecological footprint. You can go there to have lunch with MEG president Sonya Newenhouse and the group, and then get a grand tour of their green office space, located on the same floor as L'Etoile Restaurant. While you're there, check out their innovative Fullcircle Furniture line made from landfill-bound doors found in a hospital deconstruction site. See their Web site for dates of lunches, served at a Fullcircle-designed table.

The *Madison Museum of Contemporary Art* has world-class art exhibits, like the works of Chuck Close, Jasper Johns, and Robert Rauschenberg, and its gift shop is filled with top-notch local art. Next door at the *Overture Center for the Arts* you can see everything from the Madison Symphony Orchestra to Broadway productions to regional art in the James Watrous Gallery to wall exhibits that support the more immediate local art scene, including the work of area elementary and high school students.

Farther down State Street, *State Street Gallery/Wine Shop* and *Fanny Garver Gallery* are two more State Street venues that support local and regional artists in a range of media.

If taking in an independent film means to you sitting in a vintage theater—reuse at its finest—State Street's historic *Orpheum Theatre* is the total package. Its urban setting provides a spectacular downtown Madison experience with its *Lobby Restaurant* offering locally grown produce and locally brewed beers (Lake Louie from Arena, Spotted Cow from New Glarus, Ale Asylum from Madison) as a prelude to an indie film or concert. Plus, it just might have one of the best bluegill (Canadian) fish fries in the city.

The East Side

Foodies who are in Madison on the first Wednesday of the month are in luck. That's when *CHEW (Culinary History Enthusiasts of Wisconsin)* holds its monthly meeting, complete with fascinating speakers, interactive activities, and demonstrations. Past speakers include Dale and Cindy Secher of Carandale Farm in Oregon, Wisconsin, on "Aronia, Ubileen, Saskatoon, Sea Berry: Future Fruits of Wisconsin?"; Mary Carpenter on "The History of the Dane County Farmers' Market"; and John Motoviloff on "Four Seasons of Foraging in Wisconsin." CHEW was founded by noted regional food writer Terese Allen and other food enthusiasts. It's a casual group, meetings are open to the public, and they welcome visitors. Membership is open to all and encouraged but not required to attend a meeting. Check their Web site for the meeting location (often at the Willy Street Co-op) and for more information.

Atwood Avenue begins where Williamson Street ends at the Marquette-Schenk-Atwood neighborhood. This area is known for its bohemian roots that include the vintage *Barrymore Theatre*. Largely an acoustically acclaimed music venue, it also hosts independent films, stand-up comedy, flea markets, children's talent shows, and plays.

If you follow Atwood Avenue about six blocks east of the Barrymore and head north on Waubesa Street, you'll find the *Ironworks Cafe*. Set within the

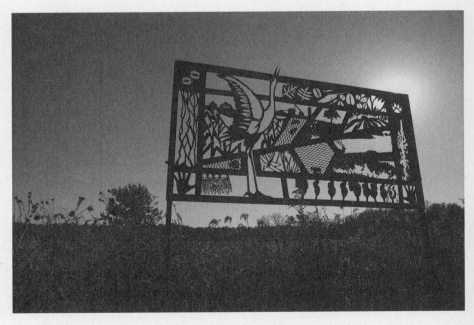

The University of Wisconsin Arboretum is home to 1,260 acres of ecological communities that are the oldest restored ecosystems in the nation. (photo by Kate Galantha)

Goodman Community Center, an architecturally and environmentally cutting edge community center that does an amazing job of creating cultural and community events and activities that reflect its neighborhood's diversity, this cafe fits the center's mission of social responsibility. The center's Web site lists its many sustainable features, including major reuse of an existing building and its contents, rain gardens, and domestic solar hot water to name just a few. Its Ironworks Cafe has its own sustainable vision. It serves breakfast and lunch using local and seasonal ingredients and employs kids from Madison East's alternative high school program who run the whole deal as a way to garner business management experience.

Head back to Atwood Avenue and go east past Fair Oaks Avenue to *Olbrich Botanical Gardens*, directly across from Lake Monona. It's a lovely sixteen-acre destination that's known for its Thai Pavilion, a gift to the University of Wisconsin–Madison from the Thai government and the Thai chapter of the Wisconsin Alumni Association (the university has one of the largest Thai student populations of any university or college in the United States). Olbrich's larger purpose is to provide beauty through teaching the importance of plants in a sustainable world. In 2005 these gardens won the prestigious Award for Garden Excellence from the American Association of Botanic Gardens and Arboreta. To you, it's a leisurely meander down wonderful paths that wind through native plantings and fifteen display gardens. In the enclosed Bolz Conservatory you can experience humid tropic air while viewing exotic plants and orchids, a waterfall, and uncaged birds. Olbrich Gardens offers a variety of classes and workshops, like butterfly walks and garden jewelry making. Its Web site has a complete list and schedule.

Next, take the bike path east to Dempsey Road and then south to Cottage Grove Road to get to *Habitat for Humanity ReStore*. After this stop you might want to return with a car. One of eight Habitat ReStores in Wisconsin, it resells salvaged goods from deconstructed residential and commercial buildings. This place has more doors than you'll open in a lifetime (OK, not quite, but lots) and other interior stuff like cabinets and maybe even a new hot tub that didn't fit but couldn't be sent back to the manufacturer. Not everything is quality, but you're bound to find something of value.

Follow the lake loop bike route along John Nolen Drive to Lakeside Street and head west to one of the sweetest spots to stop for food and fiber in Madison. As you bike by, you might not realize there's a cafe behind *Lakeside Fibers*, but set in the space adjacent to this friendly, high-quality yarn shop is the *Washington Island Hotel Coffee Room*. Named for owner Leah Caplan's hotel in Door County, all of the cafe's baked goods come from the Washington Island Hotel Culinary School and are made from organic, local, and seasonal ingredients. The menu calls out the farms used, like Sugar River Dairy and Fountain Prairie Ham. Its location overlooking Monona Bay makes it a lovely spot to stop, sit, and knit if you'd like, or just enjoy some simple, local cuisine. To return to John Nolen Drive, backtrack on Lakeside Street.

The West Side

The west side of Madison is not without its impressive green landmarks. The Meeting House at the *First Unitarian Society* on University Bay Drive was not only Frank Lloyd Wright's place of worship but it was designed by him too. It now has a twenty-one-thousand-square-foot addition, designed by Kubala Washatko Architects (think Aldo Leopold Legacy Center in Baraboo as well as Milwaukee's Urban Ecology Center and Schlitz Audubon Nature Center) with environmentally responsible innovations, such as a geothermal heating system and a built-in, natural cooling system—a spectacular sedum-planted roof that minimizes storm-water runoff and acts as a natural coolant. Call the church office for a tour or just walk the grounds, located directly across the street from the American Family Children's Hospital.

Farther west, at the intersection of University Avenue and Midvale Boulevard, is the newly renovated Hilldale Shopping Center, where you can take in a film at *Sundance Cinemas*, which supports Madison's commitment to simple, alternative recreation and lifestyle. Since Madison is home to a major forward-thinking university and the highly regarded annual spring Wisconsin Film Festival, it stands to reason that this would be the site for Sundance Group's first concept-to-completion theater. This six-screen independent film house was built with sustainable materials and reclaimed wood from the bottom of Lake Superior. Its concessions include locally roasted coffee and Wisconsin dairy products. Its interior's "rough elegance" design also supports the work of local artists.

Annual Events

Downtown Madison has loads of seasonal events to which you can bike. And if you're like many Madisonians, you won't let the snow retire your bicycle for the season. Here's a short list, but check the City of Madison Web site for the long version:

Madison Area Open Art Studios is an annual fall event during which you can see artists at work in their galleries and studios. *MMOCA Gallery Night* is a spring and fall event organized by the Madison Museum of Contemporary Art during which you can visit galleries and art studios around the city, meeting the artists and the people who support them. Or be one. *Art Fair on the Square* is another MMOCA organized event that brings hundreds of artists and scores of art buyers to the Square for a weekend in July.

Concerts on the Square is a Wednesday night summer evening event during which the Wisconsin Chamber Orchestra performs a free concert outside the Capitol to an audience of summer evening picnickers. Tables can be reserved for a fee and donations to the Chamber Orchestra are encouraged. *Jazz at Five* is another free summer evening concert series. When the weather cooperates, it's held at the 100 block of State Street. On rainy evenings it's held in the Overture Center Lobby.

The *Madison Winter Festival* is a February cross country ski event that began as the Capitol Square Sprint, the first North American race of its kind held in an urban, downtown setting. It was so popular it morphed into an international, family-oriented festival of winter events and competitions that are designed to advance healthy, outdoor winter activity.

The *Food for Thought Festival,* an annual event put on by Research, Education, Action, and Policy (REAP) Food Group, celebrates the connection between farmers and the people and businesses of Madison. The festival promotes slow food and sustainability through keynote speakers like Michael Pollan, author of *The Omnivore's Dilemma* and *In Defense of Food,* who spoke in 2009. There are also events and discussions with local farmers like John Frieze of Fountain Prairie Farm and Inn, and a payoff of samples of sustainably grown and produced food and products from Dane County.

In October, the City of Madison and the Wisconsin Humanities Council host the *Wisconsin Book Festival,* five days of readings and discussions by some of America's finest writers. In 2008, for example, the presentation by naturalist Terry Tempest Williams, author of *Finding Beauty in a Broken World,* was followed up by an open forum that addressed ideas, interests, and concerns about the environment. Events and discussions covering a wide spectrum of literary and current topics are held at venues all over the city.

The Gaylord Nelson Institute for Environmental Studies at the University of Wisconsin hosts *Tales from Planet Earth,* a three-day festival of films from around the world and outreach events that explore "stories that shape understanding of nature and inspire action on behalf of environmental justice and diversity of life." The films and related community outreach events are held at various campus and downtown theaters and venues. It's a free festival and is open to the public on a first-come, first-served basis. But donations are accepted at the door.

If you're an independent film lover visiting Madison in April, look into the *Wisconsin Film Festival*, which in past years has attracted thirty-two-thousand-plus viewers. Ten Madison venues have been the annual site for one hundred-plus feature films and almost as many short films. This festival is well respected and attracts the work of local, national, and international filmmakers. Past films have been as light and local as *Being Bucky*, a film about the students who don the University of Wisconsin Bucky Badger costume, and as far-reaching and dramatic as *Departures*, a Japanese film about a cellist who finds meaning in life through funeral work.

Bike the Barns is an annual September event that raises much needed funds for the Madison Area Community Supported Agriculture Coalition's (MACSAC) Partner Shares Program, which provides fresh local food to low-income families. The ride began in 2007 and the route changes each year. The 2009 ride enticed more than five hundred riders to bike fifty-four miles, with a lot of nibbling along the way, in the rolling countryside west of Madison. For the fifty-five dollar fee and a modest fundraising effort, they ate and learned about local food and farms all day. Breakfast at Elver Park was by Madison's Café Soleil. Riders then toured three CSA farms, where they were served artisan local food by Madison's *Underground Food Collective*, a catering co-op that uses only top-quality local foods. At the end of the day there was a party back at the park, with live music, grilled pizza with

Environmental and Spiritual Renewal

The *Holy Wisdom Monastery* is an ecumenical community run by the Benedictine Women of Madison, whose purpose is to "weave prayer, hospitality, justice, and care of the earth into a shared way of life." A big part of that life is environmentalism, which is evidenced in its ninety acres of restored prairie and now in its thirty-thousand-square-foot, LEED-certified home that is a contender as one of the greenest built structures in the United States. Individuals and groups of all religious convictions come for spiritual renewal and environmental programs. Located on County Road M, just north of Lake Mendota in Middleton, the monastery is also designed for personal retreats spent in solitude, contemplation, and prayer; for groups or individuals to receive spiritual guidance; or for a week-long hermitage retreat in a private one-bedroom cabin at the edge of the woods. Guests join the community for prayers and meals that include its garden produce and bread baked fresh every day.

locally raised toppings, and beverages, including local beer. The ride sells out, so register early.

All Around and Out of Town

Madison's bike paths are legendary. People here bike to work and to play. They walk, too. And when they can't get there fast enough on bike or foot, some hook their bike onto a Madison Metro bus, of which six are hybrid-electric powered, to pick up a path across town. You can get around Madison easily on almost any on-street route (some have designated bike lanes) or get the whole picture on a *City of Madison Bicycle Map*, which shows on-street and off-street paths. Maps can be found online or at local bike shops, of which there are plenty. Two interesting routes are a nearly thirteen-mile trek around Lake Monona and the Capital City Trail, which starts from the Olin-Turville parking lot and links up to the Military Ridge State Trail on Madison's west side. Here you can pedal all the way out to Dodgeville, a forty-four-mile ride, if you have the time and energy and wanderlust.

The Military Ridge State Trail skirts the town of Mount Horeb. A good time to bike or drive the area is during the *Mount Horeb Area Arts Association Spring Art Tour* when artists open up their studios to the public. In downtown Mount Horeb you'll find businesses doing their part for the local and global good. *Kaleidoscope Marketplace* is sustainable shopping where you can buy functional art: hand-spun yarns from locally raised sheep knit into soft hats and scarves as well as clay unearthed, shaped into drinking vessels, glazed and fired for days for strength. There are also a number of antique shops and one vintage clothing shop right on Main Street. Before you leave town, you can guiltlessly fuel up at *Trillium Natural Foods Community Co-op*, a greengrocer connected to its farming community.

But whatever you do, make sure you've got the gear, the stamina, and the route defined.

Bike It, Hike It, Like It

Milwaukee Area

One of the spiritual risks of not owning a farm is the danger of supposing that breakfast comes from the grocery.

—ALDO LEOPOLD, *The Sand County Almanac*

As you approach the city of Milwaukee via I-94 from the west, the Menomonee River Valley rests to the south as a seemingly tired ravine of old industrial ghosts and a river that's taken it on the chin. But don't be fooled by what you know about outsourced industry and the polluted waterways and communities it leaves in its dust. This is one region that has enjoyed a resurgence, now a proud part of Milwaukee County's ample revitalized green space, much of which can be seen by bike or by a hike, with many of its parkways bordered by waterways that can be paddled. But it's a big city, so where do you start?

Milwaukee's plan for sustainability includes bike paths that can lead you either into the city's more gentrified east side, which begins where the white mast of the world-class Calatrava-designed addition to the Milwaukee Art Museum rises regally over Lake Michigan, or into the south side's working-class neighborhoods, which show off the city's true blue-collar grit.

Michigan Avenue at the Milwaukee Art Museum connects you to Lincoln Memorial Drive to the north and Harbor Drive to the south. At this point the Oak Leaf Trail goes to the north and the Hank Aaron State Trail to the west, the beginning of city parkways and bike paths that link to some of Wisconsin's most amazing examples of sustainability: the Urban Ecology Center, the Schlitz Audubon Nature Center, and now the Menomonee Valley Community Park.

A Milwaukee bike map showing all the on- and off-street paths is available at area bike shops and libraries and from Milwaukee's Public Service Ambassadors, who walk the streets carrying informational brochures and generally being helpful. The City of Milwaukee Bicycle and Pedestrian Coordinator also has maps—just call (414) 286-3144.

You can take a slow tour of revitalized neighborhoods such as the Historic Third Ward, where the Milwaukee RiverWalk leads to a microbrewery that may lack an old Milwaukee brewmaster name but is an inspiring replacement—it is the first certified green brewery in the United States and it also works hand in hand with central city farmers.

Or climb the steep streets of the historic Brewers Hill neighborhood, which is home to the city's greenest restaurant with the meanest skyline view, rivaled only by its fabulous field-to-fork menu.

Or you can head north along the lake's shoreline into other historic neighborhoods that were once home to beer barons, sausage makers, industrial moguls—household names that often meet at neighborhood backyard parties. Pabst, Schlitz, Cudahy . . .

To the west are multicultural neighborhoods near the industrial valley where the now defunct railway smokestacks and the remaining brick and steel structures recall this city's hardworking laborers and their taste for local beer and brats and that highly celebrated midwestern silent sport—bowling. This valley is now a successful restoration project of cleaned-up water, native plant–restored watersheds, and a forty-acre nature preserve built to reroute runoff while providing a variety of silent sports, an arts venue for kids, and new businesses vowing economic sustainability for employees.

Whichever direction you choose, Milwaukee is a mixed bag of cultural arts, beautiful parks, and historic homes in ethnic neighborhoods—German, Polish, Italian. Some small family businesses still exist, such as the Italian families of Brady Street who sell homemade breads and hand-rolled pasta out of storefronts set up generations ago. The central city even contains an organic farm that grows produce for local restaurants and markets and gives city kids a place to stick their hands in the dirt and call an heirloom tomato their personal best.

This is a city with sprawling stretches of open space, from sandy beaches to rocky shorelines to waterfront marinas, all connected by a bike path designed to encourage locals to slow down and see the city as they travel through it. Tourists also benefit from this alternate route to sightseeing Milwaukee's many cultural and sustainable offerings.

Where to Stay

Mason Street, which stretches for eight blocks from Prospect Avenue to the Milwaukee River, is in the heart of downtown and therefore not without its historic landmarks. The elegant Pfister Hotel and Milwaukee's celebrated Karl Ratzsch's German restaurant are the street's most noteworthy. The *Hotel Metro* on Mason Street is Milwaukee's first hotel to be certified by Travel Green Wisconsin. Housed in a 1930s art deco limestone office building that was renovated in 1998, this boutique hotel is a member of Historic Hotels of America and is truly unlike any other in the city. The interior, designed by the late, legendary Madame Kouny, mixes sustainable, simple, and elegant features, such as the bamboo floors, mint green English linen walls, and Italian silk chandeliers.

Every wall is a gallery of postimpressionistic work by a Wisconsin artist whose interpretation closely resembles Cezanne and Matisse. Added interior walls have soothing organic lines and curves. The furniture designs follow the same principle, while the carpet patterns are geometric and earth toned. Guest room baths have earth-friendly Aveda products stocked in wicker baskets; bedside trays are made of bamboo. And for mindfulness seekers, the top-floor spa opens out onto a rooftop Zen garden where meditation ponds are surrounded by native grasses—not to mention a marvelous view of Milwaukee's downtown rooftops.

Hotel Metro's Zen garden overlooks a peaceful night in downtown Milwaukee. (photo supplied by Hotel Metro)

As a bonus, bikes are available to hotel guests at no charge. From here you can easily get to a bike path trailhead. Your quandary might be deciding which one to take—the lush green parkway along the lake or the urban-industrial route. Either way, having Milwaukee's only Travel Green Wisconsin–certified hotel as your starting point already puts you at an advantage.

Where to Eat

When fast food spun out of control in the 1980s and '90s, one little bulk food store that opened its doors in the '70s stayed true to its natural food convictions. *Beans and Barley* on North Avenue is now a cutting edge (but modest) cafe and market with its longtime principle of serving local and natural intact. The restaurant might be the healthiest place in Milwaukee for lunch, and its grocery store stocks local produce, humanely raised meats, and mainstream organic products.

Slow food dining can be over way too fast, as you'll find when dining at *Roots Restaurant and Cellar* in historic Brewers Hill. You'll want this perfect experience in sustainable and seasonal dining to go on all night. The simple truth is that the food is consistently amazing—where their food comes from is just the icing on the cake. Using produce grown at Cedar Creek organic farm in Cedarburg is just part of this restaurant's commitment to green cuisine. The other part is its dedication to using locally and humanely raised meats. And its herbs are grown right on the property's hillside, a Hubbard Street location where the southern view of Milwaukee rates as showy as the food. To say you haven't lived until you've tasted one of chef John Raymond's soups alongside an appetizer or entrée from his ever-changing menu might be an overstatement, but not much of one. Wash it down with a glass of Organic E.S.B. from Lakefront Brewery, and local dining doesn't get much better than this.

The organic beer brewed at the *Lakefront Brewery* (the first Travel Green–certified brewery in Wisconsin) is not what brands this place "green." But the story about how Lakefront Brewery took on Anheuser Busch, which tried to diminish the standards for organic brewing (and succeeded), shows just how green it is. Take an environmental tour of this riverside brewery, given on Fridays by owner Russ Klisch, and you'll see firsthand his commitment to sustainability. It begins with a process that saves water and energy by turning city water used to cool one batch into the next batch of beer. But that's just the surface. Then there's the building's energy-saving, heat-reflecting white rooftop. And Klisch's effort to encourage local organic growers to add hops to

Braise on the Go

Chef David Swanson's *Braise on the Go Traveling Culinary School* may be just one
of the most inventive concepts in culinary education. Swanson demonstrates his
passion for buying local by taking his school out to farms where he holds
cooking classes and seasonal dinners right in the fields where the food is
grown. His motivation is to bridge the gap between chefs and the local farmers
supplying their food, and in 2008 Chef Swanson was awarded a Buy Local, Buy
Wisconsin grant to start up the first Restaurant Supported Agriculture (RSA)
system. Some Milwaukee area restaurants affiliated with Swanson's Braise RSA
are *Meritage* on the west side, *Le Rêve* in Wauwatosa, *Cafe Manna* in Brookfield,
and *La Merenda*, a tapas restaurant in Milwaukee's Walker's Point neighborhood.
You can find a schedule of traveling culinary classes at Braise Culinary School's
Web site.

their crops. With Michael Field's Agricultural Institute, the Roots Restaurant
and Cellar's farm in Cedarburg, and other state farms trying to grow this
once indigenous vine, Klisch says he wouldn't mind seeing the state restore its
reputation as the place that has it all—hops, grain, great brewmasters (German or otherwise). But backing community efforts to bring sustainably
grown food to all families is what makes this brewer rise to the top. Each week
Lakefront Brewery sends fifteen thousand pounds of spent grain to Growing
Power (see sidebar) for conversion to supersoil: two tons of worms and
microbes in a cornmeal hash and five-hundred-million-year-old green sand
culled from an algae pond that's converted into nutrient rich soil that provides growing power for this inner city farm. After your brewery tour, sit at
the Palm Garden Bar and down a frothing, compostable, polymer cupful of
Organic E.S.B., one of the few beers in America brewed with true organic
hops. Lakefront Brewery gives daily tours, except Sunday, and serves food
only on Friday nights—a traditional Wisconsin fish fry.

Here's a no-guilt, caffeine-loading pit stop. You can fill up on the energy
produced by a great home-roasted cup of Joe, but when it's *Alterra Coffee*,
a local fair trade roaster dedicated to sustainable growth, it's hard not to
also load up on information about its zero-energy policy. For instance, its
nine cafes throughout the city, plus all of its corporate offices and cafes, are
generated by 100 percent clean, wind-generated energy through We Energy's
Energy for Tomorrow program. And its headquarters on Humboldt Boulevard
has won numerous awards for being a neighborhood and environmentally

responsible project. It's also interesting to note that its lakefront cafe, *Alterra at the Lake*, a great bike-path destination, is housed within a historic flushing station that was restored using serious green practices to prevent the site from affecting Lake Michigan's water quality. Use the Oak Leaf Trail along Lincoln Memorial Drive to Lafayette Street to get there. You can read about the company's earth-friendly practices while dunking an Alterra-baked scone into a cup of fair trade coffee.

The Comet Café, an edgy east-side restaurant-tavern and a Braise RSA member, attracts a hip crowd to its Farwell Avenue location with an interior made up of repurposed metal works and authentic, vintage diner décor. Its use of seasonal produce and local purveyors is served up in portions not typical of slow-food service that has weekenders patiently lined up along Farwell Avenue while seated guests devour everything from meat-loaded, trucker-like specials to a vegan's spin on the old traditional.

Local Foraging

Good Harvest Market is on the corner of St. Paul and Broadway in the Third Ward. Like their Waukesha location, their claim to a 90 percent organic inventory includes wine and beer as well as the brats and sausage made on-site.

Growing Power, a Central City CSA

Will Allen, recipient of a MacArthur "genius" grant in 2008, is a former professional basketball player turned urban farmer who developed easy and sustainable methods for central city farming, a vehicle to bring healthy food to inner city youth.

Allen is cofounder of *Growing Power*, a national nonprofit organization and land trust headquartered in Milwaukee whose mission is to provide communities of people from all backgrounds equal access to healthy, high-quality, safe, and affordable food. Allen's Milwaukee farm is a hands-on agricultural training facility where community members can train in horticulture, aquaculture, poultry raising, beekeeping, vermiculture (worm castings), land conservation, food processing, and marketing. Produce from its community and school gardens throughout Milwaukee is sold at local farmers' markets as well as markets such as Beans and Barley and the Outpost Natural Foods co-op. You can also visit the organization's national headquarters, an inner city sustainable farm located on Silver Spring Drive. Here you can meet the farmers and support their movement by purchasing produce grown right in the heart of the city.

But they also back their organic certification with a dedication to working with local growers of sustainably and humanely raised meat and poultry. Fish comes from environmentally responsible fisheries, and produce is locally and organically grown. Using local farms and promoting awareness of buying local, the cafe offers vegetarian and vegan entrées, an all-organic salad bar, and two organic soups daily. Classes promote spiritual, emotional, and physical wellness. This is a very smart harvest market.

On Saturdays from June to October, vendors at *East Town Farm Market* sell farm-grown produce, baked goods, specialty foods, and arts and crafts. The market includes free musical entertainment and children's activities. It's located in Cathedral Square Park at Kilbourn and Jefferson streets.

East Side Open Market, just a few blocks east of Hotel Metro, is held Thursdays and Saturdays from late June through late October at the Beans and Barley parking lot. This urban marketplace features organic produce and flower bouquets, farm fresh produce, plants, maple syrup, dairy products, eggs, special seasonal items, breads and sweets, arts and craft items, weekly live entertainment, and children's crafts.

What to Do

On Lake Michigan, a short distance from Hotel Metro, is the *Milwaukee Art Museum* with its four floors and forty galleries of rotating art collections that include some of the world's most important artists, from fifteenth-century Europe to twentieth-century America. The museum boasts a comprehensive Georgia O'Keeffe collection, along with one of America's most respected collections of American decorative arts, German expressionism, folk and Haitian art, and American art after 1960. Presently you can view an installation by Milwaukee native (and Roxbury resident) Martha Glowacki called "Loca Miraculi—Rooms of Wonder." Here Glowacki and the Chipstone Foundation participate in the international celebration of the "curiosity cabinet" by exploring the intersections of early modern science with the design of everyday objects from the seventeenth to the nineteenth centuries. This intricate and amazing exhibit mixes Glowacki's sculptural work with archival pieces owned by the Chipstone Foundation. The exhibit will be up until 2014.

A highlight of this lakefront museum is the Santiago Calatrava–designed Quadracci Pavilion with its ninety-foot vaulted ceiling that seems to jettison you out over the whitecaps. Its most notable feature, the Burke Brise Soleil, is a massive sunscreen with a 217-foot wingspan that folds and unfolds three times daily. MAM's slogan "Art Lives Here" is an understatement.

Next door, learn how Wisconsin native Les Paul advanced music with his signature Les Paul Gibson electric guitar and the electric sound system as we know it today. Okay, not energy efficient, but a historically cool claim to fame. MAM's neighbor, *Discovery World*, has Les Paul's mojo on display. Here you can see a room representing his childhood Waukesha home where it all began and instruments that helped ramp up sound around the world. But that's just a tidbit inside this museum that merges science and technology with imagination and adventure. With its hands-on educational, cultural, and environmental programs and exhibits, adults and kids can go from the Les Paul exhibit to fresh and salt water aquariums, distance learning labs, theaters, and other earth-awareness activities.

From there, bikers can take the *Oak Leaf Trail* and head north to Riverside Park, which is one of forty-two unmarked Oak Leaf Birding Trail destinations. This park is fifteen acres of wooded and natural areas on the east side of the Milwaukee River that began as a central city social hub in the early twentieth century—and by the end of the century was a crime-ridden patch of unused land along an industry-ravaged river. With the vision of a neighborhood resident (a science specialist at nearby Riverside High School) this neighborhood slowly reclaimed its piece of central city paradise. Out of that movement came the *Urban Ecology Center*, which grew from a double-wide trailer as the park was being cleaned up to a remarkable twenty-thousand-square-foot green building designed by Cedarburg-based Kubala Washatko Architects, Inc. (the same firm that designed the Aldo Leopold Legacy Center in Baraboo and the addition to the First Unitarian Society of Madison's Meeting House). This center's earth-friendly design has won numerous awards for the use of recycled and renewable materials, such as recycled slate blackboards from a church, sustainable lumber donated by the Menominee Tribal Enterprises, and furniture made by the La Lune Collection from fast-growing willow and poplar trees. But this just skims over the self-supporting qualities of this beautiful urban centerpiece. Go there to tour the remarkable building and to participate in a plethora of environmentally enriching activities, programs, and classes. For a small membership fee, you can borrow a bike or take a kayak or canoe up or down the Milwaukee River, right into the heart of downtown if you like. Sign kids up for a nature program while you canoe the river. Or take them along.

If you're up for the ride, the Oak Leaf Trail has both on- and off-road routes that lead to the *Schlitz Audubon Nature Center* on Lake Michigan in Milwaukee's north shore Bayside neighborhood, roughly a twelve-mile trek. Here

The Urban Ecology Center is a national model for sustainability set in Milwaukee's central city along the Milwaukee River. (photo by Pat Dillon)

you'll find another six miles of hiking trails throughout 185 acres of pristine land. The center is housed in yet another award-winning LEED (Leadership in Energy and Environmental Design) green building designed by Kubala Washatko Architects. The center offers a huge selection of nature programming, some on a one-day basis, such as trips to state-designated natural areas, while others are ongoing, like weekly yoga classes. But the programming options are plentiful and are led by naturalists of all kinds—raptor-handlers, spiritualists, storytellers, or nature educators who discuss everything from birding to butterflies.

The Menomonee River Valley was once home to wild rice marshes and natural areas but succumbed to landfill for a railway and foundries that became Milwaukee's primary source of middle-class economic stability. Many of those original businesses have since folded. Today that stretch of land has been restored to a natural area and a new business community, and it lies adjacent to the *Menomonee Valley Community Park*, perhaps one of Milwaukee's most successful revitalization efforts. If you head west from downtown on the *Hank Aaron State Trail*, you not only get a feel for the once thriving industrial valley, but you get a look at what happens when local and state governments get on the same page about neighborhood renewal. Managed by the Department of Natural Resources, this trail runs along a forty-acre stretch (also nicknamed Storm Water Park for the storm ponds designed to prevent storm water runoff from ending up in the river's watershed). Cited as one of the top projects in the county by the Sierra Club, this gritty historic trail is now home to a labyrinth of bike and foot paths. Interpretive markers tell the valley's history, plus native plantings, woodlands, and artwork created by school kids flesh out the ride. You'll also find an observation deck made of recycled milk bottles, interpretive markers made of recycled glass, and a business community dedicated to economic sustainability through paying its employees a living wage. This trail connects to the Milwaukee Art Museum, Discovery World, the Summerfest grounds, Miller Park, and to the Oak Leaf Trail at the Milwaukee–Waukesha county line. By 2011 an extension to the trail will link to the historic Soldiers Home and State Fair Park.

For biking in the city, take Mason Street, a designated city street bikeway, to the Milwaukee River, lock up your bike, and take the stairs down to the river. Once there you can saunter the *Milwaukee RiverWalk*, a three-mile riverside thoroughfare that has helped revitalize Milwaukee's downtown and the river that runs through it. Head north to find a myriad of restaurants, microbreweries, Schlitz Park, Pere Marquette Park, and the Marcus Center for the Performing Arts. Or get on your bike and follow Water Street south to the Historic Third Ward, a warehouse and manufacturing district turned arts district. This revitalized area has art galleries, restaurants, and theaters. From June to September, you can take the *Milwaukee Trolley Loop* from downtown pick-up points, including the Milwaukee Art Museum and Mason and Jefferson streets near the bike path.

Great Outdoors Weekend

Hold a raptor. Follow a screech owl at midnight. Take a wildflower walk. *Great Outdoors Weekend* was designed by area naturalists to get people outside and loving it by participating in some of best nature activities in Milwaukee County. And they're free. The event is held in September, so log onto www.greatoutdoorsweekendsewi.org to find a park or nature center that has the activity that'll get you excited about being in the great outdoors.

Milwaukee Bike and Skate Rental is the place to rent a surrey, a skelter, a turbo, or just a bike or in-line skates. Almost anything you think will get you there smoother than your tennies can be rented here. It's right across Lincoln Memorial Drive from Alterra at the Lake in Veteran's Park on Milwaukee's lakefront.

Tour Milwaukee's Green Industry

Mario Costantini runs a furniture outfit in Milwaukee's Riverwest neighborhood called the *La Lune Collection*. He's worked as hard to sustain the health of this once gang-ridden neighborhood as he has to grow his thirty-year-old business. From the first, Mario has used sustainable woods to build furniture pieces so popular they're coveted by celebrities like Oprah and organizations like Disney. But the real celebrity here is Mario, who first negotiated with the gangs to let him move his business into their territory and then opened a youth center to snuff them out. It worked. So has his under-the-radar, earth-friendly furniture business idea that uses unwanted, fast-growing trees and builds a livelihood rooted in sustainability. The La Lune Collection is fashioned from weed trees like poplar (also known as aspen) and willow, both harvested from Wisconsin's Northwoods on public and private lands. These are resources that would otherwise be poisoned and burned, two huge hits to the environment. You can call Mario for a tour of the factory or a list of local vendors that carry his collection. He sells primarily through wholesalers, but a few Wisconsin retailers carry his line, such as Home Expressions in Minocqua.

Cream City Ribbon is one of only two companies in the U.S. that make nontoxic ribbon, that is, packaging ribbon made of renewable, biodegradable cotton fiber grown and processed responsibly in the U.S. with water-based dyes and without chlorine bleaches. It uses soy inks and nontoxic adhesives that are approved by the USDA for indirect food use. That's not all: the packaging and spools are biodegradable, with recycled content, and 25 percent of its energy sources is renewable. And the product is pretty. It comes in all kinds of colors and designs. And you can special-order organic or recycled cotton ribbon. Unfortunately, they don't sell direct (outside of some mill ends sold on-site) but you can tour the factory if you call ahead, and people on staff may stop and give you the lowdown on their vintage (1922), German-made equipment and other points of interest. It's located near the Brewers Hill neighborhood on Vliet Street, just a few blocks southwest of the Lakefront Brewery.

The Ice Age Trail's
Youngest Legacy

Waukesha County Area

Life is divided into three terms—that which was, which is, and which
will be. Let us learn from the past to profit by the present, and from
the present to live better in the future.

—WILLIAM WORDSWORTH

The Waukesha County area is a trip to continental glaciation bounty. This
rolling kettle moraine area holds the amazing geological scars of thousands
of years of being pushed and crushed and stacked and tumbled by layers of
glacial ice. Now that may not sound glamorous, but the natural patina the
glaciers left in their wake is to you, at best, a lovely meander through a natural prairie grassland leading to a crystal clear lake near Nashotah or golfing
a naturalized golf course outside Erin; and at worst, a tough push through a
deeply kettled terrain on a mountain bike at the John Muir and Emma Carlin
trails near Eagle and Palmyra.

And what's remarkable is that, at least in this neck of the woods, it all
happened as recently as ten thousand years ago. This may not be yesterday,
but compared with some glacial formations in Wisconsin that are a billion
years old, this county's landscape is a mere toddler. But what travelers really
need to know is this: the area's commitment to land conservation is stellar
and can be seen through its park systems and natural areas and the portion
of the Ice Age Trail that connects its northern end in Monches to its southern
end near East Troy.

Visit the north side of Waukesha County and you will find rustic, hardwood-
lined winding roads leading to quiet remote lakes where you can drift in a
canoe on a charming millpond at a millhouse-turned-inn that might have
made William Wordsworth file for American citizenship. Visit a garden nursery where its eclectic charm is eclipsed only by the owners' dedication to a

sustainable lifestyle. Choose the softly rolling west end and follow the Ice Age Trail in the Kettle Moraine Forest. Stay at bed-and-breakfasts along the way while documenting your footpath as you gently explore the hills and dells of Wisconsin glaciation.

Where to Stay

You're more apt to find the *Monches Mill House* on a drive down a rustic road to trek the Monches Segment of the Ice Age Trail than you are to pull it up on a Wisconsin lodging search engine. There's no loud advertising its lot in life; it seems happy to keep a profile as quiet as its pastoral country setting is serene. This 1842 stone millhouse sits on a small pond fed by the Oconomowoc River and is truly as English a countryside setting as any in Wisconsin. Once a functioning millhouse, it has been restored to preserve the integrity of its original nineteenth-century purpose, with the original plank floors intact and thick stone walls exposed. The décor takes an eclectic route with owner Elaine Taylor's taste for period antiques and both Haitian and American folk art, making a walk through feel more like a visit to a historic art gallery than the affordable, charming bed-and-breakfast that it is.

From the Monches Mill House Tea Room, hostess Deborah Clifton, the "Tea Room Lady," has been serving a variation on the same fixed, seasonal menu for over seventeen years. Lunch, on Wednesdays and Fridays from spring through late fall, could be a nonalcoholic apéritif and hors d'oeuvre in the historic canopy bedroom or soup, salad, quiche, and dessert on a three-season porch overlooking the Monches millpond or other patio areas. You need reservations for lunch (but your room includes a continental-plus breakfast).

Deborah chooses the ingredients for her lunches as if she's picking produce from her own garden—and sometimes she is. She says one of her guilty pleasures is to take her "wad of cash after the tea room closes and run over to Monches Farm" (see below) to stock up on herbs to plant in her own garden, which end up in the Monches Mill House kitchen. She also shops local, sustainable markets like the Fondy Market in Milwaukee's central city. What doesn't get consumed at lunch becomes dinner for her worm compost at her home or the chickens at the Mill House.

For recreation, you can drift in a canoe, play tennis on the grounds, or take a Jacuzzi in a solar-driven outbuilding. Monches Mill House is an Ice Age Trail Inn-to-Inn Hiking partner, so for a ten dollar fee you can arrange for transportation from the Monches Segment of the Ice Age Trail back to this otherworldly country landmark.

Deborah Clifton's Chilled Borscht

1 cup cooled, roasted beets
½ cup small onion, sliced
1 teaspoon salt
¼ teaspoon fresh ground pepper
2 tablespoons fresh lemon juice
1 medium boiled potato, peeled and diced
1 cup homemade chicken or vegetable stock (your recipe)
1 cup sour cream
1 cup cracked ice
¼ cup fresh dill, or one handful pulled from garden

Combine ingredients and blend until smooth. Sprinkle a little dill over top to your
visual liking.

With his three dogs—Stray Boy, Molly, and Ruby—Bill Livick runs the
Eagle Hostel, an Ice Age Trail Inn-to-Inn lodge between Eagle and Palmyra
just west of the Southern Unit of the Kettle Moraine State Forest headquarters. For just twenty-five dollars a night, you get a room in a refurbished
farmhouse set just steps away from the Ice Age Trail and less than a mile
from the Emma Carlin trailhead. Bill isn't set up for transporting Ice Age Trail
hikers, bikers, or skiers, but for a nominal fee he makes a dandy continental
breakfast using vegetables from his organic garden and eggs from neighbor
Dave Friewald's free-roaming chickens. He's open Friday and Saturday nights
but guests are required to leave the premises from 10 a.m. to 5 p.m.

The *Kettle Moraine State Forest–Southern Unit*, in the southwest corner of
Waukesha County, has a number of options for camping. Just north of Eagle
and east of Dousman, two campgrounds, Pine Woods and Ottawa Lake, are
just a few miles apart. Combined, they have two hundred sites. Some are

Ice Age Trail Inn-to-Inn

All along the Ice Age Trail, bed-and-breakfasts have signed on to help
trailblazers feel they have a home to relax in once they've logged their miles
either locally or across the thousand-mile state path. Book with one of nearly
fifty inn-to-inn participants across the state, and they might arrange to
transport you from their inn to your trailhead and back again for a nominal fee.

side by side with pit toilets and showers; others are walk-to sites that give you more of a sense of isolation. From your sites at Ottawa Lake Campground you can access nature trails or swim at the Ottawa Lake beach. About eight miles southwest of Palmyra, you can rough it at the Whitewater Lake Campground with its sixty-three primitive sites with pit toilets but no shower. You can also swim at the beach here. Equestrians have their own campground that is central to the forest where you and your horse will find thirty-five back-in sites, twenty pull-through sites, one group site accommodating up to twenty people, a picnic shelter, horse shower, manure deposit stations, drinking water, and pit toilets. There is a fee for camping in the Kettle Moraine Forest, and you'll need a state forest admission sticker. Trail fees may also apply.

Where to Eat

If your destination is the Retzer Nature Center (see below for more information) don't pass up *Good Harvest Market*, Waukesha County's largest natural food store, and its *Good Harvest Cafe*. It's just a short jog off of I-94 (exit 293) to the south. As at their Milwaukee location, they claim a 90 percent organic inventory that includes wine and beer and Good Harvest–made brats and sausage. They back their organic certification with a dedication to working with local growers of sustainably raised meat and poultry. Their fish comes from ecologically responsible fisheries and their produce is locally and organically grown. The Good Harvest Cafe serves vegetarian and vegan entrees, an all-organic salad bar, and two organic soups daily. The ingredients are purchased at area farms and the buy-local concept is promoted throughout the store and cafe.

Eleven miles south of La Grange, eleven miles southwest of East Troy, and sixteen miles south of Palmyra is the town of Elkhorn. The motto at the *Wildflower Cafe* is "As the garden grows, so changes the menu." At this six-table cafe, co-owners Sandy Fisher-McKee and Margaret Kowaleski serve a menu that revolves around the growing season. Sandy believes everyone should own a little square of land on which to plant a garden, and she carries that philosophy through at her restaurant where at least half of the items on the menu come from her backyard gardens and hoop house, plus a little patch of land she gardens in a neighbor's yard. And what she doesn't grow she tries to get locally and sustainably—even if it's purchased at a local grocery store. Think vegetarian lasagne, butternut squash soup, and bison burgers. The cafe furnishings are an eclectic blend of secondhand everything, reflecting their belief that it's better to fill the space with things that already have a history but can still be put to good use. Sandy knows they'd make better money if she served up a traditional short-order breakfast and lunch, but this is about sharing experience and high quality food with customers. The Wildflower Cafe is open for lunch Tuesday through Friday and Friday nights for a nontraditional fish fry.

Local Foraging

Their chickens may drop eggs of a different color but what they all have in common is a happy home life at *The Robin's Nest.* Owner Robin Gedney raises happy chickens just off Highway 83 on County Highway E, just southeast of Lapham Peak and northwest of the Kettle Moraine Forest. You can have yours blue-green, brown, or white, but regardless of your color preference, these eggs all hail from cage-free, grass-fed, happy-as-a-clam chickens. Call Robin and tell her that you're coming first, since she's a soccer mom to three small kids.

You may not necessarily want to meet the cow you're taking home wrapped in paper, but knowing the people who raised it is a great idea. Ten years ago Will and Sue Halser at *Prairie Hill Farms* in Palmyra switched from conventional farming to rotation grazing, and they welcome visitors to come see how healthy and happy their animals really are. Go there for beef, lamb, poultry, eggs, and rabbit. They recommend you call ahead to make sure they're home.

Greg and Pat Kummrow raise bison and beef on the land that once belonged to Greg's grandfather, and they live in the house in which Greg was raised. At *Battle Creek Beef and Bison,* the Kummrows use a tractor that dates back to 1948. Their newest one was purchased in 1966, probably not too long after Greg was born. Today their farming practices have switched from conventional to sustainable, with a herd that's grass-fed in warm months and, in winter months, fed on chemical-free hay grown right there. You can buy their good beef and bison on the farm Thursday through Saturday, or anytime you catch them when they're home. Plus you can pick up some Battle Creek–made sausage and a dozen of their farm fresh eggs. On Memorial Day the farm is open for animal viewing and customer education. They call it Baby Bison Viewing Day. Repeat baby-bison gawkers come in droves every year, but maybe it's for the local FFA-grilled bison burgers. They're located just off I-94 on Delafield Road. Go south at the Willow Glen exit.

If you'd prefer to meet your fish grower and see how cushy a life your trout really has, bikers on the Emma Carlin Trail can easily visit *Rushing Waters Fisheries* in Palmyra, where the trouts' lives are as green as their gills. These rainbow trout and salmon are raised in very cold water (49 degrees) in a certified organic environment and are fed non-animal byproduct feed. If you order your salmon or trout twenty-four hours ahead of time, it will still be trying to swim upstream when your order is taken. That's about as fresh as a fish dinner gets when it wasn't caught on your own line.

Here's perhaps the mother of all meet-your-grower opportunities. Visit the Fields Neighborhood, which is located next door to (but is a separate entity from) the Michael Fields Agricultural Institute, south of Palmyra in East Troy. This might be the healthiest community on earth—certainly in Wisconsin. These lucky condo-dwellers live in homes designed to be the greenest in the state, with community interaction as a core value and community gardens as part of the plan. After walking their prairie trails, tour the *Michael Fields Agricultural Institute*, a teaching farm next door that trains individuals how to work the land organically and biodynamically—that is, in very simple terms, the farmer composts the manure from the animals on the farm to use as fertilizer in the fields that grow the food that feeds the people and the animals on the farm who create the manure.

Next door at *Local Industry*, East Troy native Tom McCormick bakes and sells artisan breads and bakery. On Fridays Tom makes pizza using produce he picks out next door at Stella Gardens and Farm, the six hundred acre organic/biodynamic instructional "classroom" at the Michael Fields Institute. Tom also promotes local farmers and businesses by stocking his bakery with local items like produce and flowers, Sasha's Salad and Sandwich Dressing, Anodyne's fair trade coffee, and local art. His long-term goal is to create a network from which local businesses can sell their goods. So get your baked goods there and then saunter through the Fields Neighborhood prairie gardens, which include 8,500 native plants and over a hundred species with many trails throughout. One leads to Honey Creek, whose watershed is protected from the neighborhood's runoff through a delicate retention pond system that includes rain gardens and wetlands. The institute and neighborhood encourage visitors to come to their community, walk their gardens, and possibly leave more environmentally enlightened.

Just north of Elkhorn on County Trunk ES in East Troy, *Quednow's Heirloom Apple Orchard*'s farm stand sells produce and apples from an orchard where conventional harsh pesticide use has been replaced with integrated pest management, as well as peaches, apples, and blackberries from a smaller orchard where no synthetic pesticides have been used. They also grow produce for the Wildflower Cafe in Elkhorn.

The *Delafield Farmers' Market* features locally grown vegetables and fruit, fresh and dried flowers, perennials and bedding plants, homemade bakery products, and a variety of arts and crafts. It runs from May through October every Saturday in the Fish Hatchery parking lot, just west of Genesee Street (County Road C), 514 West Main Street.

The *Waukesha Farmers' Market* is located on the banks of the Fox River in historic downtown Waukesha between Broadway and Barstow, just east of 332 Riverfront Plaza. It runs every Saturday from the second weekend in May through October.

The *East Troy Farmers' Market* is held every Thursday from June through October at the East Troy Village Square.

What to Do

More Wordsworthian beauty calls out at *Monches Farm*, a stone's throw from Monches Mill House on Monches Road, where no garden stone has been left unturned. Scott Sieckman and Matt Kastell own and operate a fourteen-acre nursery not of your ordinary cottage garden variety. Thick sprigs of Russian sage and knotty yellow yarrow shoot up tall alongside tossed bronzed pots and clay pots and garden angels and concrete garden benches. Woven baskets and painted urns and cherubic angels meet head-on with an eclectic weaving of architectural salvage–turned–yard ornaments. And that's just for starters. Their greenhouse has had many lives. First it was part of a large wholesale commercial greenhouse business in Brown Deer that was shut down. Then it was salvaged and reassembled in another location about a mile west of Monches Farm. From there it was reincarnated at Monches Farm, about fifteen years ago. Scott reconfigured it somewhat but it "remains true to its old roots, so to speak." The property is also home to a flock of sheep whose wool ends up woven into blankets that are sold in the Monches Farm's gift house.

But there's more. At home, Kastell and Sieckman live holistically and largely off the land. Their homestead sits on 120 organic acres where Kastell and Sieckman have relocated and restored historic structures that were about to tumble. Materials such as timbers, doors, stone, and brick were reused. And if that is not enough hunting and gathering, Kastell, a German immigrant who brought with him to America his hardy German traditions, says they grow a lot of their food, which makes for a summer of intensive canning, from pickling cucumbers to fermenting beans in stone crocks (see sidebar recipe on page 69).

Future plans might include an open house, as a model that personifies living in harmony with the land. Stay tuned! Meanwhile, check the farm Web site for special classes and spring and fall open houses.

Up the road, environmentally conscious golfers will find reason to lace up their cleats and head for *Erin Hills*. This green golf course is designed around the land with the purpose of connecting golfers to the natural landscape. It is a critically acclaimed course, considered to be a world class act that will host a world class event when the U.S. Amateur Championship is held there in 2011.

"Green" has loads of meaning at Erin Hills, located outside the little town of Erin, just six miles north of North Lake on County Road O. Here green can refer to the rolling fairways of the barely touched terrain that makes up this naturalized, eighteen-hole golf course. It can symbolize the area's Irish settlers who chose to farm on land that most closely resembled their homeland (or that's the theory). Or it can stand for owner Bob Lang's own Irish sensibility. Or its fieldstone-and-cedar clubhouse, which has the feel of an Irish inn, housing an Irish pub and seven charming European-style guest rooms where guests are served breakfast made from ingredients sourced at local markets. But perhaps most significant is its low environmental impact and the sensitive land management that went into the site's design and excavation, like the decision to move as little of this glacially toppled land as possible. In keeping with the management's sustainable sensibility, chemical herbicides are used on an as-needed rather than a preventive basis, meaning less than half the amount of treatments are applied than at conventional courses. And because the fairways and rough are planted with drought-resistant native fine fescue grasses, little water and fertilizer are ever used, making this a logical site for Audubon certification. You golf while sandhill cranes saunter the greens, call out from the marshland, or fly overhead—just one frequent wildlife sighting at these amazing, no-guilt links.

Erin Hills boasts a grand view of Holy Hill from its eighteenth hole. But you'd be doing yourself a favor by having a close-up look at this minor basilica, which stands eighteen hundred feet above sea level, for its spectacular views of the lush and rolling hills of Washington County. The *Basilica of Holy Hill*, a historic sacred site and a registered state and national landmark, is a multitiered cathedral with a 178-step tower overlooking four hundred acres of pristine forest, the height of which some think puts you closer to the very source with whom they pilgrimage there to convene. Whether your quest is spiritual, historical, or geographical, the place is an architectural wonder of steeples and shrines, biblical-themed stained-glass windows, and one heavenly view.

Seven miles east of Elkhorn is the *Northwind Perennial Farm*. This ten-acre garden nursery is beyond expectation. Its sustainable gardening practices are a special bonus to its storybook charm that reflects the sometimes mind-boggling creativity of its three owners, each of whom has a hand in its success. Roy Diblik is best known for his work growing and installing thousands of plants at the Lurie Garden at Chicago's Millennium Park. Steve Coster runs the environmentally responsible landscape design element. And Colleen Garrigan runs the garden shop in the nursery's hundred-year-old barn. Its Web site has a list of events and workshops that can help you plan a garden with native plants and perennials or create something artistic from objects found in nature. It's also worth just roaming the property on a gorgeous day or to turn an unremarkable day gorgeous.

Waukesha County's *Kettle Moraine State Forest–Southern Unit* is a formidable twenty-one thousand acres that include the Scuppernong River Habitat Area, just northwest of Eagle, the largest wet prairie (thirty-five hundred acres) this side of the Mississippi River (and that's no adage). Because the ride is a rugged tour of kettles, kames, and eskers left behind by bull-dozing

This greenhouse had many lives before being salvaged and reassembled at Monches Farm in the mid-1990s. (photo supplied by Monches Farm)

glacial ice sheets more than ten thousand years ago, literally thousands of mountain bikers flock to the forest's John Muir Trail and Emma Carlin Trail, located just outside the Waukesha County line in La Grange (Walworth County) and Palmyra (Jefferson County), respectively. But to put traction on these trails, all you really need to know is that they are a gritty rustic ride. These one-way trails provide a sense of privacy and are well marked, preventing a collision course for hikers and bikers. The forest also offers hikers a rare opportunity to meander through native flowers and grasses and the wildlife that thrive within them at the Scuppernong River Habitat Area's two natural areas, the Kettle Moraine Low Prairie State Natural Area and the Scuppernong Prairie State Natural Area, both located just outside of Eagle. With only 1 percent left of what was once millions of acres of Wisconsin prairieland, this is one hike on which you should stop to smell the, well, *Liatris spicata*. If you're really lucky, you may spot a rare two-sided skipper. Motor vehicles will need a state forest admission sticker.

If you're headed to the Kettle Moraine Forest via I-94, take the County Road C exit and stop at *Lapham Peak State Park* for twenty-one miles of hiking trails, seventeen miles of cross-country ski trails, and five miles of mountain bike trails. In fall, the forty-five-foot observation tower provides a view of the spectacular autumn palette sweeping across Waukesha County's lake country.

East of the Kettle Moraine Forest and west of the city of Waukesha you'll find the *Retzer Nature Center,* the ninety-acre homestead that Florence Retzer donated to Waukesha County. This is where she and her husband, John, had already restored their once barren farmland to a native prairie on a grand scale. Her vision for her beloved homestead was "to conserve the scenery, natural life, and wildlife, leaving the land unimpaired for the enjoyment of future generations." Over thirty years and three hundred more acres later, the Retzer Nature Center has accomplished that goal. The Environmental Learning Center uses itself as a model for conservation and how to connect people to the land. Visitors will find an eight-hundred-foot paved trail designated for people with disabilities that traverses grass prairie restoration sites and woodlands. There are also thirty interpretive Braille and raised-letter signs. The center's Charles Z. Horwitz Planetarium and the Environmental Learning Center offer programs throughout the year.

Lack of gear is no excuse for avoiding the *Ice Age National Scenic Trail* or the Kettle Moraine State Forest with *Backyard Bikes and Ski* located in the La Grange General Store west of East Troy, just two miles from the John Muir Trail or seven miles from Emma Carlin Trail. These guys are serious about getting you active with rentals on everything from skate skis to mountain bikes to snowshoes. They also have a weekly schedule of organized rides that leave from the store, and some good healthy food in the cafe-deli. You can sign up on their Web site for the annual Fall Color Festival sponsored by Trek, Wheel and Sprocket, and La Grange General Store/Backyard Bikes and Ski. This festival has mountain bikers signing up in droves to raise money for maintenance of the John Muir Trail. Once it's been groomed, the remainder goes to the Southern Kettle Moraine Forest DNR.

If you're closer to Lapham Peak, you can get your rentals and maps of area trails at *Wheel and Sprocket* in downtown Delafield, less than a mile north of I-94 on County Road C, the same road that leads south to Lapham Peak.

Sauere Bohnen (sour/fermented beans)

This recipe is from the Rhine area in Germany. People there have used this method of preserving for hundreds of years. These beans make a wonderful fall or winter meal, serve with mashed potatoes and smoked pork chops. This is my grandmother's recipe. I hope you will enjoy it.

Fresh green beans need to be washed and ends cut off. After cleaning the beans shred them coarsely the long way.

Take a stoneware crock and wash it out with hot water.

Per 10 pounds of beans use 300 grams (1 cup) of salt.

Mix the salt into the shredded beans. Create a layer of organic grape leaves in the bottom of the crock and add beans and savory (a couple sprigs of fresh savory per pound of beans) in layers and press them down.

After all the beans are in the crock, cover them with a layer of organic grape leaves and then with a flour sack towel. (This towel needs to be washed out once a week or so.)

Place a round piece of hard wood, slightly smaller than the crock, onto the beans. Weigh it down with a heavy rock and cover the crock with a lid or plate. Liquid from the beans should cover the wood after a couple days; if not, cook a salt brine, let cool and add to the crock.

A natural fermenting process will take place, similar to sauerkraut. The beans should be done within four to six weeks. Store them in a cool basement.

To cook the beans, glaze onion in some butter and add the beans, a couple pieces of bacon, and some water. Cook the beans until tender. To finish them off, make a sauce by mixing some flour in water and add it to the beans. If the beans are very sour add a little sugar.

—Matt Kastell

Lake Michigan's Harbor Towns

Port Washington and Sheboygan Area

Everything in nature transforms itself from one form into another as nature's way of recycling.

—NEK CHAND, self-taught artist

If you take I-43 straight up the eastern side of the state to the tip of the peninsula, along the way you pass exits leading to Wisconsin's Lake Michigan coastal towns. While this drive may initially feel like a flat straight shot to nowhere, don't be fooled. It doesn't have the peaks and valleys of Wisconsin's western Driftless Area because the eastern and central part of the state is where the glacier did much of its bidding. But if you take the roads east you will hit the luscious lake and a couple of its sweet harbor towns, Port Washington and Sheboygan. Go west and you will find sustainable agriculture in many forms, small historic burgs, and state and county parks with multiple trails serving as many purposes.

When the sun ramps up temps in the rest of the state, these little coastal towns promise air cooled by one of the largest fresh water lakes on earth. In winter months, they're a few degrees warmer. Their shorelines promise the squawking of sea gulls above the clanking of moored boats colliding with chunky piers. There are vintage lighthouses to be toured, and when humidity rolls out the fog layers, the combination of cool lake air and the call from a distant fog horn can stir chills from head to toe.

Both of these towns enjoy healthy marine activity, show off vintage architecture, and offer museums celebrating Great Lakes sailors and their storm-lost rigs. Each is also linked to other towns and attractions by county- and city-sponsored bike trails.

Sheboygan, once primarily known as a sausage capital of the Midwest, has shaken that cheesy title with its impressive Kohler-backed cultural attractions.

And its natural attractions stand today as ever. Ripe with some of Wisconsin's most celebrated natural areas—the sand-duned Kohler-Andrae beaches and the Ice Age National Scenic Trail, which links over a thousand miles of terrain tossed and tumbled by glacial ice—the area is a hiker, biker, paddler paradise. Stay in Port Washington, home to one B&B whose owners' longtime understanding of energy efficiency benefits the earth and their business. Then eat, bike, and play in Sheboygan and the surrounding area. Tour a family farm, then eat slow food at a restaurant where the fruits of many other Wisconsin sustainable farm laborers will likely end up.

Where to Stay

Perched atop a hilly street overlooking the Port Washington harbor is the *Port Washington Inn*, a bed-and-breakfast so clean you might not hesitate to eat off its third-story laundry room floors—equipped with two Energy Star–certified front-loaders. This clean sensibility carries over in most of the decisions made by owners Rita and Dave Nelson, starting with the many energy-efficient details they've incorporated into their daily maintenance of this 1903 structure of eclectic design. With as many as three different window treatments on windows throughout the inn, the Nelsons are able to benefit from or eliminate the passive solar energy produced daily throughout each season. Guest rooms and common areas offer ambient and task lighting using compact fluorescent lights wherever possible. Guests enjoy the results of the innkeepers' "behind the scenes" environmental efforts.

Hailing from Iowa, the Nelsons are seasoned backyard vegetable growers, known as respectful land stewards in this residential neighborhood for their composting and mulching of flowerbeds and vegetable and herb gardens. Several years of gardening and inn keeping convinced them to focus on flowers and to frequent the local farmers' markets (highlighted on their Web site blog) for vegetables.

Herbs, rhubarb, and onions still find their place in the inn's gardens and are well utilized in the energy-efficient, state-of-the-art kitchen where full breakfasts are prepared for guests. Gourmet, "from scratch" picnics are also offered from May to October for guests to take with them on the Interurban Trail or to local parks or nature preserves.

When the Wisconsin food cooperative that supplied many of the Nelsons' cooking staples ceased operations in 2008, finding alternative sources for high quality ingredients became a process of research and discovery. One of their favorite resources is Frontier Natural Products Co-op (www.frontiercoop.com), from which they order personal care products that are easy on the senses and on the skin. Guests whose lives are plagued by allergies find the Port Washington Inn a hospitable environment.

The Port Washington Inn has three guest rooms and two guest suites, one on the second floor and the largest on the third floor. The bonus for most travelers might not be the Nelsons' natural sensibility about good business and environmental stewardship but their spacious rooms and tasteful décor. The inn is simply and handsomely decorated, sans the frilly Victorian details so common to Wisconsin B&B's. Each room exhibits a blend of nineteenth- and turn-of-the-twentieth-century antiques, vintage pieces, and furniture reproductions crafted by Dave and son Aaron out of decades-old walnut harvested from Iowa farms.

As the Nelsons strive to cut down on their carbon footprint, grass (and the need to mow it) is increasingly replaced by a mix of perennials, shrubs, groundcovers, and bricked walkways. They've even found new homes for the rock and stone that were unearthed as they landscaped. Certified by Travel Green Wisconsin, the inn lives up to its claim of being one of the Milwaukee area's greenest overnight stops amid scores of competitors.

Where to Eat

The *Java Dock Cafe* is a little Port Washington coffeehouse that gets kudos for its contribution to sustainable practices. Here fair trade or locally roasted organic Alterra coffee is served along with conventionally grown roasts. But its real global greater good is in the fair trade imported merchandise sold here. Bracelets, pens, hair ties, jewelry, and other handmade merchandise carry information on their country of origin and the families that will benefit from your purchase.

While many of the ingredients of chef-owner Stefano Viglietti's three Sheboygan restaurants—Trattoria Stefano, Il Ritrovo, and the Duke of Devon—come straight from the fields of Italy, and they really do, he doesn't overlook the neighborhood farmers. His fourth restaurant, *Field to Fork*, keeps things very local, helping to offset those carbon emissions. As a member of Home Grown Wisconsin and a supporter of the International Slow Food Movement, the Field to Fork menu comes from the fields of twenty-five family farms that have adopted a system of getting their food to their members' tables in less than a day. Stefano's Market, the little grocery shop that's tucked in between Il Ritrovo and Field to Fork, also features local artisan cheese and in-house baked bread and other sustainably produced canned and packaged foods. The Trempealeau Hotel walnut burger at Field to Fork is among the best this side of the Mississippi River, next to the hotel's itself.

Local Foraging

Beechwood Cheese Company is located twenty miles west of Cedar Grove in the town of Beechwood on County Road A. Established in about 1894, the company passed through the hands of many cheesemakers until Norbert Heise took ownership in 1956 with his wife, Evangeline. Today their son, Mark, and his wife, Kris (famous for her chicken soup cheese), run the small family business and buy their milk from area family farmers. On the first Saturday of every month people flock to "Almost Famous Cheese Curd Day" when Beechwood Cheese unloads fifteen hundred pounds of cheese to loyal customers. And while their flavors aren't locally grown, the Heises do claim they're all natural.

Autumn bikers along the Old Plank Road Trail can take a short detour west on County Road E to the *Log Cabin Orchard* in Plymouth for minimally sprayed Cortland and Macintosh apples, pears, plums, fresh apple cider, maple syrup, apple syrup, honey, and apple butter.

Port Washington Farmers' Market, located at North Franklin and East Main streets, runs from early July to late October on Saturday mornings.

What to Do

At the end of Port Washington's breakwater is an art deco lighthouse, built in 1935 (you can see the top of it from the Port Washington Inn). While not open for viewing, its exterior architecture is unusual and worth seeing against the Lake Michigan shoreline. The historic 1860 light station is home to the *Light Station Museum* of the Port Washington Historical Society. Its tower and lantern room, destroyed in 1934, have been reproduced to their original configuration. Part of the station has been restored to 1860 and furnished with 1860–1934 furniture. It also houses a two-bedroom apartment that's leased out for a year at a time, just for the experience. The station is open from early May until mid-October, but you can tour it year round by appointment.

In 1894 the *Lottie Cooper* capsized and sank just off the Sheboygan harbor. During the construction of Sheboygan's Harbor Centre Marina, its remains were recovered and dry-docked on the shore. You can view what's left of this historic three-masted lumber schooner on the Sheboygan waterfront in Deland Park as a wonderful little slice of the Great Lakes' maritime history.

Ozaukee County is peppered with numerous historic downtowns that are linked together by the *Ozaukee Interurban Trail*, a thirty-mile path that follows the route of the former rapid transit system (purchased by the Milwaukee Electric Railway and Light Company in the 1920s), which connected Milwaukee and Sheboygan from 1905 to 1951. This trail, designated for nonmotorized vehicles only, is now a foot and bike path as well as a cross-country ski path in winter months. It's designed to link the historic Ozaukee communities of Mequon, Thiensville, Cedarburg, Grafton, Port Washington, and Belgium with the county's natural landscape. You can go online and download the *Ozaukee Trailside Birding Guide* to take along for a detailed schedule of the glorious bird habitats tucked into the path's woods and wetlands and the Milwaukee River corridor. Sensitive conservation areas are also included in this guide. This trail then continues into Sheboygan County.

Biking Sheboygan might be the sustainable traveler's best bet for reducing carbon emissions on a trip that can require time in the car and fuel to keep you moving, unless you originate somewhere between Port Washington and Sheboygan. On a bike, you can arrive in Sheboygan and pick up the *Sheboygan Urban Rec Trail*, a 4.25-mile path that takes bikers and hikers from Sheboygan's west end right down to its Lake Michigan harbor. The routes are clearly marked. It traverses parks and green spaces, winds through historic residential and commercial districts, and provides access to Sheboygan's central business district, as well as numerous scenic, historical, cultural, and recreational sites. Designated as a bicycle trail, it is also suitable for walkers and in-line skaters. At its west end, the trail connects with the *Old Plank Road Trail*, a seventeen-mile multiuse trail that connects Sheboygan with the communities of Greenbush, Plymouth, Sheboygan Falls, and Kohler.

If you'd rather see the area by boat, rent a kayak at *Expedition Outdoor Supply* on South Pier Drive, located on the Sheboygan River. *Ecology Outfitters* in Sheboygan will bring you kayaks, life jackets, splash skirts, and pumps, and teach you the ropes, such as how to save yourself if you tip and roll, and then send you out onto Lake Michigan or down the Sheboygan River for a couple of hours. Or they'll guide you for the same price. And if you're ambitious, they'll give you private lessons. In the winter months, Ecology Outfitters will deliver cross-country skis and snowshoes to tackle the paths at Kohler-Andrae State Park, the Kettle Moraine State Forest, or the Maywood Environmental Park. You can also go to their store, where they carry everything you need for silent sports, including several lines of outerwear that's organic, clay dyed, and fairly traded. They also carry a handmade and organic soap line, Healing Origins, made in Mishicot.

The *Henry S. Reuss Ice Age Visitor Center*, twenty-nine miles west of Sheboygan in Fond Du Lac County, is set within the *Kettle Moraine State Forest–
Northern Unit* in the town of Dundee. This is the part of Wisconsin that
moved Ray Zillmer, the founding father of the Ice Age National Scenic Trail,
to envision a thousand-mile footpath to follow the effects of the continental
glaciers as they moved through the state as long ago as 1.8 million years and
as recently as 10,000 years. Through educating the public about the Ice Age's
historic effects on our state, the center commemorates the Ice Age Trail's
most ardent backer, Henry Reuss, the Wisconsin congressman who advanced
the idea and promoted its development. It now links northwestern Wisconsin at Interstate Park on the St. Croix River with northeastern Wisconsin at
Potawatomi State Part in Door County.

Within the twenty-nine thousand acres of Kettle Moraine State Forest you
will find kettles, kames, and eskers that tell the story of the many glacial lobes
that carved out much of our Wisconsin landscape. At the nature center you
will find everything you need to know about this amazing geological fossil and
can join a naturalist program-sponsored walk, talk, or hike through the forest.
The northern part of the forest has biking paths. If you launch a bike on the
Old Plank Road Trail in Sheboygan, you can ride it clear out to Greenbush.
Once there, follow the Kettle Moraine Scenic Drive (marked with green acorn
signs) to the Greenbush Recreation area, a hilly trail system through the Kettle Moraine Forest that can be used for hiking and mountain biking (see the
Elkhart Lake chapter). Other larger, more irregularly shaped kettles within
the Northern Unit include the area between the Ice Age Trail and Long Lake
(see map at Kettle Moraine–Northern Unit Web site), which is said to contain
one of the most striking groups of kames (deposits left by retreating glaciers that form a hill or mound) to be found anywhere in the world. Dundee,
Johnson, and McMullen hills are some of the best known and can be viewed
from atop the Parnell Observation Tower (see the Elkhart Lake chapter).

The *Kohler-Andrae State Park* at Lake Michigan, just south of Sheboygan,
is known for its sand dunes and extensive white sandy shoreline through
which the Creeping Juniper Shoreline Trail winds. Within the park are a number of other trails, such as the Woodland Dunes Nature Trail, which explores
the park's diversified tree life; the Black River Marsh Boardwalk, which skims
over wetlands and nesting ponds and offers an opportunity for hikers to sit
and observe; and the Dunes Cordwalk, a series of boards and ropes that create
a trail through the dunes with three lookout points, including a rare inter-
dunal marsh area. Dogs are welcome here.

Ellwood H. May Environmental Park, or Maywood, is a City of Sheboygan–owned, 135-acre urban natural area in the Pigeon River corridor that promotes environmentally responsible life choices through hands-on experiences. It hosts local food fairs that promote slow food and local farmers and offers bird walks, eco-camps, and a host of other classes and activities that put people closer to the land around them and the wildlife within it. Its many trails can be cross-country skied or hiked, and it's free of charge.

Halfway between Port Washington and Sheboygan, in the town of Cedar Grove, is a five-generation family farm, the *Bahr Creek Llamas and Fiber Studio.* Originally a Holstein ranch, Bahr Creek has branched out and is now also dedicated to their new love of raising llamas. Here you can buy fiber spun almost right off the backs of their beloved herd or you can learn how to spin it yourself. Owner Bridget DeMaster offers spinning and weaving classes that are largely self-designed. Call her or check out her Web site to take a class or workshop using materials grown and harvested right on the ranch. You can even get on your bike in Port Washington and take it all the way to Cedar Grove via the Sheboygan County leg of the Interurban Trail.

Dear Old Books in downtown Plymouth is a destination along the Old Plank Road Trail. This is a full-service used bookstore that has fifteen thousand rare and gently used books in stock and offers free book searches. Then head over to the *Exchange Bank Coffeehouse* in the historic Exchange Bank Building. Here you can get a cup of Milwaukee's responsibly roasted Alterra coffee and a slice of quiche made from local organic eggs. The place is filled with quality local art.

Local Arts

In Sheboygan, the *John Michael Kohler Arts Center*'s mission may be to preserve our artistic landscape while inspiring others to culturally and creatively prosper, but its permanent collection of Wisconsin outsider art is perhaps the most stunning example of reclaim and reuse of both natural and manmade materials around. From the scrap iron bird sculptures of Tom Every that greet you at the center's entrance walkway to the concrete and stone castles that lead you, circuitously, into the center's front door, this collection illustrates concrete and fabric artist Nek Chand's belief that "everything in nature transforms itself from one form into another as nature's way of recycling." He and other artists in the center's collection imaginatively incorporate found or used objects, like scrap iron, rock, boulders, ceramic, glass shards, and building waste—in Chand's case, contents from destroyed villages in India—into the spaces in which they lived, their homes, yards, and personal surroundings. The center also offers classes and workshops for children and adults. Between the center's organic architectural design and its fabulous contents, this is one spot near the Lake Michigan shoreline that shouldn't be missed.

Just south of Sheboygan, James Tellen spent the last ten or so years of his life sculpting his legacy out of concrete. What he left when he died in 1957 was thirty life-size sculptures that now make up the *James Tellen Woodland Sculpture Garden*. It surrounds his modest cabin near the Lake Michigan shoreline and has been restored by the John Michael Kohler Arts Center. Tellen was a self-taught artist and used nature-derived images that depict simple country life—men on horses, men chopping wood, people gathered for devotion—all set where Tellen left them. You'll have to call the John Michael Kohler Arts Center to tour this folk art exhibit, but it will be worth the effort.

The Baraboo Hills,
a True American Relic

Wisconsin Dells Area

> Failing this, it seems to me we fail in the ultimate test of our vaunted
> superiority—the self-control of environment. We fall back into the
> biological category of the potato bug which exterminated the potato,
> and thereby exterminated itself.
>
> —ALDO LEOPOLD, *The River of the Mother of God*

Some know the Baraboo Hills in Sauk County as the Last Great Place, as
the Nature Conservancy called it for being one of the most important areas
for biological diversity in the Western Hemisphere. Others know it for its
quartzite escarpments, one of the most ancient rock outcroppings in North
America. Still others just pass through en route to the Wisconsin Dells. With
Highway 12 cutting through Sauk City and Baraboo, it can be a road or bike
trip through Wisconsin's most important ecological landscape. Or it can be
appreciated simply for its breathtaking views.

This is a trip led by a bounty of environmental stewards. Tucked inside and
out of these communities are amazing ecological landmarks and impressive
environmental institutions that celebrate and advance the health of the land
and the wildlife that depend on it, starting with a spectacular natural attraction, the Wisconsin River. This cold, fast river snakes its way right down the
center of the state before heading west to the Mississippi River. Here water
enthusiasts come from all over to paddle its whitewater rapids and camp on
its sandy islands. Ornithologists (and just plain sight-seers) gather to docu-
ment the eagles that gather to roost and fish on its open winter waters before
heading back home to the Northwoods in warmer months. Farther north in
Baraboo, you can visit the International Crane Foundation, which takes loving care of these highly valued birds. And just east of the hills, Aldo Leopold's
legacy is carried out through the care of the land on which he erected his

modest cottage (The Shack), taught his children to tread lightly, and culti-
vated Wisconsin's indigenous plants and wildlife.

Stop at Devil's Lake State Park to bike a two-mile trail into downtown
Baraboo—or the other way around. Climb a quartzite bluff or swim in a
plugged gap in the south range of the Baraboo Hills, rock deposits left there
by the gasp of an ancient glacial flow. You can visit farms devoted to promoting one of Wisconsin's most important industries, dairy production, with
sustainability as their driving force, and eat at a local restaurant that knows
that using ingredients grown just a few miles from its kitchen sustains a local
economy while giving back to the land.

This is a route that takes you to Mirror Lake, where you can rent a place
built by Wisconsin's beloved son Frank Lloyd Wright and where his organic
architecture enhances rather than fights the natural elements surrounding
it. Or, if you prefer, stay at a spa on the outskirts of the Wisconsin Dells
that borrowed Wright's philosophy and combined it with the serenity of the
eastern belief that less is more and quieting the mind creates harmony with
nature.

The ancient Baraboo Hills are called one of the "Last Great Places" by The Nature
Conservancy because they are the oldest formations of metamorphic quartzite rock
in the Western Hemisphere. (photo by Kate Galantha)

Where to Stay

As it turns out, Wisconsin Dells and sustainable hospitality are not mutually exclusive. While there are water parks that have incorporated environmentally friendly practices into their economic development plan, none has cornered the sustainable travel market in the Lake Delton area quite like *Sundara Inn and Spa*.

This is a home-grown resort conceived on the holistic lifestyle principles of its founder and former owner, Wisconsin Dells native and secretary of Wisconsin's Department of Tourism, Kelli Trumble. Achieving sustainability, harmony, and balance was Trumble's goal even before she saw her plans drawn up on paper. If this was accomplished, she felt, the rest would come. And it did. Since then Trumble has sold her interest in Sundara, but her vision is solidly intact.

Thoughtfully carved into a twenty-six-acre parcel of mature pines, Sundara has become world renowned for its advancement of inner health. It's Travel Green Wisconsin–certified and is one of a select group of North American spas (called Founding Seed Spas) chosen by Green Spa Network to lead the industry in its initiative to promote environmentally responsible practices. Every step in the development of Sundara was done with the planet in mind, starting with minimal removal of trees during construction to preserve the green space. The Cambrian sand unearthed in the excavating stage became a staple ingredient in the Sundara Sandstone Body Polish product. The building was designed to capitalize on open spaces, natural energy, and ambient light—the windows were placed to maximize and minimize the solar effects of the sun and the natural views that surround the structure. Even the turquoise infinity pool feels indigenous to the property.

The same feng shui principles of Sundara's main resort—sustainability, harmony, and balance—apply to the property's luxurious private villas. The expansive floor-to-ceiling windows hold views of nearby waterfalls, gardens, and woods. The largest units have a central three-way fireplace, state-of-the-art kitchen, wraparound veranda, and a private master suite with a featherbed, fireplace, and "bath sanctuary." Day and overnight guests are equals with access to the same amenities—the purifying bath, fresh fruit and water in the relaxation room, and the infinity pool services.

Birchcliff Resort—the first place in the Dells to be awarded Travel Green Wisconsin certification—may be in the Dells, but owners Dailene and Joseph Malacina run a peaceful country resort, not a water park. On the wooded grounds, log-style cabins sleep two to ten people. Ten newer cabins (four are duplexes) were constructed with an eye to energy conservation, a priority for the owners. The seven older, rustic cabins and original lodge yield a pleasant ambiance reminiscent of earlier, quieter days in the Northwoods.

Activities like Ping-Pong, horseshoes, shuffleboard, basketball, and tennis offer old-fashioned, earth-friendly fun, and the outdoor swimming pool is solar heated. A hiking trail provides access to the Wisconsin River, yet a substantial wooded buffer between the cabins and the river protects the river's ecosystems.

As part of their environmentally friendly approach to inn-keeping, the Malacinas use biodegradable cleaning products and detergents, have installed low-flow fixtures and compact fluorescent lights, are replacing refrigerators with Energy Star models, and have a recycling program. They plan to install solar panels for hot water heat. For themselves and their family, the owners grow their own vegetables and buy local and organic foods. For their guests, they recommend the High Rock Cafe, which features local foods.

The owners offer packages that help guests discover the natural settings of the Dells area and enjoy local and organic foods. The resort is closed in the winter, so they don't have to heat those log cabins.

In the woods of Mirror Lake, just west of Wisconsin Dells, Frank Lloyd Wright built the *Seth Peterson Cottage* in 1958. It was found in a shambles in the 1970s by the late Audrey Laatsch, a Mirror Lake cottage owner. Laatsch was instrumental in having it restored to its original splendor and served as the founding president of the Seth Peterson Cottage Conservancy, a nonprofit group organized to help save and restore the deteriorating architectural relic.

This cottage was Wright's last Wisconsin commission and was completed during his lifetime. It was the first and only Wright-designed house available to the general public for rental use when it opened in 1992. This 880-square-foot beauty, perched on a continuous slope down to Mirror Lake, embodies Wright's design principles so completely that Wes Peters, the head of Taliesin Associated Architects after Wright's death, said it has more architecture per square foot than any other building he knew of. If you're patient about waiting lists, as it can take up to five months to become available, you can experience the serenity of his simple, organic architectural style firsthand. Or you can see it when it's open for tours the second Sunday of every month. It's a Wisconsin original, now owned by the State of Wisconsin and the Department of Natural Resources.

Where to Eat

Not everything you'll find in Wisconsin Dells has as much class as the second-generation family-run *Del-Bar* restaurant on the strip. But if you're staying at the Seth Peterson Cottage, this place just might complete your travel circle. Established in 1943 as a log cabin bar, it has morphed over the years into a James Dresser–designed, Frank Lloyd Wright–inspired, Prairie-style establishment. Second-generation owners Jeff and Jane Wimmers' appreciation for simplicity and elegance comes through in the food as well as the décor. Jane says the classic Wisconsin supper-club fare includes local Country Bumpkin Farm produce, local and regional Amish-raised chicken, Neuske's pork, and a variety of Wisconsin cheeses. The food is pricey but consistently very good.

The Cheese Factory is actually a vegetarian-vegan restaurant housed in a former cheese factory. It serves Wisconsin cheese; it's just not made on site. The focus is not necessarily on local ingredients, but the quality of the food is great and the restaurant is run by a group of people whose mission is to spread their appreciation for life, defined by its daily miracles. You may not subscribe to their philosophy, but you just might subscribe to their taste and find yourself filling a to-go bag with some of their wonderful bakery items made by specific bakers who do their one thing very well. The Cheese Factory is on Highway 12 next to the Wilderness Resort, not far from Sundara Spa.

Local Foraging

Carr Valley Cheese is an award-winning, family-owned business that's as old as the hills, just not the ones that surround its factories and stores in central Wisconsin. At its Sauk City retail store, you can take cooking classes from some of the area's leaders in sustainable and slow food, like L'Etoile's chef Tory Miller. Check their Web site for upcoming classes or go to one of their seven central Wisconsin locations.

Cedar Grove Cheese in Plain has been around this area for well over a hundred years. It is family owned and makes organic and specialty cheeses using only vegetarian ingredients that are free of GMO (genetically modified organisms), including its specialty brand, Prairie Premium, a cheese made from the milk of grass-fed cows. But perhaps more important is their use of the Living Machine, an environmentally friendly way of cleaning up the cheese production wash-water so they can send it back into Honey Creek, which is part of the Wisconsin River basin. They're open for tours seven days a week. Follow County Road B west from Sauk City to Plain.

The *Sauk County Farm Connect Guide* is a list of local farmers who would be thrilled to have you visit their farms to meet the people who grow your food. They hope you come to taste their wares and maybe purchase a thing or two. It's quite the list, but if you are so inclined there are enough farms to fill a year of travel. Download it and find the food or product that you are eager to get from a hard-working local farm family. Some are certified organic, some are sustainable, and some conventional. But all are local to this region.

What to Do

Back in Baraboo, within the humble yet lovely grass prairies and wetlands just five miles north of the Baraboo Hills, the *International Crane Foundation* does a world of good. Saving cranes is an international concern, and much of that takes place here where all fifteen species are bred until they are launched into migration. This is where the whooping crane was taken from its endangered status, with a count as low as sixteen (that's birds, not species) in existence, to today's count of more than five hundred. This lovely setting includes walking paths to observation decks that overlook wetlands and woodlands filled with wildlife. The real treat, though, is the exhibition that houses the whooping cranes. These long-legged lovelies stand gracefully along the edge of a naturalized pond as if they know they're on stage and you're in the good seats. The foundation is certified by Travel Green Wisconsin and its Spirit of Africa exhibit is a 2009 Focus on Energy SE^2 (Sustainability and Energy Efficiency) Leadership Award winner.

Just two miles east of downtown Baraboo lie the magnificent Baraboo Hills that run between Sauk and Columbia counties. These hills just happen to be the most ancient (like a billion and a half years ancient) rock formations in the Western Hemisphere. You can hike their wooded hills, bike their winding trails, and climb their quartzite rock walls (at your own risk) in *Devil's Lake State Park*. You can even swim in its glacial kettle, Devil's Lake, and cross-county ski its snow-capped range. This park is nearly ten thousand acres and is a unit of the Ice Age National Scientific Reserve with a trail segment that runs through it. Some of its nearly thirty miles of trails are easy, like the Grottos Trail, which skims the bottom of the south end of the bluffs; some are not so easy, like its link to the Potholes Trail, a hike straight up that is equal parts agony (for the heart-pumping challenge of it) and ecstasy (for arriving at the top and earning the views). There are more trails when you get up there, and many throughout the park that double as cross-country ski trails. There are also eight miles of mountain biking trails. Some of these trails are not for the weak of heart, so make sure you're up for the job and know where you're going. The park's concession stand rents canoes and kayaks, including a kayak specially designed for people with disabilities. It is said that more people visit Devil's Lake State Park than Yellowstone National Park.

The granddaddy of all Wisconsin ecology sites, the *Aldo Leopold Legacy Center* was erected on the site where Aldo Leopold loved, lived, and died. Donated by his children, the center has been called the greenest building in the world, and it has their lifelong influence at its core. This is where Leopold's land ethic—that land is a community and should be loved and respected—planted its roots and spread its wings. You can visit this platinum LEED-certified building, a Kubala Washatko architectural beauty, not only to learn more about sustainable energy use, but also to revel in its sheer simplicity and beauty. It was made from some of the thousands of trees planted by Leopold and his family after the Dust Bowl left this region barren. Come for one of many programs that teach numerous ways to live with land awareness. Hike to the Shack, the Leopolds' beloved one-room cabin in the woods where his children learned the importance of land stewardship, a place that his son, Cal, was said to have chosen over his own senior prom. This place is special and well worth the ten-mile jog off of Highway 12 near Baraboo. The center is certified by Travel Green Wisconsin and has a green score of 104.

Nature's Acres Farm is set on 130 acres surrounded by Nature Conservancy land, overlooking the magnificent Baraboo Hills. This is where Jane Hawley Stevens, her husband David and their three kids, Forrest, Savanna, and Sylvie, farm healing herbs for their *Four Elements Herbals* products—soaps, body oils, bath salts, tinctures, balms, and other holistic products sold in stores and through its Web site. On the land Jane also maintains a chakra garden, a place of healing contemplation with a design that is based on the ancient Sanskrit belief that our bodies hold seven wheel-like centers (chakras) that are the receptors and transmitters of energy. The herbs grown there correspond to each system in their healing properties. You can come to Nature's Acres Farm to roam this formal garden or to attend one of Jane's many workshops or to just bask in the natural beauty of the area. See her Web site for workshop ideas, such as organic growing techniques and how to cultivate herbs to make your own healing products. Jane asks that you make advance arrangements before arriving because their schedule is busy and varied.

At the *Necedah National Wildlife Refuge*, sixty miles northwest of Baraboo, birding is big. In fact, this is where the International Crane Foundation sends its graduate whooping cranes to learn migration skills behind the wings of an ultralight aircraft, the ultimate ornithology experience. But the wildlife that roam these 43,656 acres is big, too, such as the wolves that pack around these parts. The endangered Karner blue butterflies and white-tailed deer comingle with the whooping cranes and ringed bog hunter dragonflies and flying squirrels—some cautiously, others stealthily. It's a carefully monitored ecosystem with observation fields, a lookout tour, and a network of walking trails.

The *Wormfarm Institute* is a nonprofit that links communities with art and sustainable agriculture. Its owners, Donna Neuwirth and Jay Salinas, are worker bees of an extraordinary kind. On their forty acres fifteen miles west of Baraboo in Reedsburg, they do amazing things. They grow organic produce for the Wisconsin Home Harvest, a growers collective that operates as a CSA model. In exchange for fifteen hours of farmhand labor, they invite artists to temporarily live communally and create works that speak to land and sustainability issues. The art then feeds their downtown Reedsburg art gallery, the *Woolen Mill Gallery*. Wormfarm artists also help strengthen community pride through their mural projects, which can be seen in downtown

Famed artist Tom Every has saved landfills from thousands of pounds of scrap iron by creating sculptures like these that line Highway 12 just outside Sauk City at Delaney's Surplus Sales. (photo by Kate Galantha)

The Greening of the Badger Army Ammunition Plant

In 1942 the Sauk Prairie was home to more than eighty farms and twenty-five commercial properties located on a glacial washout prairie. That year the United States government condemned over seven thousand acres to build a plant to manufacture ammunition in preparation for the United States' entry into World War II. The *Badger Army Ammunition Plant* has a sixty-plus year history that has morphed into an impressive conservation effort led by many parties including the Wisconsin Department of Natural Resources and the *Sauk Prairie Conservation Alliance*. Today this land that borders the Baraboo Range, Devil's Lake State Park, the Ice Age Trail, and Riverland Conservancy land is central to an aggressive decontamination plan that will ultimately make way for recreation, conservation, and education. The massive environmentally sensitive cleanup plan includes reuse of some existing structures, deconstruction and salvaging wherever possible—including the sale of metal works on eBay—and the reuse of Highway 78 concrete. The vision for the site includes reclamation of natural areas for biking, hiking, and canoeing; displays introducing Ho-chunk and Native American culture, a free-roaming bison farm, introduction to mound building and education on how the mounds were lost; education on farming, dairy ecology, and prairie and savannah restoration and maintenance; observation of rare and endangered bird species and their habitat reclamation; and access to the Wisconsin River. Currently the Badger property is seldom open to the public other than tours conducted by the *Natural Resources Foundation of Wisconsin*, but down the road it should offer numerous tourist attractions linked with land abutting Devil's Lake State Park. Meanwhile volunteer opportunities are plentiful through the Sauk Prairie Conservation Alliance. You can go to their Web site for this information and for updates on how the cleanup is progressing.

Reedsburg. The one on the side of the Woolen Mill building overlooks the Baraboo River; another, "Rails to Trails," can be viewed along the downtown bike path. The Wormfarm is not set up for visitors, but work that hails from their fields can be viewed at the Woolen Mill Gallery.

Easton Dreher is a twenty-something with a mission to turn the Wisconsin Dells into the kayaking and rock-climbing center that he believes it was meant to be. With his kayak outfitters business, *Vertical Illusions*, Easton went from a fleet of five kayaks a few years ago to fifteen kayaks and eight staffers. This guy has as much energy as the Wisconsin River, where you'll go if you sign up with him. He's the founder of Stewards of the Dells, a nonprofit whose mission is to preserve, conserve, and protect the Dells area, and his kayak business targets young kids so they get to know the land before they get roped into reality television and video games. He also purchased Chimney Rock Park in Adams-Friendship and saved it from development, then turned it into a rock-climbing destination. Dreher has saving the Wisconsin Dells' environment in his sights at all times and he may be just the guy to do it. He's open all year long, in winter months for snowshoeing along the Wisconsin River canyons and torchlight cross-country skiing in Mirror Lake Park among other healthful things. This is a Travel Green Wisconsin–certified business.

Outsider art lovers will be amazed at the sculpture garden along Highway 12 just after you leave Sauk City heading west. *Delaney's Surplus Sales* is a crusty old business chock full of reclaimed goods, located right across the street from the Badger Army Ammunition Plant—possibly the future home of thousands of Ho-Chunk–owned bison. For years Tom Every, better known as the scrap iron folk artist Dr. Evermor, salvaged millions of pieces of scrap metal and iron to construct his internationally famous sculptures, some two or three stories high. Along the roadside bordering Delaney's property, birds, insects, and, more famously, his science fiction pieces can be viewed. John Michael Kohler Arts Center in Sheboygan has some of his work, and numerous documentary filmmakers have followed his path. This is truly a case of Dr. Evermor's junk being everybody's treasure.

Southwest Wisconsin

Sparta

La Crosse
Coon
Valley
Stoddard
Viroqua

Cashton
Ontario
Westby
La Farge

Soldiers Grove

Plain
Spring
Green
Muscoda
Avoca   Arena
Boscobel

Mazomanie
Black Earth
Cross Plains

Fall River

Fennimore

Blue Mounds

Bagley

Mineral
Point
Lancaster

Dodgeville

Beetown

Blanchardville

Cassville
Potosi

Platteville

Argyle   Monticello

Dickeyville

Monroe

Dubuque

Browntown

Juda

Sinsinawa

N   20 miles
0

ILLINOIS

Back to the Land

Boscobel Area

Our gardens are the sum of the soil they are planted in. So too, we
are the sum of where and when we are planted, not only living
expressions of what we literally eat, but also where we were born,
raised, and our time in history.

—JEAN MURPHY, "The Compost Pile"

The Driftless Area, that lovely land of wooded hills and class A trout streams,
makes a dandy escape from city life. Out there, you're miles from any urban
center, the skies hold more stars than any city dweller ever knew existed, and
insect choruses, not sirens, fill the summer nights.

Through this land flows the Wisconsin River. Since 1989, the Lower Wisconsin State Riverway Board has protected the river valley from development.
Beloved by canoeists, the braided channels of this great river have always been
a wonderful place to spend a day or even a week. During the summer of 1887,
Reuben Gold Thwaites paddled the Wisconsin from Portage to the Mississippi
with his wife—his "fellow voyager down the river of time." His account of the
journey in *Historic Waterways* tells of the river itself and the hardships of settlers
along its banks. Three State Natural Areas along the river between Boscobel and
Wauzeka, and units of the Lower Wisconsin River State Wildlife Area, provide
outstanding wildlife habitat for nature lovers to explore by canoe or kayak.

Just north of the river, an artistic and spiritual destination is found at Saint
Isaac of Syria Skete, where monks hand-paint and sell marvelous Byzantine-
style icons.

And, best of all, when you visit this corner of the Driftless Area, you can
stay in a farm guesthouse.

Where to Stay

At *Life O'Riley Farm and Guesthouses*, halfway between Boscobel and Fennimore on a narrow winding road, two urban escapees live the country life that

they sought way back in the seventies. (Remember the seventies, when we all wanted to go "back to the land"?) Jean and Mike Murphy love the land and people they found in rural Wisconsin. After all these years away from Chicago, it's still a good life for them. When you first meet Jean, you'd swear she was born a country girl. But there's something in the way she talks farming (and runs guesthouses) that tells you she was city-bred. The way she combines these two sensibilities really works.

As she explains, "One of my great joys is sharing our lives on the farm with people who are longing for a connection back to the farm or to nature—whatever that might mean to them. Having grown up in the Chicago suburbs, I was thinking just the other day how I do not belong either here or there. Here, because I do not have the background, upbringing, and knowledge of a farm kid; there, because I have been gone over thirty years. Belonging somewhere in between, I figure I am a fairly good bridge for people from the city or suburbs who long for some way to connect to our common roots."

Reflections on being "in between" have appeared in "The Compost Pile," a column she has written for the Boscobel newspaper.

A locally handcrafted Amish quilt dresses up the Schoolhouse bedroom at Life O' Riley Farm near Boscobel. (photo by Robert Diebel)

Choose the Life O'Riley Farm if you want the peace of a remote farm, delightfully quirky guesthouses, and access to Jean's extensive organic gardens—in summer, of course. The guesthouses have full kitchens and lots of comfort. There's even Internet access (if you sit on the porch and if the signal's working) but you're probably hoping to escape that.

Without and within, Jean and Mike recycle and reuse as a way of life. They built the Granary guesthouse—which sleeps four—with the wood and other materials from an old granary on the same site. The Schoolhouse, a country school until 1960, was moved to its present location in 1970 and restored. This cottage sleeps six. The original old chalkboard runs the length of one wall of the Schoolhouse, and old desks and chairs take guests back to elementary school days. Locally made Amish quilts dress the beds, and the works of regional artists like Jura Silverman adorn the walls. The couple's extensive collection of books fills the shelves, inviting quiet reads on the porch.

Outside, you can hang out with pigs, chickens, and other animals on this working farm, hike to hilltop overlooks, and explore fifty acres of woods and two rock quarries. You can lounge on the porch of your guesthouse and write, paint, draw, or compose. Jean's many artistic guests will attest to the farm's ability to get their creative juices flowing.

Or choose the farm if you simply want a cozy, peaceful nest to return to after a day of exploring the beautiful hilly countryside.

North of the river and just south of Soldiers Grove is another green lodging option. Surrounded by 160 acres of wooded land, *Inn at Lonesome Hollow* was once a farm. It's as quiet as Life O'Riley, but more conventional and manicured. It offers three kinds of accommodations: bedrooms in the main house, a detached cabin (Cedar Cabin), and a four-bedroom house (the Homestead). Note: the inn closes for two months in midwinter.

Owners Pete and Nora Knapik are adopting green practices and are certified by Travel Green Wisconsin. From the very start, they supported local businesses by buying locally made Amish oak furniture from Cashton as well as Amish quilts and local art. The pork sausage and Canadian bacon served at breakfast come from Kickapoo Lockers in nearby Gays Mills. They installed water-saving fixtures and energy-saving sunshades; converted to biodegradable, nontoxic laundry detergents and cleaning products; use dispensers for their vegetable-based shampoo and soap; and have a recycling program. Upset by the number of plastic water bottles in the recycling bin, Nora now provides hikers with stainless steel water bottles filled with Brita-filtered water. Guests can either return these reusable bottles when they leave or purchase them.

Life O'Riley Rye

Combine:
  1/2 cup warm water
  1 teaspoon sugar
  1/4 teaspoon ginger
  3 tablespoons yeast

Stir and let get bubbly. Then add:
  1 1/2 cups warm water
  1/2 cup molasses
  2 tablespoons caraway seeds
  2 tablespoons dill seeds
  2 cups rye flour
  2 teaspoons salt
  4 tablespoons of lard, bacon fat, or butter
  2 cups white flour

Mix and let sit for 20 minutes. Then add:
  2 cups white flour

Knead for 5–10 minutes until elastic. Let rise, covered, until doubled (about 30–40 minutes). Put out on board, slap down, and cut in half. Shape into rounds or use a loaf pans or divide into 4 and make little french breads. Whatever! Bake at 350 degrees for 45 minutes if loaves or rounds. Check at 30 minutes for baguettes.

This is a quick-rising, dense, tasty bread—under three hours and always a hit. Great with our own ham, our own horseradish, and local cheese!

—Jean Murphy, Life O'Riley Farm

Nora said that birders love the fact that the inn is on a dead end; their record of bird sightings grows steadily. Another group drawn to Lonesome Hollow is dark sky enthusiasts. An astronomer who visited said the night sky show there is the best he's found in Wisconsin. The fields and woods are full of spring wildflowers. The inn also offers its guests workshops on such subjects as digital photography, cheesemaking, yoga, and scrapbooking. Two miles of trails lace the hardwood forest, and snowshoeing is excellent if you can manage the hills.

Where to Eat

Jean stocks the guesthouse kitchens at Life O'Riley Farm with coffee, fresh eggs from her chickens, and a loaf of homemade bread or a pan of cinnamon

At Life O' Riley Farm, old fashioned hollyhocks hang out with the veggies in Jean Murphy's organic garden. (photo by Robert Diebel)

rolls. She'll let you pick from her organic garden. From her freezer, she'll sell you meat from animals she and Mike raised. You won't go hungry on the farm.

If you do want to buy groceries on your way to Life O'Riley Farm, there are several food co-ops on main routes to the Boscobel area. The Pine River Food Co-op is in Richland Center, on Highway 14, about thirty miles north. The Driftless Market is in Platteville, about thirty-six miles south on Highways 61 and 81. The Viroqua Food Cooperative is about thirty-six miles north on Highway 61.

The locally owned *Our Little Restaurant and Bakery* in Fennimore offers tasty, reasonably priced diner food and baked goods. Although they don't focus on local or organic food, their meals are "homemade."

If you stay in either the Homestead or the Cedar Cabin at the Inn at Lonesome Hollow, both of which have kitchens, you can buy all your groceries at the Viroqua Food Cooperative, twenty miles north. You won't have to leave the property for your whole vacation.

Local Foraging

On the main street of Fennimore, look for a giant mouse called Igor. He stands outside the *Carr Valley Cheese Store*, which sells many great cheeses. Carr Valley owner Sid Cook is a fourth-generation, award-winning master cheesemaker. This particular Carr Valley store also bakes and packages bread cheese, a semifirm cheese similar to the Finnish cheese Juustoleipa (*hoo-stah-lee-pah*). The Finns make it from reindeer milk, but this cheese derives from cows. Bread cheese doesn't melt when heated. Bake or microwave a square until it glistens and it'll stay a square, a warm and tasty square. Finns dip it in their coffee, but Carr Valley recommends a dab of fruit preserves or honey instead. Just don't eat it cold.

Sugar and Spice Bulk Foods, south of Fennimore on Highway 61, is run by Mennonites. They carry organic rolled oats and other grains, bulk nuts, "no chemical" hard wheat that you can grind into flour on the spot, and a nice array of local fresh seasonal produce, including some unusual items such as mulberries and kohlrabi.

Speaking of bulk foods, the Saturday *Fennimore Produce Auction*, held in July and August, offers locally grown fruits and vegetables in small lots for household consumption, canning, or freezing. Produce is picked fresh just hours before the sale by growers within a hundred-mile radius of the auction. Auctions are held three miles north of Fennimore on County Road T, not too far from Life O'Riley Farm.

What to Do

With dozens of trout streams in Grant County and about a hundred miles of trout water within a fifteen-mile radius of Fennimore, fly fishermen flock to this area. The Big Green River, northwest of Fennimore, one of the most popular streams in Wisconsin, has a self-sustaining population of brown trout. Cast for brown and rainbow trout on the Blue River, northeast of Fennimore; it's one of America's most scenic trout streams, with limestone bluffs topped by stands of old-growth white and red pine. Crooked Creek, which follows Highway 61 south of Boscobel, is a good destination for trout. And there are many more, of course. Jim Romberg of the *Fly Fisherman's Lair* in Fennimore offers guide service.

For all anglers, a Wisconsin trout stamp and license are required. Always check open season dates and follow all current bag and size limits listed in the regulations pamphlet that comes with the license. Respect private property by not tearing down fences or littering. Although some parking areas are available, most parking is along roadways. Please do not block driveways or field access roads.

Paddle the Lower Wisconsin River. You won't be alone—canoeists and kayakers love this wide, sandy-bottom river with its intricate channels. Thanks to the Lower Wisconsin State Riverway Board, there's almost no development visible along the river's final 92.3 miles; instead, handsome rock bluffs flank many stretches. Abundant sandbars provide good picnic and camping sites, and landings are frequent and well maintained. Large populations of wildlife live in the bottomlands, so you're likely to spot sandhill cranes, bald eagles, herons, egrets, and kingfishers. If you camp on the river, great flocks of sandhills may wake you at dawn with prehistoric croaks as they head out to forage some farmer's field. Don't miss this awesome river. If you don't have a boat, *Wisconsin River Outings* in Boscobel rents Wenonah canoes and Current Design kayaks and provides shuttle service. If you're new to paddling, they offer guided trips. The definitive paddler's guide to the Lower Wisconsin is Mike Svob's *Paddling Southern Wisconsin.*

Explore *Wisconsin Natural Areas* in the Lower Wisconsin valley. Three are located close to the town of Woodman, on the south side of the Wisconsin River. The DNR Web site has driving directions. In Adiantum Woods, southwest of Woodman, find wildflowers and other native plants. Woodman Lake Sand Prairie, northeast of Woodman, is a dry sand prairie and sand barrens covered with native plants. Dead Lake is a shallow seepage lake that sustains muskrat, beaver, mink, and puddle ducks, and the marsh edge is good turtle habitat.

Order or download a free copy of *Great Wisconsin Birding and Nature Trail: Mississippi/Chippewa Rivers Region* from the Wisconsin Department of Tourism's Web site. It's full of maps and specific information on species, locations, and directions. The Wisconsin River valley is legendary birding territory. Marsh habitat, river bottom, agricultural fields, and bluffs host an astounding number of bird species, from owls to ruffed grouse. Wauzeka Bottoms—west of Woodman and accessible by canoe—is home to rare birds: red-shouldered hawk, yellow-crowned night heron, and cerulean, Kentucky, and prothonotary warblers. In the Lower Wisconsin River Wildlife Area, numerous sites rich with bird life are clearly identified for public access along Highway 18 in the Bridgeport/Wisconsin River Bottoms area, close to the confluence with the Mississippi. Others are located east along County Road C to Bergum Bottoms and Woodman.

Ride your bike from the Inn at Lonesome Hollow to Soldiers Grove to see *Solar Town*, a solar-powered business district built after the Kickapoo flooded the valley town one too many times. When Soldiers Grove was relocated from the floodplain to higher ground in the late 1970s, the town built twenty new commercial buildings powered by solar energy.

Local Arts

Visit *Orthodox Byzantine Icons*, the monastery business that supports St. Isaac of Syria Skete. This amazing enterprise is located in a remote valley north of the Wisconsin River at Boscobel. Here in 1987 Father Simeon founded a Bulgarian Eastern Orthodox monastery, or skete. Since then, St. Nicholas Orthodox Mission Church, St. Isaac's Orthodox School, and Monastery of St. Silouan (a monastic community for women) have been added. Icons are their bread and butter. Working in the traditional medium of egg tempera, natural pigments, and genuine gold-leaf, the monks hand-paint and sell glorious Byzantine-style icons. Visit their Web site for a preview of their work. To be sure someone is available to show you around and help you pick out icons, please call before you visit. It's about five miles northwest of Boscobel—the Web site has detailed directions and hours.

Soldiers Grove is the site of the annual *Driftless Area Art Festival*, a delightful September celebration of artists who live and create in the Driftless Area. Go for the art—both visual and performing—for the live music and dancing, and for the delicious local food and drink. It's a happening.

On Father's Day weekend, Boscobel hosts *Art by the Stream*, an outdoor juried fine arts and crafts exhibition that draws some great local and regional artists and craftspeople.

True Green

Monroe Area

> Though I do not believe that a plant will spring up where no seed has been, I have great faith in a seed. Convince me that you have a seed there, and I am prepared to expect wonders.
>
> —HENRY DAVID THOREAU, *Faith in a Seed*

Hidden in the rolling hills of Green County, just north of the Illinois border, is a truly green bed-and-breakfast. As you head west on County Road P, a road that dips and swoops like a swallow, you'll spot the Bergey wind turbine. That's the place.

And that's your first clue that the owners of this B&B are darn serious about sustainability. They've been living their green life since long before the media woke up to the quiet greening of America. Since 2003, they've been energy independent, with wind power, solar power, and wood heat. As a result of applying common sense efficiency to an ordinary farmhouse, their kilowatt usage is also 40 percent lower than the previous owners'. They're tied into the grid, which means they give power back to their local energy community. They grow their own food and serve it to lucky bed-and-breakfast guests.

Best of all, they're eager to share their pioneering experience and expertise with guests and visitors who seek the sustainable life.

The B&B can be a base for exploring the hilly countryside by bicycle. Go birding in a Wisconsin Natural Area oak forest. Visit a local fiber mill, a sheep and llama farm, or a cheese cooperative that produces the only limburger in the country.

Green County's cheese is legendary. Until about a decade ago, this mostly meant mild-mannered cheeses. But a growing movement toward grass-fed single herds, washed rinds, and cave aging is resulting in nationally acclaimed artisan cheeses. The pendulum is swinging back to the early nineteenth century when European immigrants brought their cheesemaking skills to the new land. Green County—not just swiss cheese anymore.

Just ten miles from the B&B, the historic city of Monroe boasts a stellar arts center, an authentic Ratskeller restaurant, and, in summer, an outdoor movie theater. The city is also a stop on the Badger State Trail, a bicycling route between Madison and the Illinois border.

Where to Stay

Guests at *Inn Serendipity*, Lisa Kivirist and John Ivanko's award-winning bed-and-breakfast, often simply enjoy the peace of country life by relaxing on the farm—reading or writing in a quiet garden hideaway, playing a game with the outdoor life-sized chess set, or meditating in the labyrinth. In winter, they're apt to cross-country ski on the property and end up next to the wood burner in the commons, reading from the inn's extensive and eclectic book collection.

Choose from two cozy guest rooms, both on the second floor and both decorated with themes. The Writing Room has a queen bed and an attached private bath. The Music Room has a full bed and a private bath across the hall. The house is cooled by opening windows at night and closing them during the day, eliminating the need for air-conditioning. Fans are available.

Guests often choose Inn Serendipity because they want to learn more about sustainability and to be inspired to make changes in their own lifestyles. In Travel Green Wisconsin's certification program, the inn scored 120 points, the third highest to date. It was recognized as one of the "top 10 Eco-Destinations in North America" by *Natural Home* magazine, received an Energy Star Small Business Network Award from the EPA, and have been accepted as a VocationVacation and a Green Routes destination. It was featured in the new book *Eco Hotels of the World* and on the Web site www.ecohotelsoftheworld.com.

In addition to sharing their wealth of knowledge and ideas about reducing one's footprint on this earth, Lisa and John are highly articulate advocates for social change. They've published several books on the rural renaissance and on eco-preneuring. Their latest is *ECOpreneuring: Putting Purpose and the Planet before Profits* (New Society Publishers, 2008). They are national speakers and freelance writers. Green travelers will find fascinating conversation at Inn Serendipity.

Where to Eat

A stay at Inn Serendipity includes a generous vegetarian breakfast, with fruit and veggies from the farm, local cheeses, and fair trade and organic ingredients from other sources.

Monroe area restaurants nearly always serve Green County cheeses, but it's more challenging to be a locavore here than in Madison. That said, lunch at *Baumgartner's Cheese Store and Tavern* on the courthouse square is a Monroe must. If you're adventurous, order limburger cheese—produced north of town—and red onion on rye. Smear your sandwich with sharp brown mustard from the squirt bottle on the table. (Don't worry, a breath mint is included.) Once introduced to the delights of creamy limburger, you may want to take some home. The counter guy will hermetically seal the fragrant stuff in layers of plastic, foil, *and* waxed paper so you can carry it around in public.

Right across the street from the tavern, in the center of the square, is the stately Green County courthouse, a red brick Romanesque beauty.

On the east side of the square, dessert hounds will find *Chocolate Temptation*, where hand-dipped truffles, Gertles (pecans or roasted cashews in caramel and milk chocolate), and other artisan chocolates created by the Buol family definitely tempt.

The *Garden Deli* on the square serves Chocolate Shoppe and Babcock Hall ice creams, both rich and luscious and both made in Madison.

On the north side of the square, Laura Winters's new kitchen store *Kookaburra's* offers cooking classes that highlight locally produced, seasonal foods, like Stef Culberson's spaetzle class. Laura, who grew up on an Illinois farm, loved cooking with her mother and grandma, especially at the fall harvest

---

Local Food Chase

Here's a great field trip. North of Argyle and east of Blanchardville, on a lovely little sustainable farm named the Goose Chaser, owner Steffi Culberson raises Heritage meatbirds and pigs. Stef's geese, turkeys, ducks, chickens, and pigs live as nature intended them to live, with access to dirt baths, a pasture to roam in, and a creek where they can swim, drink, and play. When it is time for their final trip, it is as humane and quick as possible.

When she isn't tending livestock or their "goose chaser" son, Seth, she's probably greeting customers for their products, like the goose and duck bratwursts sold exclusively at the farm. Stef is also a freelance food stylist who hosts seminars on how to make her food look as delicious on film as it does on your palate. Her green focus avoids food waste and chemical use and saves the corporations who hire her time, money, and resources. Stef also teaches cooking at Kookaburra's in Monroe, including an authentic spaetzle class (she's from Germany) featuring non-traditional recipes that use spelt flour or gluten-free flour.

Stef's Garden Cucumber Soup

4 cucumbers, seeded, peeled, and chopped
1 cup sour cream
1 cup buttermilk
coarse sea salt and pepper to taste
1 tablespoon lemon juice
1 tablespoon each: fresh chopped garden herbs (chives, lemon thyme, Thai basil, and dill; chervil is lovely also)

Combine cucumbers, sour cream, and buttermilk in blender. Puree until smooth. Add lemon juice, fresh herbs, and salt and serve chilled. Top with fresh chopped vegetables such as peppers, onions, and heirloom tomatoes and grilled slices of bread.

when all the women and girls cooked together. She wants to spread that value to young people, many of whom don't cook that way anymore. Laura says that Kookaburra's classes emphasize local foods and simple gourmet cooking that involves others. Embracing the locavore concept even further, Laura plans to open a restaurant in her store where she will serve local foods.

A few blocks away, the *Turner Hall Ratskeller* offers a Friday fish fry. Ask for the "never-frozen" catch-of-the-day (we know, it's not local), and do not miss the Swiss rösti, a tasty fried potato treat. On Sundays, polka or schottische to live music in the Grand Hall.

The best cuisine for miles around is in the little town of Monticello at The Dining Room at 209 Main (see the Sugar River chapter). Although a tad expensive, a meal at the Dining Room is big city quality and style in a small town original that focuses on local foods, and is more than worth the drive.

Local Foraging

For a nice stash of local foods to tote home, shop at the *Monroe Market on the Square*, held in the county courthouse parking area on Wednesday afternoons and Saturday mornings from mid-May to mid-October.

Or forage the countryside. For fresh veggies and eggs, visit the farm stand at *Christensen's Farm* near Browntown. In addition to an array of organic vegetables, Katy and Mark Dickson grow currants, a delightful old-fashioned berry that's often hard to find, and raspberries. Their egg-layers live in a chickenmobile built by Katy's father, Gene Christensen. For veggies only, look for their stand at Monroe Market on the Square.

Carrie and Eric Johnson raise grass-finished beef, grass-fed Icelandic lamb, and pasture-raised chicken and turkey (including Bourbon Red heritage turkeys) and grow potatoes and garlic on their well-known *Jordandal Farm*, about ten miles northwest of Monroe. "We're really into the soils, test them every year, add our animal compost, and remineralize with Midwestern Bio-Ag products," said Carrie Johnson. To taste the delicious results, order ahead and pick up at the farm by appointment. Their heritage turkeys sell fast, so don't delay. Provider to numerous top Madison restaurants, this place is the best.

Grass Is Greener Gardens, eight miles west of Monroe, is the sustainable farm of Rich Horbaczewski and Jackie Gennett. Using sustainable and organic methods, they raise lamb, chicken, eggs, produce, herbs, and flowers. Lamb and chicken are available year-round at the farm and they welcome visitors. Check the Web site for directions.

You can't escape cheese in Monroe. Aficionados should tour the *Roth Käse* plant to see the big copper vats. At the adjoining *Alp and Dell Cheese Store*, chat with Bruno, the Swiss cheesemaker who manages the store.

A stop at the *Historic Cheesemaking Center* will educate you about the area's Swiss immigrant cheesemaking heritage. And the biennial Green County Cheese Days finds a herd of Brown Swiss cows with bells around their necks parading through the square (followed by pooper scoopers). Cheesemakers in Swiss attire stir cheese in enormous copper vats. One local resident said it looks like "a giant family reunion on the square."

Another good side trip is to the *Chalet Cheese Cooperative* factory (where Baumgartner's limburger is born) north of Monroe on County Road N. Although they don't give tours, there's a factory store. Their baby swiss is tasty, and they might give you a sample of limburger if you ask nicely.

What's really exciting is the emergence of area artisan cheeses, crafted by Wisconsin master cheesemakers. These artisans hold certification from the nation's only advanced cheesemaking certification program, rigorous and intensive training rooted in the traditions of European cheesemaking and run by the University of Wisconsin–Madison.

The families in the *Edelweiss Graziers Co-op* use intensive rotational grazing. This means a cow must eat 60 percent or more grass, with no silage fed. The farm must provide 1.5 acres of land per cow for grazing, and fencing must be moved every twelve hours so cows have fresh grass. Combining milk produced on this diet of southern Wisconsin's grasses and flowers with limestone-filtered water, Wisconsin master cheesemaker Bruce Workman handcrafts a fabulous cheese at the *Edelweiss Creamery*. You can buy a chunk of Edelweiss raw milk Emmentaler at the creamery's plant on County Road C. Call before visiting. Bruce starts the day very early and may not be there after 10 a.m. The cheese and the co-op's tasty Maple Leaf cheeses are also available at *Maple Leaf Cheese Factory Outlet* in Juda, east of Monroe.

What to Do

Laced with quiet scenic back roads, the area is wonderful for biking. The hills are sometimes a welcome challenge for bicyclists, sometimes not. If you like your bike route flatter, choose the *Badger State Trail*. A trail stop with parking and rest rooms is located at Monroe's Twinning Park. To the south, the Badger connects with the Jane Addams Trail, which continues to Freeport, Illinois. If you ride north for twenty-seven miles, you will reach Madison's Southwest Bike Path (the final seven miles between Paoli and the path will be complete by June 2010) and the Capital City State Trail as well as the Military Ridge State Trail. Scenery along the Badger is quintessential southern Wisconsin beauty—ravines, forests, prairies, farmland, distant vistas. Between Monticello and Belleville, the twelve-hundred-foot Stewart Tunnel—dark as a dungeon—gives riders a thrill. Bring your flashlight. And remember that the Dining Room at 209 Main (see Where to Eat) is in Monticello—bring a change of clothes and stop for supper. After eating, the eleven-mile ride back to Monroe will erase any calories you acquire while dining.

Birders can hike nearby Browntown Oak Forest, a State Natural Area on the north-facing slope of a St. Peter sandstone ridge. Regularly spotted species include tufted titmouse, blue-gray gnatcatcher, yellow-throated vireo, and orchard oriole. The state-threatened cerulean warbler has also been found here. Parking is along Allen Road, just south of Highway 11.

Local Arts

In the little town of Argyle, about twenty miles north of Inn Serendipity, is the *Argyle Fiber Mill*. Three area women—Carrie Johnson, Elizabeth Wellenstein, and Kristi Langhus—renovated Argyle's oldest stone building to house the mill. This is where the growing ranks of local producers bring their fiber to be processed. Llama, alpaca, Icelandic sheep, mohair, merino—it's all fifty-mile fiber, which means that the animal lives and was shorn and the fiber processed within fifty miles of the mill. At the mill, fibers are washed with a mild, citrus-based detergent. The women recycle the water, let the fiber air-dry, and process it into clouds, roving, batts, and yarn. You'll find an earth-toned rainbow of shades. It's open for retail sales of consignment fibers and for fiber folks to gather. Call ahead to be sure someone will be there. If no one answers the front door, go around to the side.

On Jim, Sandy, and Ross Ryan's *Homestead Wool and Gift Farm* in the Jordan Valley west of Monroe, you'll find raw and washed wool, spinning fiber, shawls, ponchos, scarves, hats, mittens, hand-hooked items, and other fiber arts. The Ryans do custom spinning. All wools come from local sheep, alpaca, and llama.

Or head for Monroe. The *Monroe Arts Center* is housed in a historic Gothic Revival–style church designed in 1869 by Milwaukee architect E. Townsend Mix. According to director Richard Daniels, the building itself, with its distinctive angled corner tower, made a unique contribution to ecclesiastical architecture. Inside, find exciting regional art exhibits. The center's Artmix gift shop features original and limited edition artwork of regional artists and artisans, note cards, pottery, photography, and CDs by Wisconsin musicians. The former sanctuary is now the recently renovated Gunderson Stiles Concert Hall, presided over by a glowing Rose Window. Choose from an extensive schedule of varied musical entertainment and theater performances by the Monroe Theatre Guild. The center is three blocks from the square.

Monroe's *Sky-Vu Outdoor Theater*, a relic from 1954, is an interesting entertainment option on a nice summer evening.

Mississippi River Adventure

Cassville and Potosi Area

I do not know much about gods; but I think that the river
Is a strong brown god—sullen, untamed and intractable . . .
—T. S. ELIOT (who grew up on the Mississippi),
Four Quartets: The Dry Salvages

Green comes in many shades, including the preservation of historic architecture—restoring rather than replacing. In the southwest corner of the state, nestled at the base of towering Mississippi River bluffs, are two towns dating from the early nineteenth century, quiet little river towns with fascinating histories. Cassville and Potosi now lie along Wisconsin's Great River Road, but they began life as stops on the great water highway, the Mississippi.

The 1856 Potosi Brewing Company once depended on the river for transporting beer to Dubuque. The company's handsome brick buildings—closed for thirty-six years—have been renewed in remarkable ways. The brewery is operating again, and a national brewery museum has moved in. A new restaurant serves Potosi beer, of course, and features some tasty regional foods. By rebuilding a piece of its past, Potosi (pop. 711) is creating a sustainable future.

Cassville is also rich in historic architecture. In 1836, when the town tried valiantly to become the capital of the new Wisconsin Territory, the big brick Denniston House was built to house legislators. Converted to a hotel in 1854, the building now stands empty—gazing at the river and reflecting the town's rich history. Across the tracks, past and present merge in Riverside Park—the site of a Native American effigy mound, the landing for the Cassville Ferry (in operation since 1836), and the weekly farmers' market.

On the north side of Cassville, the farm estate of Wisconsin's first governor, Nelson Dewey, once covered two thousand acres. What remains is now a state park with spectacular bluff-top views and a historic site where visitors experience nineteenth-century rural village life.

Silent sports are popular in the valley—hiking the five-hundred-foot bluffs on state park trails, biking the hilly back roads, mountain biking on state park trails, and canoeing and kayaking, of course.

True river rats will want to visit the National Mississippi River Museum and Aquarium, just over the border in Iowa. Another green destination is the Dominican retreat in Sinsinawa. And the Dickeyville Grotto is an awe-inspiring blend of art and recycling. Near Lancaster, the Helen Anderson Gallery displays local artists' work.

The Cassville-Potosi area is a major birding destination, and a sustainable future for nature is an integral piece of the valley. Two state parks and five State Natural Areas provide habitat for wildlife and native plants. The Upper Mississippi River National Wildlife and Fish Refuge is home to amazing numbers of birds, fish, and animals. To introduce visitors to these river valley denizens, a Cassville company offers ecotours and beautifully restored nineteenth-century lodging.

Where to Stay

In a nineteenth-century brick building—with one of those cool false fronts you see in Western movies—Cassville couple Clyde and Judy Male have created a lovely getaway they call *Upper Miss Lodging*. It's easy to imagine spending more than just a night in one of these elegantly restored and comfortable apartments.

The back story: The ecotours came first, then the lodging. *Upper Mississippi River Adventures*, launched in 2005, is headquartered on the first floor. "Green travelers—that's the community of people we're interested in reaching," said Judy, "and lots of our business is local people who grew up here loving the river and want to show it to their guests. We took one ninety-nine-year-old woman out who was 'in heaven' on the river. She said to Clyde, 'I'll remember this for the rest of my life.'"

With their river tours finding an eager market, the couple decided to devote the rest of the building to overnight guests. At the end of a day exploring the river valley, you can retire to the comfort of a fully furnished townhouse. The kitchens are nicely furnished and the beds very comfortable. The building's two units are rented separately but may be combined for larger groups. A great blend of historic and modern—these apartments make you want to move in.

The building was in bad shape when Clyde and Judy bought it at auction. They did all the remodeling themselves, recycling as many materials as

Clyde and Judy Male offer lodging in this restored historic building; the office for their ecotours of the Mississippi River is there as well. (photo by Robert Diebel)

possible. Although there is air-conditioning, good cross-ventilation from the windows is the green alternative. (Burlington Northern trains rumble through town several times a night, a few blocks away, so light sleepers may want to close the windows.) Refillable liquid soap dispensers, a recycling program, and a refurbished claw-foot tub are other green touches.

Wyalusing State Park and *Nelson Dewey State Park* have campgrounds, with tent, electrical, and group campsites; showers; and toilets. Tent campers will be pleased to learn that Nelson Dewey's four walk-in tent sites have some of the best bluff-top views in the whole park. Both parks have prairie restoration projects and programs to prevent invasive species. The parks also use recycled paper and paper products.

Where to Eat

For an out-of-town treat, drive or bike seventeen hilly miles along the Great River Road to the *Potosi Brewing Company* restaurant. Just inside the restaurant door, you step onto a Lexan floor window. The vigorously bubbling spring that provides the brewing water is visible beneath your feet. And seeing the ornate wood bar—created by artist and Potosi native Gary David, a major player in the restoration—is worth the trip. The menu recommends pairings of regional artisan cheeses with Potosi's standard and seasonal beers, on tap in the restaurant. Or you can order a tasty Potosi root beer, brewed with cane sugar and also on tap. Wisconsin cheeses are named on the lunch and dinner menus, and the ground Angus beef for the popular Good Old Potosi burgers comes from Weber Processing in Cuba City. And according to Greg Larsen, executive director of the Potosi Brewery Foundation, the restaurant's focus is shifting to traditional foods of the Great River Road, embracing the brewery's connection to the larger river community. Plan your trip around a tour of the brewery museum. And leave time to explore the Rustic Road that heads up the Brewery Hollow Road hill then down to the river on Slazing Road and River Lane.

Local Foraging

If you like to cook, the Upper Miss Lodging units have full kitchens and an outdoor grill. In season, eat locally with produce and Amish baked goods from the *Cassville Farmers' Market*, Saturday mornings from May through mid-October. If you're coming into town through nearby Platteville, stop at the new *Driftless Market* co-op and stock up on regionally produced food. The *Platteville Farmers' Market* is held on Tuesdays and Saturdays from May through October.

What to Do

In 1852, Gabriel Hail and John Albrecht built the Potosi Brewery to slake the thirst of local lead miners. Squeezed out by the big brands, the brewery closed in 1972. Credit for its phenomenal comeback in 2008 goes primarily to energetic local folks who value their historic buildings and heritage (and hops). Grants, generous donors, and a partnership with the American Breweriana Association (ABA) did the rest. In its quest to be the site of the ABA's *National Brewery Museum,* little Potosi beat Milwaukee and St. Louis. Village president Frank Firenzo, paraphrasing Frank Lloyd Wright, said, "Our buildings should be an extension of the history and heritage of the community." You needn't be a beer fan to enjoy the museum's vast collection of rare memorabilia, to eat at the restaurant, or to peruse the gift shop's selection of locally produced cheeses, wines, syrup, and honey. And you needn't be a lead miner to drink the beer.

You can tour the remains of the *St. John Mine,* right there on Main Street Potosi. The tour operator also rents canoes.

Back in Cassville, take yourself on a historic walking tour. Contact *Cassville Tourism* for a copy of the town's brochure or print out the online version. Its Web site also has historical information on the Cassville Ferry. While you're exploring, stop by Mike and Char Udelhofen's *Unique Creations* on Amelia Street to see their handmade log furniture. Hours are limited, so please phone ahead to be sure they're open.

Tour the river with an expert. When Clyde Male of Upper Mississippi River Adventures takes visitors on a "Natural Wonders Ecological Tour" of the Upper Mississippi River sloughs, he does so with thirty years of experience in natural resource management, fisheries and wildlife biology, predator and waterfowl research, river resource management, and conservation law. He not only knows where herons and egrets fish and where to spot a bald eagle nest, he can tell you all about these three and all the other species of bird, mammal, and fish that call the river home. Everybody is issued a pair of binoculars for the adventure. The couple chose the quietest, most environmentally friendly motor to power their six-passenger pontoon boat and also have a recycling program.

Explore nearby *State Natural Areas*, including Cassville Bluffs–Roe Unit, which protects a rare expanse of undeveloped bluff and sand terrace overlooking the Mississippi River. There's no highway between the river and the bluffs of this large preserve. The best prairie lies on the steep south-facing slopes in the southeast portion of the preserve. Gasner Hollow Prairie has a series of Native American mounds on the bluff summit. Rush Creek Natural Area features a two-mile-long series of "goat prairies."

Birders love the Mississippi flyway. Potosi Point is especially good for spring birding. In spring and summer, go to Closing Dam Road, a gravel road north of Cassville and Nelson Dewey State Park. The bluffs of Cassville Bluffs–Roe Unit Natural Area and Nelson Dewey are good places to watch the fall migration. From December to late February, watch bald eagles fish. Top viewing locations include a wildlife observation deck at Riverside Park as well as nearby Nelson Dewey State Park. Cassville's *Bald Eagle Days* features outdoor viewing with the help of knowledgeable guides and indoor educational exhibits and programs.

In *Wyalusing State Park*, twenty-five miles north on the Great River Road, rent a canoe from the park concession and follow a loop water trail through the Mississippi sloughs. Hike 500-foot bluffs for great views of the confluence of the Wisconsin and Mississippi rivers. Two forested State Natural Areas are inside the park. Wyalusing's two mountain bike trails—one 3.2 miles through

Five Great Field Trips

Down the road in Dubuque, Iowa, the *National Mississippi River Museum and Aquarium* is a fantastic introduction to the complex ecosystems in the river valley. Interactive exhibits explore the river's environmental history and ask tough questions about the river's future and the consequences of human choice. And huge catfish in the aquarium tanks make the museum a must-see. Nearby *Cafe Manna Java* is a good choice for lunch, with artisan breads and wood-fired pizza made from scratch.

The *Dominican Sisters of Sinsinawa* offer seminars on topics like simple living, as well as trails for hiking the mound (a remnant of Niagara Escarpment dolomite caps Sinsinawa Mound, as well as Belmont, Platte, and Blue Mounds) and an outdoor labyrinth. At the gift shop, buy bread baked daily by the sisters and shop for fair-traded import goods. Their sustainable farm provides fruit and vegetables for the convent.

Plan a trek to the *Dickeyville Grotto*, an amazing blend of art and recycling built from 1925 to 1930 by Father Matthias Wernerus on the Holy Ghost Parish grounds. You can take a guided tour or just walk through on your own. It's right on Dickeyville's main street.

Make a journey to the *Helen Anderson Gallery* in the rolling countryside outside Lancaster. Helen Anderson's photographs, many of which were taken on the Mississippi near Cassville, are all about wildlife, raptors (especially eagles), landscapes, wildflowers, songbirds, and butterflies. The gallery also features the work of other local artists. Call ahead for hours and directions.

Visit *Switchback*, ninety acres of wildlife preservation land on Five Points Road, six miles southwest of Lancaster, where prairie, wetland, and woods are open to hikers.

---

woods and prairie grassland; the other, 3.0 miles of heavily wooded terrain—are rated easy to moderate. And 6.9 miles of cross-country ski trails make the park a good winter destination.

The nearby Grant and Platte rivers, swift and winding, are popular paddling destinations. The Grant flows past beautiful rock outcrops, and Mike Svob, author of *Paddling Southern Wisconsin*, calls it "one of the most delightful paddling rivers in the state." Canoe rentals are available at the *Grant River Canoe Rental* in Beetown, nine miles from Cassville, or from *St. John Mine and Canoe Rentals* in Potosi.

Hike three miles of trails at Nelson Dewey State Park, where you'll find ancient effigy mounds, a native prairie, and breathtaking views of the river.

In winter, check the schedule for candlelight hikes. Across the road, visit *Stonefield Village*, an interactive Wisconsin History site.

Road biking fans, the byways of this hilly countryside are prime territory for challenging rides. Gorgeous scenery is the reward for your hard work. Pick up a Southwest Wisconsin Bicycling Map from the Great River Road brochure rack at the Potosi Brewery or order it online from *Cycle Southwest Wisconsin.* Then head out on one of five local loop rides, ranging from seventeen to twenty-seven miles. Loop maps are also available online along with links to great biking events, like the Potosi Great River Road Bicycle Tour—"Oktoberfest 100." And Upper Miss Lodging (see Where to Stay) participates in their Bed and Bike in Southwest Wisconsin program, with special online offers for cyclists who stay there.

Excellent cycling maps of Wisconsin's *Great River Road* are also available online for download from the Wisconsin Department of Transportation Web site.

Coulee Hideaway

La Crosse Area

To preserve and interpret the natural environment and cultural heritage of the region, to make people aware of and sensitive to these resources and to provide educational opportunities at all levels through its arboretum, nature and heritage centers, and staff—both volunteer and professional.

—Norskedalen's mission statement

Tucked into one of the countless coulees, or steep-sided valleys, in the Driftless Area, Norskedalen, which translates to Norwegian Valley, is only eighteen miles from the busy university town of La Crosse. Once you leave Highway 14 at Coon Valley and head north on County Road P, however, you gently slip off the modern treadmill and into a timeless world.

Since 1977, the University of Wisconsin–La Crosse Foundation has evolved Norskedalen from an arboretum and natural laboratory into a place where past and present intersect. Norskedalen's mission is living history—touring a restored pioneer homestead, attending a natural history lecture, hiking in the creek with a guide to learn what flooding has done to the coulee, or taking a flintnapping course to learn the Native American art of shaping arrowheads.

The Norskedalen Center is philosophically dedicated to preserving the nature and heritage of the area, what you might call Green 101. On a practical level, the staff is committed to natural resource conservation. Recent initiatives include a rain garden, compact fluorescent lamps, recycled carpet, and energy-saving film on the windows of the Thrune Visitors Center.

Sometimes the modern world intrudes. During the summer of 2008, Hollywood came to Norskedalen. *Fort McCoy,* a historical period drama set during World War II in and around the military base at nearby Fort McCoy, was filmed in the woods and fields of the center.

Where to Stay

Whether you want to spend a weekend learning to sew a Norwegian bunad (a traditional regional dress), casting for trout in a local stream, or snowshoeing on nature trails, the place to stay around Coon Valley is *Paulsen Cabin at Norskedalen.* The cabin, which sleeps six, is big enough for a family or group gathering. It's also quiet and private enough for those seeking a getaway.

Your stay in this authentic log cabin from the 1880s will give you a taste of homesteader life. But nineteenth-century primitive it's not. Modern (but simple) kitchen fixtures, propane heat, compact fluorescent lamps, and a new bathroom and washer-dryer in the 1982-vintage basement take log cabin living to a nonhomesteader level.

There's no TV or radio to break the old-fashioned spell in this hideaway. There's also no air-conditioning, but every evening, about six or seven o'clock, a cool breeze sweeps down narrow Poplar Coulee. Log cabin comfort without frills.

Authenticity extends to the sleeping quarters. Guests climb a ladder-steep stairway to the loft, where a queen-size bed, a twin bed, and a dresser provide simple comfort for three people. Two unauthentic but comfortable sofa beds in the sitting room downstairs sleep three more. Rosemaling adds charm to

At Norskedalen, you can vacation in a historic log cabin. (photo by Robert Diebel)

A Brief History of the Paulsen Cabin

Although the cabin has been rented to visitors for only a short time, it has been around for more than 120 years. Norwegian immigrant Peder Paulsen Rognhulet built the log house in Timber Coulee in 1887 and lived there with his wife, Anne Fredricksdtr, and their two sons. After he died in 1916, his son Paul lived there until his death in 1932, when it passed to Paul's brother, Fredrik.

When Fredrik held an auction to sell the household goods, it's said that Martin Smeby of Spring Coulee paid one dollar for a kubbestol (a traditional chair carved from a solid log) and enlisted Philip Stakston to help him carry it over the hill to Spring Coulee. When Martin's son Alf Smeby later sold the kubbestol at his own auction, the Norwegian ambassador to the U.S. bought it for $585 and took it back to Norway. Apocryphal perhaps, but that's the story.

For a few years, a neighbor family by the name of Vatland rented the building from Fredrik as a place to dry seed corn. Alf and Sophie Olstad, who bought it in 1939, had more respect for this historic structure. When Sophie sold the farm, she gave the cabin to Norskedalen to be preserved.

In 1982, Norskedalen caretaker Brian Olson, along with Ardell Olson and Myron Storbakken, took the house apart and reconstructed it on the hillside where it now stands. Brian lived there until he married, and the house was subsequently rented to several other long-term tenants. In 2006, the Norskedalen board decided to renovate it as a vacation rental.

many surfaces, and ceiling boards between the exposed beams are stained with real walnut stain, not a petrochemical imitation. A pioneer family of six would have thought this cabin luxurious.

Where to Eat

Guests at the Paulsen cabin are likely to stay put, not search for a new restaurant every evening. The simple kitchen—with an electric stove, microwave, and toaster—makes it easy to fix in-house meals. The refrigerator is only counter high, however, so don't bring too much that requires refrigeration.

If you do want a restaurant meal, local, sustainably raised food is served at restaurants in La Crosse and Viroqua, both within twenty miles of Norskedalen. In La Crosse, you'll find the *Root Note*, a downtown restaurant with an all-vegetarian menu. It's a cozy, casual place, where you order at the counter. The menu is small but tasty; homemade build-your-own pizzas with all-local toppings are a favorite choice. Customers also love the homemade granola. You'll find Kickapoo Coffee, espresso, teas, fruit smoothies, local microbrews,

and Wisconsin wines. Local art on the walls changes monthly. Don't be surprised to find a knitting group or the German Club meeting there. As you
might have guessed from their name, there's live music on their stage on
weekends.

Root Note co-owner Corrie Brekke said, "The direction we're headed in is
to become a sustainable downtown business, filling a niche." It's a big niche.
The Root Note buys from several local farms, a local orchard—they have
a local exclusive on Hoch Orchard organic applesauce—and a local dairy
(Castle Rock organic milk comes in reusable glass bottles). They offer an
organic catering service, with meat options. The restaurant is the drop-off
point for the Small Family CSA. Root Note's kitchen waste is composted at
the Driftless Farm, one of its vendors, and Root Note was among the first to
buy a share in the Driftless Farm's CSF (see Annual Events for translation).

Also in La Crosse, upstairs from the People's Food Co-op, *Hackberry's Bistro*
serves delicious local, organic, and conventional foods with white tablecloth
elegance. Open for lunch, dinner, and weekend brunch, Hackberry's features
live music on many weekend evenings.

Local Foraging

If you're headed to the cabin through La Crosse, shop at the *People's Food
Co-op* on Fifth Avenue. You'll find local, organic, and conventional produce;
bulk foods; fair trade and organic chocolates and coffee; gluten-free foods;
organic and local poultry and meats, including elk; Organic Valley eggs,
cheese, yogurt, milk, and other dairy; an extensive deli and in-store bakery;
and regional beers.

On Friday afternoons and evenings in season, La Crosse's *Cameron Park
Farmers' Market* is the place to find sustainably raised local food and local arts
of all kinds. It's La Crosse's only farmer-run market. (The Root Note shops
here.)

What to Do

There's no excuse for boredom at *Norskedalen Nature and Heritage Center*.
Guests have the run of the property—about four hundred acres of varied ecosystems, including wetlands, prairie, and woodland in the Helga Gunderson
Arboretum. Norskedalen is laced with five miles of nature trails and bisected
by quiet little Poplar Creek. Fed by twelve clear springs, the creek is eminently
wadeable. In winter, explore Norskedalen on snowshoes or cross-country skis
(trails are *not* groomed).

Anglers will find plenty of world class trout water. Nearby Timber Coulee Creek, with many access points and fishable tributaries, provides Class I fly fishing. The Spring Coulee Public Fishing Area is located along County Road P, on the route from Norskedalen to Coon Valley. Contact the Driftless Angler, a Travel Green Wisconsin–certified business in Viroqua, for eco-oriented guide service (see the Viroqua chapter).

You can take a fascinating peek into fisheries management by signing up for a field trip held annually in Bohemian Valley near Coon Valley by the Natural Resources Foundation of Wisconsin (see the NRF sidebar for more information). Watch experts electro-shock a stream to assess fish populations. The trout and other fish rise to the surface and then swim away unharmed.

Norskedalen special events are seasonal celebrations—a spring maple syrup boil with an organic pancake breakfast and craft classes; a midsummer bonfire with food, live music, and old-time fun; a fall threshing bee; and an old-fashioned Christmas. A stay at the Paulsen Cabin includes free admission to the Thrune Center exhibits, tours, programs, and special events. Tour the Bekkum Homestead and the Skumsrud Heritage Farm. Go to Saturday Smorgasbords, a nice mix of family programs that range from making birdhouses to baking lefse. Attend an Always on a Sunday program; speakers include regional authors, world travelers, and experts on nature, heritage, and history. Norskedalen Nights invite children (and the young at heart) to evening programs about bugs, birds, pioneer life, and Native Americans, among other topics. The Thrune Center's heritage classes are available to guests, but tuition is extra.

For strong, experienced cyclists who can handle the hills, La Crosse is within peddling distance, a twenty-mile ride on the back roads. Take County Road PI (steep), State Road 162 (steep), State Road 33, County Road F, which becomes Bliss Road (steep), which becomes Main Street as you head toward the historic downtown. Be sure your brakes are in good condition and be ready to use them going downhill.

Explore the green side of La Crosse—marsh, forest, and bluff top—on over twenty miles of hiking and biking trails that link the city's Riverside, Red Cloud, and Myrick parks and Hixon Forest. The five-mile River to Bluff trail starts at Riverside Park on the Mississippi River, wanders through the La Crosse River marsh and Hixon Forest—great birding territory—and then climbs over four hundred feet, ending with amazing views from the native prairie atop Grandad Bluff, the highest bluff in the area. Every spring, *Myrick Hixon EcoPark* holds the River to Ridge run/walk, an annual fundraising event, on this trail. The city grooms seven kilometers of Hixon Forest trails for cross-country skiing. And the new green-built Myrick Hixon EcoCenter has trail maps, environmental education exhibits and programs, and snow-shoe rentals.

Atop Grandad Bluff, you'll find thirteen miles of shared use (mountain biking, hiking, cross country skiing) trails. The trailhead is next to the National Weather Service Station on County Road FA, less than a mile north of County Road F. You'll spot a kiosk and a gravel parking area. The three miles of easy prairie trails, the ten miles of steep, challenging forest trails and the "dirt park" for kids on mountain bikes were built and are maintained by a local nonprofit called *Human Powered Trails* (HPT).

HPT's Judson Steinback said that the organization, under the visionary leadership of Dan Luebke and Mike Charron and with the help of many other volunteers, values equally the ecological integrity of the land and a great recreational experience. The group works closely with the Department of Natural Resources, the Mississippi Valley Conservancy, and Myrick Hixon EcoPark, and members attend workshops on building trails that minimize erosion. To raise awareness and build community, HPT hosts Trail Fests several times a year. These free, family friendly events feature guided rides for all ages and abilities, guided nature hikes through Hixon Forest, and free food and drink. It's also a chance to meet the generous volunteers who built the trails. Check the HPT Web site for dates.

River enthusiasts should make the trek to La Crosse for one of the evening paddle group outings offered weekly by *Three Rivers Outdoors* (3RO), a family-owned outdoor store in the historic downtown. River Divas (women only) is on Monday evenings, and Paddle Time (for men and women) is on Tuesday evenings. For a small fee (ten dollars in 2009), 3RO supplies the boats, the paddles, the personal flotation devices and a little instruction.

If you visit the area in the fall, consider signing up for Migration on the Mighty Mississippi, a field trip offered annually by the Natural Resources Foundation of Wisconsin (see the NRF sidebar for more information). The trip is held in this globally important bird area during the peak of fall migration, so you can expect to see up to 250 bald eagles and over 100,000 waterfowl. The outing begins in Brownsville, Minnesota. Cross the river on Highway 14 and follow Minnesota Highway 26 about seven miles south. The date is announced early in the year, prior to NRF's spring registration.

Those interested in alternative architecture and renewable energy will want to schedule their visit around the annual October *Driftless Farm* open

Explore Wild Wisconsin with the Experts

Wisconsin has more than its share of natural beauty. Sample the wealth on field trips that connect you to what Jeffrey Potter of the *Natural Resources Foundation of Wisconsin* (NRF) calls the heart and soul of Wisconsin. For more than twenty years, the foundation has worked with citizens, businesses, nonprofit organizations, and the government to promote the protection and enjoyment of Wisconsin's public lands, waters, and wildlife. NRF field trips offer expert guides, one-of-a-kind experiences, and remarkably low prices, making these trips among the best outdoor activities in the state. We love these outdoor adventures.

Trips are led by Wisconsin Department of Natural Resources conservation biologists and others who share their love and knowledge of the state's natural resources with participants. Nearly one hundred trips are offered statewide between April and October each year. Registration for all trips opens in the spring and continues throughout the season, but space is limited and some trips fill quickly. Members can register for members-only trips and have priority during registration. You can become a member, learn more about the program and register for field trips on the foundation's Web site.

---

house. The Driftless Farm, located about ten miles from Norskedalen, collects power through photovoltaic panels, obtains water with a water ram, and uses composting toilets. Buildings include a house, studio, greenhouse, and guest-house constructed from whole trees and featuring passive solar, straw-bale construction, and green roofs. *Whole Trees Architecture and Construction* is the sustainable firm of Driftless Farm owner and architect Roald Gunderson. "We grow people's homes, so to speak," said Roald. The Driftless Farm is also home to the first Community Supported Forest (CSF). Members can forage freely in the farm's 140-acre forest for oyster, puffball, chanterelle, and other mushrooms, as well as watercress, spring water, medicinal herbs, and maple syrup trees. They also choose from other forest products (like garden plots, firewood, sustainably milled lumber, and landscaping stone), services and workshops. The October event is part of the Midwest Renewable Energy Association (MREA) *Wisconsin Solar Tour*. Other area homes and businesses on the tour are listed on the MREA Web site.

Sylvan Workshop

Mineral Point Area

Woodlanders Gathering extends and elaborates people's positive thinking
about sustainable living; it builds community; it's a way to recharge.
—DANIEL MACK, artist

For years, Mineral Point has been all about historic preservation and local
art. So it's no surprise that area folks would be naturals in the sustainability
department. From the conservation of resources and land implicit in their
historic preservation to their amazing outdoor market to restaurants serving
local foods, Mineral Point is growing green.

From up on Military Ridge—that east-west height of land that divides
the Wisconsin River valley from the Rock River watershed to the south—the
terrain around Mineral Point appears gently rolling. Drop off the ridge to the
south, though, and you're into some serious hills and valleys. To the north,
the grades are even steeper and more dramatic.

Wisconsin's history is rooted deep in these hills, where early lead miners
discovered rich mineral deposits. The first miners lived in crude shelters
known as "badger holes," hence the state's nickname. Later immigrants from
Cornwall, England, brought the area's distinctive stone building style, still
well preserved today. And it was in Mineral Point that Henry Dodge was in-
augurated in 1836 as first governor of the Territory of Wisconsin.

Touring the Pendarvis historic site concentrates the area's heritage for visitors, and just wandering the steep winding streets of the town is an architectural delight. Some visitors come for the workshops at Shake Rag Alley
Center for the Arts. Artists have found shelter in the aging structures of this
old mining town for over half a century, forging an extensive arts community.
The range and quality of galleries and studios in and around Mineral Point
are legendary. You'll find summer theater at Alley Stage and year-round performances and films at the Opera House. And it's all happening in quirky
salvaged buildings.

The countryside is as much a lure as the town. Consider exploring on bicycle—state trails make riding easy, and two popular state parks lie along the trails. The more intrepid bicyclist will want to tackle the many quiet back roads, challenging hills that test even the strongest biker. If paddling sports are your choice, canoeing and kayaking are good on a little river south of Mineral Point.

Several local eateries embrace the eat-local movement. From May through October, the outdoor Mineral Point Market features just-picked, locally grown food of every stripe and color. (In winter, finding locally raised groceries means a trek to a food co-op in Spring Green or Mount Horeb.)

Where to Stay

Four miles northwest of Mineral Point, down a long gravel drive that runs through a farmyard, find a quiet retreat at *Maple Wood Lodge*. You won't have any neighbors; the lodge is rented to only one group at a time. And if you're like previous guests, you won't want to leave.

"Time and time again, whether it's adults or families with children, they come with all these plans for excursions, then decide that they just want to be here," said lodge co-owner Coleman.

The lodge at Maple Wood is landscaped with native plants. (photo by Robert Diebel)

"Just being here" means walking the trails; visiting Pedlar's Creek (a tributary of the Pecatonica); watching birds; playing volleyball, tetherball, horseshoes, or croquet in the yard; or simply swaying in the hammock. If you stay during morel season, Coleman will tell you where to hunt. The ridge path is thick with spring wildflowers. In winter, you can cross-country ski or snowshoe the trails. Star gazing is popular.

"They ask, 'Where did all these stars come from?'" said Coleman. This is dark sky country, far from city lights.

Inside, three second-floor bedrooms with sloping ceilings sleep six in cushiony comfort. Window and ceiling fans cool the rooms in summer. In winter, passive solar design keeps their propane bill down to less than four hundred dollars.

Locally made art objects are everywhere, from Brewery Pottery mugs to twig furniture from Longbranch Gallery to papier-mâché art created from discarded books. And every piece of furniture has a story that Coleman will happily tell, like the one about chairs salvaged from the burn pile at the dump.

Coleman, producing director of Alley Stage, and his partner, John Fetters, live on the adjoining twenty acres. They chose this place for the quiet countryside, the great bird populations, and the maple trees. Every spring, they tap about twenty-five trees and boil down the sap into syrup. They've restored five acres of prairie and created extensive bird habitat.

Another country option less than a mile south of Mineral Point and its delights is Harriet Story's *Bluebird Hill Country Cottage*. Perched on a hilltop with a great view of the town, the prairie-style cottage is surrounded by eighteen acres of prairie reserve laced with mown hiking paths and dotted with lots of bluebird houses. Harriet grows a big organic garden, does a lot of composting, and encourages guests to participate in adding to the composting process. Each group of guests receives a basket of organic fruit and vegetables upon arrival. The cottage has a full kitchen and, with three bedrooms and two bathrooms, can accommodate six people.

Harriet's an artist whose love of original local art and locally produced rustic furniture is reflected in the décor. Her pottery is sold in her Mineral Point store, Story Pottery, and she also owns Leaping Lizards Toy Store. Harriet lives near the cottage, above her pottery studio, housed in an environmentally conscious, energy-efficient remodeled barn. According to Harriet, her standard poodle is also supporting her sustainability efforts by producing wool for her sweaters (she wears a lot of black).

In town, choose the *Mineral Point Hotel* for the organic bedding and spa robes and for the handcrafted organic pastries you'll eat for breakfast. Molly Walz and Jay and Diane Homan bought the restored historic stone hotel in early 2008, are paring away the Victorian décor in the four guest rooms, and have installed a recycled Marmoleum floor in the lobby. They use Zum's nontoxic, biodegradable cleaning products and sell these and the organic bedding line in the lobby. Breakfast is homemade with local ingredients, including fruits from Tippy Top Organic Orchard at the market and organic flour from Great River Organic Milling in Fountain City, Wisconsin.

All three lodgings participate in the Cycle Southwest Wisconsin Bed and Bike program (see What to Do).

Where to Eat

Cafe Four at the Chesterfield is a modern addition to a historic stone inn. The new building has an elegant coved ceiling and clerestory windows. Their

The land around Harriet Story's Bluebird Hill Country Cottage is quintessentially southwestern Wisconsin. (photo by Harriet Story)

specialty is tasty handmade pizza baked in a wood-fired oven that's framed with a relief sculpture made by local artist Bruce Howdle. On the menu you'll find Uplands Cheese Pleasant Hill Reserve and Roth Käse cheeses. They use New Century eggs, Valley View meats, Green Spirit and Shooting Star produce, Blue Marble milk, and Kickapoo coffee. Wollersheim wines are served and local brews are on tap. In other words, they're on board with the local food movement.

The *Walker House*, owned and restored in a highly energy-efficient way by Joseph and Susan Dickinson, offers casual dining in the Cornish Pub (with typical Cornish pub décor as well as "badger holes" furnished with tables, chairs, and candlelight). There's also what Joseph calls Civilized Dining in the dining room. Chef Craig Thompson uses local foods as much as possible, including Rink DaVee's great veggies. In June 2009, the Dickinsons opened an inn in their stately 1830s stone building, with nine guestrooms sharing four bathrooms.

Local Foraging

The *Mineral Point Market* is held every Saturday morning from May to October under the water tower at Business 151 and Madison Street. One of the best small farmers' markets in Wisconsin, it's a social gathering spot as well as a source of great food. This popular Saturday morning event dates back to 1996. Rain or shine, cold or hot, breezy or calm, they'll be there. Market co-managers, who are also full-time vendors, maintain an organized and informative Web site with vendor profiles and a weekly newsletter with updates and messages from each vendor. You will find Rink DaVee and Jenny Bonde at the Mineral Point Market selling their gorgeous produce. The couple's three-acre *Shooting Star Farm* is twelve miles east of Mineral Point.

In an unassuming building that was once a blacksmith's shop in Mineral Point, Julie and Tony Hook of *Hook's Cheese Company* make award-winning cheeses with milk exclusively from local farms. In 1982, Julie's Colby won an international award, and their ten-year cheddar won a first in its category at the 2006 American Cheese Society judging. Their blue cheeses—Tilston Point and Blue Paradise—are glorious. Several restaurants in Mineral Point serve Hook's cheeses. Visit their factory on Friday mornings only, and please call ahead.

What to Do

Stop by the *Mineral Point Chamber of Commerce* to pick up a "Historic Mineral Point Architectural Driving Tour" booklet, and then walk or bike the route instead of driving. The tour takes you all over town to see thirty-five beautiful examples of historic architecture, including the Pendarvis State Historic Site. You'll learn a lot. Note: Private homes on the tour are not open to the public. Please respect their privacy.

Farm Tours

Visit an artisan cheese cave, home, and business powered by solar and wind— and you can get there from Mineral Point by bicycle. At *Bleu Mont Dairy,* northwest of Blue Mound State Park, artisan cheesemaker Willi Lehner transforms the milk of rotationally grazed cows into award-winning cheeses. His credentials are impressive. He learned the craft from his father, a Swiss cheesemaker who immigrated to Wisconsin in the 1950s. Willi also studied cheddar making in the UK. His Bandaged Cheddar, wheels of white cheddar aged in a traditional cloth-wrapped method in their simulated cave, took first place in its category at the 2006 American Cheese Society. Also impressive is his dedication to terroir (simply translated as intensely local flavor). Using raw organic local milk and microbes from the soil on his farm, he crafts a brine-washed soft cheese that he calls Driftless Select Earth Schmier—truly local cheese. He also produces gouda, farmstead Käse cheese, and gruyere-style cheese he calls Li'l Will's Big Cheese. Bleu Mont cheeses are produced in small batches. To create these magical cheeses, Willi uses the facilities of four other cheesemakers, three also in the Driftless Region. For the all-important process of aging the wheels, he built a 1,600-square-foot, vaulted subterranean cave on his farm. A straw-bale greenhouse is home to his first small affinage (aging) cave. Visitors to Willi's farm will learn about more than cheese—a 10kW wind generator and 1000-watt photovoltaic panels power the farm and return the excess to the grid. You can ride your bike from Mineral Point to the dairy via Shake Rag Trail, Military Ridge State Trail, and a county road. Visits are by appointment only. Another option is to register for an interactive culinary farm tour through an organization called *Learn Great Foods.* Tours include a cheese tasting and dinner in Mount Horeb. See their Web site for a schedule and more information.

After several years of being washed out on their farm near Viola, Joel and Jai Kellum of Avalanche Organics moved to *King's Hill Farm* south of Mineral Point during the summer of 2008. They're now at the Mineral Point Market. They welcome visitors to their farm and ask that you make an appointment to visit and learn about their use of permaculture principles in their farming. They farm forty acres of vegetables for their CSA and have added perennials and bees, as well as ducks, geese, turkeys, and pigs. The Bonner branch of the Pecatonica runs through their land but stays out of their fields.

Silent Sports

Paddle the Pecatonica River. It's a quiet little stream, and there's a nice eight-mile stretch that runs from Calamine (about ten miles south of Mineral Point) to Darlington. Midweek when ATV traffic is minimal, you can run a bicycle shuttle on the Cheese Country Trail that parallels the river. For more information, see Mike Svob's *Paddling Southern Wisconsin*.

If you're a bicyclist, check out the *Cycle Southwest Wisconsin* Web site for twenty-eight loop routes totaling over a thousand miles, to order a free Cycle Southwest Wisconsin Bicycle Trail map (also available for download), and for links to great local biking events like the Horribly Hilly Hundreds. All three of the lodgings in this chapter participate in the Bed and Bike program, with special offers for cyclists.

Cycling on Shake Rag Trail and *Military Ridge State Trail* is a good way to get long, fine views of the countryside without riding up and down steep hills. The six-mile-long Shake Rag Trail heads north from Shake Rag Street in Mineral Point to the south side of Dodgeville. The Military Ridge State Trail runs forty miles from Dodgeville to Madison. Along the route, connector trails lead to *Governor Dodge State Park* and *Blue Mound State Park* and some interesting side trips. All state trails require a trail pass.

Explore a *State Natural Area*. Within Governor Dodge is the Pine Cliff Location Natural Area, an unusual southern pine relict community perched atop several sandstone cliffs. (Pine relicts are southern Wisconsin pine forests that have persisted since the last glacier receded some twelve thousand years ago when a cooler climate was favorable for the growth of pine forests.) All three species of pine native to Wisconsin—red, white, and jack—grow here, out of their typical ranges. The pines are habitat for more northerly bird species, including black-throated green and Blackburnian warblers.

Further east on the bike trail, Ridgeway Pine Relict State Natural Area is a spectacular site containing eight separate pine relicts set among soaring sandstone cliffs, numerous rock outcrops, shallow caves, and rock shelters on 187 acres. It's on County Road H, less than a mile north of Ridgeway.

Local Arts

If you're on the trail of local art—and in Mineral Point, who isn't—*Gallery Nights* are held the first Saturdays of April, June, August, and December.

These citywide art parties get everyone out visiting galleries, of which there are many. Hunt for the perfect piece to take home or just admire the area's creative wealth.

For gallery visits at other times, call ahead. Just a few representative galleries are mentioned here—there are lots more to explore. *High Street Gallery* is an artists' collective and staffed by the artists themselves. *Green Lantern Studios* exhibits the works of one artist at a time or an exhibition based on a theme, like art created from found objects. The *Longbranch Gallery*, which was once an automotive garage and still sports a concrete floor, has a sizable collection of twig furniture and other local art. It displays the work of more than a hundred artisans.

Don't miss the *Fall Art Tour*, a chance to meet area artists and artisans. Some of Wisconsin's best invite you into their studios, in town and tucked away in the hills, to watch demonstrations, chat, and sell their work. You may go home with a one-of-a-kind piece of local art. Even if you don't buy a thing, you'll leave with a deeper sense of Mineral Point's strong artistic spirit. For low-impact, consider biking to the studios.

Just across Commerce Street from the Mineral Point Hotel, *La Bella Vita* fiber gallery has its home in the Set in Stone Bookstore. You'll find a collection of locally raised alpaca, llama, angora, and sheep fibers—sourced from less than twenty miles away (as well as internationally produced fibers from fair trade women's cooperatives). The shop also sells functional hand-blown glass knitting needles made by local artisans. They offer classes on a

A Field Trip to Folklore Village

For forty years, the nationally recognized *Folklore Village* east of Dodgeville has celebrated folk arts and culture with art, music, dance, and food. The message on its Web site reads: "Study with a master fiddler, sing with a gospel choir, dance until midnight, learn to spin wool, feast on jambalaya, join a back porch jam session, plant prairie flowers, or picture yourself as a student in a real 1890 schoolhouse . . . pass it on." So we are . . .

At Folklore Village all ages are welcome and invited to jump into the activities—song, dance, eating, art. There's something happening every weekend, from Saturday Night socials and old-time barn dances to special events for all ages and especially for kids and families. Admission is charged for events, but it's fun just to visit, walk the restored prairie, wander through the buildings, and meet the people who work at this inspiring place.

wide range of needle arts, and the shop's Thursday evening group is open to the public.

Foundry Books is housed in the 1847 stone Lanyon Iron Foundry. Among owner Gayle Bull's fascinating offerings, you'll find a number of works by Wisconsin authors. Regional titles may include *The History of Mining in Iowa County* by Stanley Holland.

The *Mineral Point Opera House* is one of the city's wonderful restoration projects, now returned to its 1914 glory. Today it is the venue for the local Shake Rag Players, the *Mineral Point Film Society*'s monthly screenings, national live theater, dance, and music performances, and daily presentations of quality mainstream movies. It's a gem.

Arts and Crafts Classes

Shake Rag Alley Center for Arts and Crafts, a nonprofit arts education center, offers an amazing schedule of workshops from April to August. Classes are held outside and inside nine restored historic miners' cabins on Shake Rag Street. Touring the campus is like going back in time. And when you see the wide range of opportunities for creative fun, you won't be able to resist registering for at least one class. Sign up early as class sizes are limited. The campus also includes the outdoor *Alley Stage*, an intimate theater (120 seats) featuring live performances from June through August. You can picnic in the gardens before the performances.

Every July at Shake Rag Alley, Daniel Mack's *Woodlanders Gathering* draws over two hundred participants to work with natural and found materials like debris, brush, and small saplings. From these elements come furniture, baskets, wood carvings, and other creations of the imagination. It's all about low-impact living. An artisan from Warwick, New York, Mack started doing this work in 1978; in 2009 the Mineral Point event was in its fifteenth season. You can sign up for a single day or the whole three-day happening.

Art and Ancient Heritage

Muscoda Area

The hills,
Rock ribbed and ancient as the sun.

—WILLIAM CULLEN BRYANT, *Thanatopsis*

As you wander the wooded hills just south of the Lower Wisconsin River, the world feels remote, uninhabited, and beautifully wild. Steep valleys, narrow roads, the occasional house, a small farm—all converge in a feeling of having left the modern world behind. And in a sense this corner of Wisconsin has turned its back on unchecked growth. The river valley, protected from development since 1989 by the Lower Wisconsin State Riverway Board, adds mightily to this sense of wildness.

The spirit of long ago inhabitants of this land can be sensed in the effigy mounds—sacred to Native Americans—near Muscoda. The Ho-Chunk Bison Prairie I Ranch near Muscoda reconnects the modern tribe spiritually with the bison that once roamed this land and which their ancestors hunted west of the Mississippi.

Artists have been inspired by the land for decades, urban refugees with studios hidden away in the woods or cunningly disguised as farmhouses. On one of these former farms, adult students can spend a day, a weekend, or longer, learning and creating art. And spending time on this farm can be about more than art. It's the kind of peaceful setting that nourishes creativity of all kinds. Between scheduled workshops, small groups may also rent the farm's three thoughtfully designed buildings for retreats of their own devising.

It is primarily the recycling of buildings that makes this destination notable for green travelers. Kathy and Bill Malkasian first lived in the hundred-year-old farmhouse, and then added their own low-profile, energy-efficient home near the studio buildings to free up lodging space for workshop participants. The art workshops are held in a building designed and built to fit naturally into the original farmscape. In planning the interior, Kathy reflected artist Virginia Huber's assertion that a studio should be colorless and have balanced light, so as not to distract from the creative process. Found objects and recycled art form the general theme of several of the studio's workshops. Kathy has used rustic elements like logs, branches, stone, and native plants to create an artful garden space—and a recycling statement of sorts—which greets you as you turn off the county road.

Where to Stay

For workshop participants at Kathy Malkasian's *Valley Ridge Art Studio and Retreat Center*, the most convenient option is to rent a room in the studio's historic Farmhouse. The two-story building is a classic American foursquare, original to the property and remodeled to house four people, each in a private bedroom. The four occupants share two bathrooms—bed linens and towels are provided—as well as the living room, dining room, and kitchen. There's also a large screen porch and a deck with a view. It's an attractive, spacious, comfortable place to stay.

If all rooms are full when you sign up for a workshop, a farm eight miles west rents two guest cottages. Jean Riley at Life O'Riley (see the Boscobel chapter) is used to accommodating overflow from Valley Ridge, and it's a lovely place to stay.

When workshops are not in session, individuals may rent a room or a group may rent the whole Farmhouse.

Where to Eat

When you register for a workshop at Valley Ridge, you can make reservations for catered lunches. A substantial lunch of fresh, mostly organic foods—a variety of salads, cheeses, fruits, dessert—is served for lunch each day of the workshop for an extra fee. (Beverages are included in the workshop registration fee.)

Culinary adventurers will definitely want to reserve a Saturday evening seating at Isaac and Havvah's *Milkweed*, unforgettable outdoor dining in the hills about twenty-five miles east of Valley Ridge. June to October, by appointment only.

Local Foraging

Since the Farmhouse kitchen is fully fitted with gas stove, full-sized refrigerator, dishwasher, microwave, and coffeemaker, life on the farm can be self-contained. On your way, stock up for your stay at one of the great area co-ops—Madison's Willy Street Co-op, Mount Horeb's Trillium Natural Foods, the Viroqua Food Co-op, Richland Center's Pine River Food Co-op, Platteville's Driftless Market.

The Wisconsin River town of Muscoda, twelve miles north of Valley Ridge, has the title of Morel Capital of Wisconsin. In celebration of this woodland delicacy, the town holds a *Morel Mushroom Festival* every spring the weekend after Mother's Day. Just so you know how many morels we're talking about—the average morel weighs just a few ounces, and sometimes gatherers bring in and sell over two thousand pounds of these coveted fungi for the festival.

What to Do

Valley Ridge Art Studio is all about making art and forging an arts community, but it's not necessary to have extensive art experience to sign up for a workshop. Workshops are taught by world class instructors (bios are on the Valley Ridge Web site). The list of workshop topics, which reflects Kathy Malkasian's passion for book arts in particular, includes mixed media, metals, fiber, and other arts. Kathy also typically schedules several open studios each year, where artists work on individual projects.

A garden framed with a rustic art installation greets you at Valley Ridge Art Studio and Retreat Center. (photo by Robert Diebel)

Recent two- to three-day workshop offerings were Altered Fabric Collage and Book; Working with Wire; Open Book: An Artist Journal Weekend; Captured! Bezel Setting for Found Object Jewelry; Print, Pattern and Paper; Found Object Alchemy; and the Painted Page, a two-day workshop on creating a visual journal.

Several retreats are longer and more intensive. One of these, a five-day retreat titled Beyond Precious Little, focused on found objects. Instructor Keith Lo Bue is a jeweler, sculptor, and teacher whose work is featured in the Smithsonian Institution in Washington, D.C., and the Museum of Arts and Design in New York.

A preliminary program list for the coming year is typically posted online in September. By December, the schedule is complete and registration begins. By March, about half the year's classes are already filled.

The shared strong connection to the arts at Valley Ridge builds community. A remarkable 80 percent of students return year after year—some have

---

Ho-Chunk Tribal Heritage Field Trips

Near Muscoda, effigy mounds were built by ancient peoples about a thousand years ago. "Effigy Mounds Grand Tour," a fascinating brochure with a map and directions to each mound site, is available from the *Lower Wisconsin State Riverway Board* office in Muscoda. The brochure, created by *Cultural Landscape Legacies*, includes recommended reading about the insights the mounds offer into the ideas of these early peoples. The relatively recent discovery of cave paintings in Tainter's Cave has provided archeologists with new clues in the mystery of the effigy mound builders' fate. Please remember that the mounds—sacred to Native American tribes—are almost always burial sites and must be accorded proper respect. Mounds are protected under state law.

On the Ho-Chunk *Bison Prairie I Ranch*, about fifteen miles north of Valley Ridge, a herd of 115 bison graze on the prairie grasses of tribal land along the Wisconsin River. The herd's presence renews the tribe's ancient connection to the bison, spiritually important as their traditional source of food, shelter, and clothing. There's also a modern motivation—tribal members reap the health benefits of eating this tasty, low-fat, grass-fed meat. The ranch uses sustainable agriculture practices—rotational grazing, prairie restoration, and organic hay production for winter feed. You can visit the herd by arranging a tour of the ranch. Call a week ahead and leave a phone message for herd manager Richard Snake.

During the Morel Festival in May (see Local Foraging), you can get a free bus ride from Muscoda to the ranch and effigy mounds.

---

been coming since the studio opened, and several attend eight to twelve workshops each year. Although the majority of students are women, men report feeling quite comfortable in this female-dominated environment and a few attend regularly.

When a workshop is not in session, Valley Ridge Retreat Center rents any or all of the buildings to groups of twenty or fewer for their own studio needs, retreats, reunions, or conferences. The center is generally available midweek and on holiday weekends. In addition to the Farmhouse and Classroom, the Community Building has a large meeting room, kitchen, and bathroom.

Valley Ridge workshops end each day at 4:30. A lovely way to end the day is to explore the farm's 120 acres of forest, prairie, and meadows, hiking or snowshoeing as the seasons dictate. The land is home to considerable wildlife, including hawks, eagles, turkey, pheasant, deer, and coyote, and a trout stream runs though the valley below.

If you time things right, you may be able to combine your stay at Valley Ridge with an annual field trip offered by the *Natural Resources Foundation of Wisconsin* (NRF). This is a chance to explore two quite different State Natural Areas (SNAs) along the Lower Wisconsin. Blue River Sand Barrens SNA, a remnant of Wisconsin's "desert," is home to cacti and other arid-loving plants. In Avoca Prairie SNA, you can explore the largest wet prairie east of the Mississippi. The trip date is announced early in the year, prior to NRF's spring registration. Visit NRF's Web site for more information on this and other NRF field trips.

Flowers offer natural inspiration. At *Blooming Valley Perennial Nursery*, gorgeous perennials are the stars of the show. Visitors are welcome to explore Douglas and Ina Lukas's perennial, ornamental grass, and native plant nursery. They offer landscape design and garden coaching services. Ina and organic farmer Roger Reynolds teach on-site gardening workshops, and Ina also teaches children's programs, which she calls Radicle Sprouts Workshops (a radicle is the rudimentary root of a seedling). These short, playful workshops—Edible Flower Taste Testing and Garden Tea Party, Faerie Magic, and Monarch Magic—are offered only once a season and have limited enrollment. Blooming Valley is a beautiful place—and a sustainable operation as well. They recycle, conserve water, and use integrated pest management and organic sprays and fertilizers. It is located about twenty miles east of Valley Ridge—within biking range if you can do the hills.

Head for the Hills

Sparta Area

When we see the land as a community to which we belong, we may begin to use it with love and respect.
—ALDO LEOPOLD, *The Sand County Almanac*

For those who live and farm in the hills of the Driftless Area, nature sometimes seems to hold most of the cards: steep fields to work, river floods that wipe out farms and even whole towns, and a landscape that both inspires and discourages. Visitors to this land are entranced by both the glorious natural beauty and by the human stories they sense in weathered houses and barns.

In the past few decades, an agricultural revolution has transformed the coulees, now home to countless sustainable agriculture farms and farmers who seek to work with the land, not against it. This new breed of farmers feeds not only Wisconsin's demand for local, sustainably grown food but the urban markets of the Twin Cities and Chicagoland. With this and other changes have come a new cultural optimism and sense of community with each other and with the earth.

Some changes came early. The Elroy-Sparta State Trail is Wisconsin's oldest (and many would say best) bike trail. The first of those great "rails to trails" projects that repurpose abandoned railroad beds, the trail opened in 1967. Since then, the popularity of bicycle tourism has spawned a network of connecting trails: the "400" State Trail, the La Crosse River State Trail, and the Great River State Trail.

The Cashton area is home to a large Amish settlement—farmers and artisans who make a living selling their products. And some lifelong residents, loath to leave the land they love, have chosen to open their farms to guests who want to sample the Driftless Area. Their guests share the sentiments of the woman at Justin Trails Resort who said, "I'm sick to death of staying in hotels. They're all alike. I want connection, to meet the owners."

They want to meet the land too, through eco-friendly outdoor fun like biking, hiking, cross-country skiing, and snowshoeing. That's what this adventure in the hills is all about.

Where to Stay

Along Interstate 90 at Sparta, the land lies flat in the La Crosse River valley, and wooded hills rise to the south. Back in those hills, Donna and Don Justin have transformed their family farm into *Justin Trails Resort*, a bed-and-breakfast resort based on outdoor fun.

The couple still lives in the American foursquare home that Don's grandparents Gustave and Appolonia Justin built in 1920. And Justin Trails is still a farm, with llamas and goats in residence and fields of oats, barley, and rye bordering the yard.

But since 1985, the machine shed has become an office and restaurant lodge, the granary a guest cottage, and the chicken coop a massage and meeting center. The upper levels of the farmhouse have been remodeled into three guest rooms, with Donna and Don's quarters on the lower level. Their guests choose from those guest rooms, two log cabins, and a cottage, all decorated in relaxed country style and furnished with very comfy beds. Extensive gardens are planted in part with native plants. Rethought and sustainably recycled, these buildings reflect the changes in their owners' lives.

Guests can also hike a third of a mile to a tent campground with toilets, picnic tables, and fire pits. (The Justins' land restoration project has yielded lots of firewood for the fire pits.) For more remote camping, hike a half mile into the wilderness camping area or to primitive sites on the wooded ridge top.

Although 71 acres are tilled—using strip cropping, grassy waterways and a runoff pond to prevent erosion, and small grain crops to eliminate the need for chemicals—the 213-acre farm is two-thirds wooded coulee. Every ten years with the help of a professional forester the couple sustainably harvests the birch, aspen, shagbark hickory, black walnut, and oak. The first cutting yielded some of the wood for the floors in their remodeled buildings, and a later harvest, trees for a log cabin. Ten miles of trails now snake through the woods for hiking and mountain biking, cross-country skiing, and snowshoeing.

Hilly pasture land became a disc golf course and, in winter, a fabulous sledding hill. Two kilometers of trail are devoted to skijoring, where a skier is pulled by a dog. Pets are welcome, and all the outdoor fun makes Justin Trails ideal for families.

Snowshoes for guests to use for winter fun cover the lodge wall at Justin Trails Resort. (photo by Robert Diebel)

Locally made furniture and crafts, recycled furnishings, and local art (including Donna's nationally recognized photos) are an integral piece of the couple's conservation-minded approach to life, as is doing much of the work themselves. The former dairy barn is Don's woodworking shop, where he has built much of the furniture. When they need outside help—as with building the log cabins—they hire a local builder. The bigger log cabin, raised in 1993, sleeps six people.

In the energy conservation department, heat and air-conditioning come from Trane energy-efficient units, and the front-loading washer and commercial dishwasher are equally energy efficient. The resort participates in a program of buying electricity from renewable sources and uses compact fluorescent lights. Donna and Don shovel and sweep rather than snow-blow the walkways, and they own only one vehicle.

The Justins also schedule old-fashioned work days, which they announce in their e-newsletter. In return for four hours of helping with Don and Donna's ambitious land restoration project, workers get a night's lodging for a greatly reduced rate or camping for free. Everyone works together, everyone eats the gratis lunch and dinner together, and the next morning's breakfast is included in the lodging. "It's about building community as well as improving the land," said Donna.

Where to Eat

The full breakfast served by the Justins to all guests is homemade, using ingredients from the *Northwood Country Market* in Sparta, from food co-ops in Viroqua and La Crosse, and from Donna's gardens. Donna offers vegetarian, gluten-free, nondairy, and nut-free options on request. This is a big country breakfast—four courses and plenty of delicious food to keep you going during a day outdoors. Donna serves breakfast in the Lodge or brings it to your cabin or room.

The Lodge is also a restaurant, where Donna will make lunch and dinner for groups who make advance reservations. The kitchenette in each cabin and room has a small refrigerator, coffee maker, microwave, dishes, and silverware, but no pots and pans. Two cabins have grills.

In Sparta, seven miles north, locally owned *Ginny's Cupboard* serves homemade soups, chili, sandwiches, and Wisconsin ice cream. It has an espresso bar and features a fully functioning 1957 soda fountain. Located less than a mile from the bicycle trail depot, Ginny's would be a good choice for a post-ride meal.

You can dine at locally owned *Angelini's Pizzeria and Ristorante* in Sparta or have your order delivered to Justin Trails for a small charge.

For ambitious bicyclists, a great eating adventure involves a ride on the La Crosse River and Great River state trails from Sparta to the Mississippi River town of Trempealeau, a seventy-five-mile round trip. Your reward is a tasty lunch at the Trempealeau Hotel, in the dining room or on the sun deck or screened porch overlooking the Mississippi River. Try their famous Walnut Burger.

What to Do

"Go outside and play," said Mom. And it's easy to play without leaving Justin Trails.

Hike the trails to watch hawks soar the thermals, for the distant views from hilltops, or just for the peace of this quiet coulee. One ridge top climbing destination is a tall rock outcrop with a dolostone cap—you'll see Sparta seven miles away. Or hike to the spring-fed pond, a 1961 watershed management project that's home to bullfrogs and water birds.

Mountain bike the grassy ski trails—ten miles of single track and ten miles of double track trails.

Go llama trekking—that means walking a llama on a halter lead, a hike with a new friend, so to speak. The llamas, Dusty and Rusty, are gentle creatures and fond of humans. Either Donna or Don goes along on llama treks.

Play one of the professionally designed eighteen-basket disc golf courses. The Classic course, a one-mile hike on steep hills, takes a foursome about two hours to play. The new Big Brother course is even tougher—three steep miles and about three hours of play. The courses are open year-round, and there's an Ice Bowl Tournament every winter. Justin Trails also hosts an annual summer tournament and is a stop on the PDGA Wisconsin Tour.

Winter playtime means some great snow tubing. There's no lift on the big hill, so you'll really get a workout. George and Heidi, the Justins' Siberian huskies, will join you if you wish, on leash, of course. Skijoring is another chance to hang out with George. The skier wears a harness, the dog wears a harness, the harnesses are hooked together and the dog pulls the skier. Donna will teach you this novel sport. With a little help, Heidi and George will also pull a kick sled in a modified form of dog sledding. Silent (except for the barking) sports are the norm at Justin Trails.

At the end of a long downhill run, Heidi the Husky is ready for more. (photo by Robert Diebel)

Native Prairie Walks with Bob Lee

Railroad right-of-ways are sometimes prairie remnants, small samplings of the great prairies that once covered this part of the state. Along the bicycle trail east and west of the town of Rockland, native wildflowers and grasses still grow in abundance and are now protected as a State Natural Area. Those who love true prairie, and those who simply want to experience its beauty, should schedule their visit to Sparta around one of a series of guided prairie walks.

Each year since 1991, local naturalist Bob Lee has led walks to follow the seasonal changes in this remnant prairie. The area's rolling landform features several ecosystems, everything from dry prairie knobs to wet prairie. Bob did a plant survey, finding about 350 different native prairie or oak savanna plants. From the emergence of the spring pasqueflower to the fall glory of big bluestem grasses, he tells the story of the prairie and oak savanna that once was. Bob also tells stories about the people who put names on plants, about local history, and about how he came to know and love this beautiful bit of land.

Bob's prairie walks are always on a Sunday afternoon, from late April to early October. For a current schedule, visit the Sparta Depot or call Wildcat Mountain State Park Work Unit (608) 337-4775. Meet at the trail crossing on Commercial Street (County Road J) in Rockland.

On National Trails Day in June, Bob leads a morning walk that starts at the Sparta Depot to explore several prairie remnants. For details, call the Sparta Chamber of Commerce.

There's a whole wall of plastic snowshoes (made in La Crosse by ORC, which hires disabled workers) at the resort for trekking on marked trails through the woods. And if you love the sport, they'll sell you a pair to take home. Bring your cross-country skis. Ten miles of groomed Nordic ski trails—varying in difficulty and length—run through wooded and open land. The Bambi-eze trail gives beginners and kids an easy option.

About fifteen miles from Justin Trails and two miles east of Cashton, *Down a Country Road* is a Travel Green Wisconsin–certified business owned by Kathy and Chuck Kuderer. Here you can browse five charming little shops for products made by Amish families as well as by local non-Amish crafters. Amish families in the area craft quilts, furniture, baskets, and rugs and make jams, jellies, maple syrup, candies, and other foods. Some sell their products from their farms. For those who would like to visit Amish farms and learn more about the Amish way of life, the business offers tour guides who will accompany you or motorcoach tours (non-Amish driver), depending on the size of the group.

Over a hundred miles of connected state bicycle and hiking trails can be accessed seven miles from the resort. Take Highway 27 across I-90 to the intersection with Highway 16 and turn right. Go a half-mile to Water Street and turn right. It's another half-mile to the *Sparta Depot*, the west end of the 32-mile *Elroy-Sparta State Trail* and the east end of the 21.5-mile *La Crosse River State Trail*. If you're over sixteen, a trail pass is required.

If you didn't bring your own bike, reserve one in advance from *Speed's Bicycle Shop*, next to the trail in Sparta. The shop also does bike repairs and shuttles.

The Elroy-Sparta Trail heads southeast and hooks up with the "400" State Trail at Elroy, running through three dark, cool tunnels along the way. The longest of these is three-quarters of a mile—bring your head lamp and a jacket. The La Crosse River Trail heads west, joining the Great River State Trail north of La Crosse. The town of Rockland is about six miles from Sparta. To both the east and west of Rockland, the *La Crosse River Trail Prairie State Natural Area* stretches about 2.5 miles along the trail. Look for signs that alert you to a really nice array of native prairie plants and scattered young bur oak openings along these five miles.

Along the Lower Wisconsin

Spring Green Area

All my life I've loved listening to rural people tell their stories. What interested me about Arena is that it is not a township sold out to urban interests; it is an agricultural township true to its original conception. They have a true identity. They believe in themselves. They represent what all of us consider to be a good life.

—DICK CATES, author of *Voices from the Heart of the Land*

The Lower Wisconsin River valley is a land that inspires. The gentle wooded hills are home to Frank Lloyd Wright's Taliesin and the American Players Theatre. These two cultural icons have lured visitors for decades. You'll find local arts communities in Spring Green's many galleries, annual art fairs, and tours; Taliesin's Hillside Theater; and the Spring Green Literary Festival. And of course there's BobFest, a raucous spring celebration of Bob Dylan's music.

The river towns have been greening up over the last decade. In Spring Green, two restaurants and a cafe proudly feature local foods. North of town, a master cheesemaker makes fabulous artisan cheese and cleans the plant's wastewater with an innovative system. An award-winning grass-fed beef farm south of town is run by a local author and his family.

The Lower Wisconsin State Riverway Board protects the broad river valley from development. Canoeists paddle the free-flowing Wisconsin in great flotillas, camping out on the many sandbars. (Fortunately, those seeking a little solitude can find it on river reaches less paddled, those downstream of Spring Green.) Four State Natural Areas within just a few miles of Spring Green protect a total of almost fourteen hundred acres of environmentally significant land. Bicyclists love riding the valley's quiet byways.

And the owners of a local B&B are helping preserve the nature of this beautiful place.

Where to Stay

Find lodging at the *Hill Street Bed and Breakfast*, housed in a Queen Anne Victorian in a quiet residential neighborhood of Spring Green. Antique furnishings and traditional décor are featured throughout the downstairs and the seven attractive and comfortable guest rooms.

Historic buildings and furnishings are earth friendly simply by virtue of being recycled rather than replaced. What also makes this B&B notable is that Kelly and Jay Phelps, owners since 1994, are adding green practices. They're steadily replacing incandescents with compact fluorescent lights. They buy shampoo in bulk, use earth-friendly cleaning products, and have installed low-flow showerheads. Waste reduction is a big priority; they recycle everything they can and compost food waste and the biodegradable throwaways to which they've recently switched. (Their attractively planted yard, which includes some native plants, is the compost beneficiary.) They use biodegradable detergent in their Energy Star front-loading washer. Kelly plans to install a programmable thermostat and a rain barrel.

Kelly noted that some guests use eco-friendly transportation to travel to Spring Green. Some bicycle in, and one canoed. Spring Green is on the Greyhound route, so bus travel is an option. Once in residence, transportation can be carbon-neutral. A short walk takes you to downtown galleries and eateries. You can bike to many area destinations.

Tower Hill State Park has a small, quiet campground south of Spring Green on the Wisconsin River. Fifteen sites are available on a first-come, first-served basis. The campground has water and pit toilets.

Where to Eat

A five-block walk from the B&B will take you to what used to be the State Bank of Spring Green. Now Spring Green's latest culinary addition—*The Bank Restaurant and Wine Bar*—the place still feels like a bank, a very swanky bank. This is an impressive recycling project. Many architectural features of the 1915 building are intact, from the ornate neoclassical revival façade to the coffered ceiling in the main dining area. Have a glass of wine next to the teller cages in the lobby wine bar. Then reserve a table for six in the vault (the door still closes) or one of several other dining areas. Sounds formal, but since they cater to the American Players Theatre crowd, many diners are casually dressed. The Bank serves lunch during summers only and a special 4:30 dinner before theater performances. According to Bank manager Danielle

Belanger, the restaurant's new menu focuses on hot and cold tapas, with only a short list of entrees. Offerings are based on locally sourced food. In summer, she says, up to 50 percent of their food comes from area farmers, all listed on the Bank's Web site. Witness tapas like Cuban Beef—the beef comes from nearby Cates Farm—and Bank Rolls stuffed with Cedar Grove cheeses.

During a hard day at BobFest (see Annual Events) a bite to eat at Karin and Todd Miller's *Spring Green General Store* (sponsor of the event) is the way to go. Once a cheese warehouse, it's now a cafe serving home-cooked ethnic food—breakfast, lunch, and weekend brunch for eating in, eating on the porch, or carrying out—and a variety of beverages, including local microbrews. And it's an event center: In addition to author events, Saturday Afternoon Musical Performances, and Mostly Mondays Poetry Society meetings, their entertainment schedule includes Paul Bentzen Day (you'll have to ask), St. Patty's Day, and BobFest. And it's a hippy boutique, with everything from scented candles and tie-dyed dresses to exotic spices. A general store indeed.

The dining room at the *Riverview Terrace Cafe* overlooks the broad Wisconsin River from inside the Frank Lloyd Wright Visitor Center, two miles south of Spring Green off Highway 23. Local ingredients—including beef from Dick Cates—dominate the ever-changing menu. It also serves local microbrews. Open May 1 to October 31 for breakfast and lunch.

Hitting all the galleries in nearby Mazomanie (see What to Do) can add up to an all-day trip—which means lunch at the *Old Feed Mill* on Cramer Street. If you're still there by evening, *Wall Street Gallery and Bistro* serves good homemade pasta and pizza, although service can be slow when they are busy. They're open Thursday through Saturday.

Local Foraging

Nineteen miles east of Spring Green on Highway 14, in the town of Black Earth, *Black Earth Meat Market* puts an ecologically aware new face on the old fashioned butcher shop. Not only do they sell retail cuts of locally, humanely and organically raised grass-fed beef, hogs, lambs, and goats, but they are the only remaining abattoir in Dane County. This is not anonymous meat.

What to Do

Pack a picnic and head for the hills south of Spring Green. *American Players Theatre* (APT)—world-class open-air theater in a natural amphitheater—is the reason many folks go to Spring Green in summer. APT is a good steward to its 110 acres of wooded hills. There's a volunteer spring garlic mustard pull and the oak trees are managed to protect against oak wilt. Patrons can hike through an oak savanna restoration, several acres of managed prairie, and one prairie remnant. Dundee McNair, APT director of operations, said he has spotted ornate box turtles (a Wisconsin endangered species) in the prairie and that red-headed woodpeckers are also in residence.

In 2009 APT celebrated its thirtieth anniversary with the opening of the intimate indoor Touchstone Theater. All two hundred seats are reclaimed and refurbished. The Touchstone and the prairie restoration that surrounds it replaced a former employee parking lot. The new theater's shuttle, known as the Touchstone Tram, is an electric vehicle. Madison patrons have the option of purchasing a bus ride with their tickets to selected Friday performances, one for each of the five summer productions. Call the box office for details.

If you're a Frank Lloyd Wright buff, set aside a whole day for a guided tour of *Taliesin*, his residence and studio. Wright is famed for his organic architecture—buildings that follow the landscape, rather than changing the landscape to suit the building. An alternative is to use the directions and map

Grapes hang overhead and tropical plants thrive in the bubbling water purification system that is Cedar Grove Cheese's environmentally friendly Living Machine. (photo by Robert Diebel)

on the Chamber of Commerce Web site for the *Architectural Driving Tour* and tour by bike instead. The eight-hundred-acre estate's Travel Green certification is based on native prairie restoration (five prairie remnants), sustainable forestry, and organic farming managed by the Otter Creek Foundation. Half the estate is left natural and managed for ecological integrity.

Ride your bike north to Plain and tour the Living Machine at *Cedar Grove Cheese*, seven miles north of Spring Green. In a greenhouse up the hill from the cheese plant is master cheesemaker Bob Wills's ingenious solution to the wastewater problem that all cheesemakers face. (It involves tropical plants and microbes.) The end result is pure water flowing into Honey Creek. Tours are Monday to Saturday mornings. While you're there, buy some cheese. The Prairie Premium line is made with the milk of pasture-grazed cows and the cheddar is outstanding. Best of all, they have squeaky fresh curds daily.

Canoe the Lower Wisconsin Riverway between Spring Green and Boscobel. This reach is less popular than Prairie du Sac to Spring Green, so you won't have to share the river with rowdy crowds. You'll see the real wildlife instead. Rentals and shuttles are available in Spring Green from *Wisconsin Riverside Resort* (formerly known as Bob's Riverside) on the south side of Spring Green. For the complete scoop on paddling the Wisconsin, read Mike Svob's *Paddling Southern Wisconsin*.

Bicycling the hills around Spring Green is quite popular. A lovely twenty-mile loop through the wooded hills starts at the Highway 23 bridge south of town and heads down County Road C toward Tower Hill State Park. Turn right on Golf Course Road and pass American Players Theatre. Make the long climb on High Point Road to Coon Rock Road, then Amacher Hollow Road. Head south on County H and west on County T and north on County Z. A bike path along Highway 23 near Taliesin skirts the highway for about a mile and takes you over to Unity Chapel.

Explore one of four *State Natural Areas* (detailed descriptions and directions on the Web site) within easy biking distance of Spring Green.

Tower Hill Bottoms is 125 acres of undisturbed floodplain forest in Tower Hill State Park along County Road C, south of Spring Green. You can reach the forest by park trails or by canoe. Bird life includes pileated wood-pecker, tufted titmouse, prothonotary warbler, and the state-threatened red-shouldered hawk.

Look for desert plants, birds, snakes, and spiders in the Spring Green Preserve, about two miles northeast of Spring Green. Rare open country birds like the dickcissel, grasshopper sparrow, and lark sparrow are common here. This 1,011-acre rolling sand prairie is best known for its spiders and insects, including the black widow and several wolf spiders; five species of cicada; eight species of tiger beetles; and predatory wasps. Reptile populations include the rare bullsnake, the six-lined racerunner, and the blue racer.

In the 160 acres of Bakken's Pond natural area, about four miles west of Spring Green, are a cold, spring-fed stream, a wet sedge meadow, and flood-plain forest. In these habitats, look for cricket, green, chorus, and leopard frogs; tiger salamanders and eastern newts; northern water snake; and eastern painted turtles. The state-threatened Blanding's turtle is also found here. Wear your waders.

The Arena Pines and Sand Barrens covers eighty acres northwest of Arena. Dry prairie species include little blue-stem, June grass, three-awn grass, flowering spurge, hoary puccoon, Venus' looking-glass, blue toadflax, lyrate rock cress, and prairie coreopsis, as well as the only Wisconsin population of button-weed.

Hemlock Draw, a Nature Conservancy property north of Spring Green near Leland, is worth the longer ride (or drive). Hemlock and yellow birch, normally seen in northern Wisconsin, grow in a long, narrow valley between rock formations. Look for more than forty species of breeding birds, including barred owls, ruffed grouse, wood thrush, black-capped chickadee, six species of warblers—including the rare worm-eating warbler—and four species of woodpeckers. Spring wildflowers are numerous.

Art lovers will find a mother lode of galleries in Spring Green. At the *Jura Silverman Gallery*, one among almost a dozen galleries, huge lilacs frame the front door. During May, the air is scented outside and in. Inside, you'll see the work of over seventy-five Wisconsin artists and artisans. The regional Fall Art Tour includes Spring Green artists (see Mineral Point chapter).

The *Spring Green Literary Festival* held at Taliesin in September is an opportunity to hear noted authors talk literature in a natural setting.

On Sunday of Memorial Day weekend, *BobFest* celebrates the life and talents of Bob Dylan at the Spring Green General Store. The party is held outside (weather permitting) with the back porch as the stage for hours of Dylan songs performed by a wide variety of musicians. A special menu and local microbrews are featured.

If you'd like to know what a truly ethical beef operation looks like, make an appointment to visit the *Cates Family Farm*, about six miles south of Spring Green. The farm was the first in Wisconsin to be certified by the Animal Welfare Institute and by Food Alliance Midwest. The Cates family's Angus and Jersey steers are completely grass-fed and receive no growth hormones or

BobFest performers rock out on the back porch of the Spring Green General Store. (photo by Robert Diebel)

antibiotics. Farmer Dick Cates based his book *Voices from the Heart of the Land: Rural Stories That Inspire Community* on interviews with more than thirty families living in and around Arena Township.

Microbrew fans, make an appointment for a short and entertaining Saturday tour of *Lake Louie Brewery*, about ten miles east of Spring Green. In the late 1980s, Tommy Porter bought land north of Arena from his Uncle Louie. On the land is a quarter-acre pond. When Tommy decided in 1999 to take his weekend brewing hobby to the next level, Lake Louie beer was born. He's a mechanical engineer, so he bought used brewing equipment that he knew he could work on himself. He knew he had a good product. "The reason the beer is so good is that the water here is so darn good," says Tommy. He installed holding tanks to recycle the wastewater. Grain comes from Chilton, Wisconsin. His catfish logo was the invention of an artist friend with a carpenter's pencil, a scrap of paper, and fifteen minutes. His mission: to produce quality beers for local people. And to entertain, we might add.

Head for artsy little Mazomanie, sixteen miles east of Spring Green. If you arrive on Highway 14, you'll pass Wisconsin's first solar photo panel factory at the edge of town. Downtown, thirty-three of Mazomanie's buildings are on the

Historic Register. Careful restorations of these beautiful old buildings and a strong arts community have helped the town thrive. It's all about high quality local art and reclaiming, reusing, and recycling what was already there. The Old Feed Mill restaurant owner Dan Viste is the catalyst and driving force behind much of the restoration, including an entire block between Crescent Street and the new Promenade Park. The Mount Horeb Area Arts Association's Spring Art Tour includes studios in Mazomanie (see the Madison chapter).

If it's a weekend afternoon, your first stop should be the *Mazomanie Historic Art Center* on Crescent Street. In an elegantly rehabbed blacksmith shop, ongoing shows feature the very best of local artists, many of whom paint *en plein air*. Then head to the Brodhead Street galleries. The *Hembrough Gallery* displays Doris Hembrough's nature photography. The *Woven Palette Weaving Studio* has beautiful hand-woven scarves, and, in the same building, the *Creative Edge Gallery* cooperative features the fine art and jewelry of local artists. Shop for high quality, stylish recycled apparel at *Halle's Vintage Shoppe*.

The River Alliance of Wisconsin

If you join only one Wisconsin environmental group, make it the *River Alliance of Wisconsin*. First and foremost, they are effective. Their work has led to the removal of small obsolete dams throughout the state, returning rivers like the Baraboo to their happy free-flowing natural selves. They got the word out when the massive and ill-conceived Grand Cambrian, a proposed waterfront development, threatened in unprecedented ways the unique geology of the Lower Dells of the Wisconsin River, and they worked with other concerned groups to successfully stop it. They help small watershed groups with river protection projects, help farmers keep their manure out of the rivers by pushing for education and funding, advocate changes in groundwater law and educate the public about its importance, strive to keep agriculture and high capacity wells from draining rivers like the Little Plover out of existence, and are leading the fight against invasive species that threaten our rivers. Their innovative Project RED (Riverine Early Detectors) trains interested citizens to canoe or kayak their favorite streams looking for invasive species.

And in between these battles, they find time for "dates with rivers"—highly enjoyable canoe trips on rivers like the Wisconsin, the Kickapoo, and the Baraboo, with interesting and informative guides along to interpret the river. They take hikes along riverways, up the Mississippi bluffs, or along the St. Croix–Bois Brule Portage Trail. They sponsor environmental films at Sundance. And they hold an annual meeting and party called the Spring Confluence where you can get together with like-minded river folks.

Twenty-five miles east of Spring Green, the interesting village of Cross Plains is developing its ecological awareness. From the green-built Rosemary Garfoot Public Library (LEED silver certified) to the new green-built head-quarters of the Ice Age Trail, the community grows greener every year. At the *Crossroads Coffee House*, owner Mary Devitt serves fair trade coffees and teas and local products like Sassy Cow milk from Columbus. Local art is on display. (Cross Plains is on Mount Horeb's Spring Art Tour—see the Madison chapter.) What makes this coffeehouse stand out is that Mary hosts Science Tuesday programs. She invites noted researchers to speak on such topics as Wisconsin's Ice Age landscapes, the science of Black Earth Creek, Wisconsin's wild mushrooms, and farmland preservation; a group discussion follows.

New Ideas in the Old Hills

Viroqua Area

There are no flat places on this farm—so we're not used to walking on pavement.
  —ROSEANNE BOYETT, organic farmer and innkeeper

Eat local. Eat slow. Swallow.
  —KAY O'BRIEN, The Driftless Cafe

If you've never explored the area around Viroqua, Westby, Avalanche, Ontario, and La Farge, you'll be delighted by the wild beauty you find there. It's a land laced with coulees—narrow curving valleys where spring-fed trout streams race, flanked by steep, wooded ridges.

Industrial farmers find these coulees too confined to cultivate with their big machines, and floodplains are prone to washouts. Thus the narrow strip fields and pastureland of small organic and traditional Amish farms—the agricultural models best suited to coulees. These farms produce an amazing bounty of sustainably raised food for farmers' markets all over southern Wisconsin, Minnesota, and northern Illinois.

Not all land is farmed. In Vernon County alone, vast tracts of public land—8,600 acres in the Kickapoo Valley Reserve, 3,600 acres in adjacent Wildcat Mountain State Park, 707 acres in a county forest, 150 acres in a state natural area, 890 acres in two county parks—will never be farmed or developed. Ho-Chunk Nation tribal land occupies 1,200 acres in the Reserve. Habitat for wildlife and birds, these preserves are there for you to explore and enjoy.

Near Viroqua—center of all things alternative—you'll find a folk art and sustainable living school, an arts retreat with a spiritual focus, and a country life school that also connects you with visitors of other nationalities.

Human-powered recreation is right at home in the hills. The crooked Kickapoo is a favorite with canoeists. Every fall, the Kickapoo Dam Challenge gives amateur triathletes a chance to show their stuff. Wildcat Mountain has hiking trails, cross-country ski trails, and snowshoe trails. Bicyclists pedal challenging routes through the steep hills. And the trout fishing is legendary.

But when those little trout streams and the bigger Kickapoo flood, as they often do, everyone is hit hard. Farming the steep coulees without polluting the streams means controlling erosion. Limestone karst, or sinkhole, formations demand great care to protect the groundwater. Land stewards rather than simply farmers, this new breed of family farmer works hard to reduce the runoff that feeds the floods. What visitors can do to help preserve this beautiful landscape is to choose sustainable lodging and food.

Where to Stay

West of La Farge, *Trillium Cottage* gives you a chance to sample life on a rambling organic farm. You can choose from two cottages—a 1929-vintage shingled cabin and a stuccoed cottage built in 1988 by innkeeper Roseanne Boyett and her family. A stay in one of these unpretentious, homey cottages feels like visiting Grandma on the farm.

In fact, the farm's former owners moved the little shingled cabin onto the property for their Grandma Nordeen to live in from 1929 to 1943. The two-story cottage up the hill is bigger, with enough room for a family of six. Some families return to Trillium year after year.

You'll meet—and may feed—the Boyetts' various sheep, goats, ducks, rabbits, cats, chickens, cows, and potbellied pig. If you hike the wooded acres of the eighty-five-acre farm or sit quietly on the cabin's front porch swing in the morning, you may also spot some of the farm's undomesticated inhabitants, like a wild turkey, strutting by.

Each morning, Roseanne brings you warm, freshly baked breads wrapped in a tea towel—she says you can stay there up to three weeks and get two different breads every day—accompanied by jellies and jams she makes with the farm's fruits. The refrigerator is stocked with cheese, butter, and milk from the Westby Creamery and eggs from the farm's chickens. Breakfast at Trillium is a feast.

Antique country furniture and recycled building materials add to the earth-friendly nature of the place. Land conservation measures include planting the perimeter of the farm with a windbreak of trees, rotational grazing for the cows and sheep, sustainable harvesting of trees from the woodlot, a runoff pond to control erosion, and organic gardening practices. Big trees shade the cottages in summer, so there's no air-conditioning; and both cottages have wood-burning fireplaces as well as conventional furnaces. The old-fashioned bathrooms have tubs rather than showers. Roseanne has replaced all the lights in the cottages with compact fluorescents, and she uses biodegradable cleaning products. She provides compost buckets with snap-on lids in both cottages, which she empties daily, and composts all waste from her own kitchen.

At *Hidden Springs Bed and Breakfast*, owned by Brenda and Dean Jensen, you can stay on a working sustainable sheep farm and creamery east of Westby, in the heart of Amish country. This is where Brenda crafts her amazing award-winning cheese (see Local Foraging). It's a lovely setting, high on a hill and named for the hidden springs down the slope. A little stream runs through the seventy-six acres of hilly land.

To house the new B&B, the couple's Amish neighbors built an addition to the farmhouse with a private entrance. (Local Amish carpenters also built the house, the barn, and the creamery.) There's one unit open and more planned. It has a full kitchen, a sleeping loft, a full bath, and a living room with a gas stove. A private back deck features a great view, and there's a fire pit as well. Watch the sheep graze from the porch swing.

As a guest on the farm, you can meet "the ladies," as Brenda affectionately calls her herd of gentle East Frisian and Lacaunes. "The ladies like visitors," said Brenda. You can even help milk if you wish; she uses a waist-high pipeline for these petite, docile animals. You can also visit her cheese-curing caves, built into the hillside near the creamery. And you will no doubt want to meet

The cozy Hill Cottage at Trillium has room for a family of six. (photo by Robert Diebel)

Beauty and Chief, the Percheron draft horses—not tractors—that provide all the power for plowing the fields. Rotational grazing paddocks provide fresh grass for the herd all summer and protect the land from erosion. Donkeys guard the sheep from coyotes and other predators.

The Jensens work closely with the Amish and have built a strong community with neighboring families; bridges across the fences connect them physically as well. With the knowledge gained from eight years of raising sheep—their herd now numbers about 250—they're helping other families in the area start sheep farms. As her herd's milk production slows in the fall, Brenda adds milk from Amish neighbors' cows to her cheeses. In winter, she feeds the herd with hay raised by the Amish.

Before she began sheep farming, Brenda spent twenty-five years in the corporate world. Now she's immersed in the age-old cycles of farming. In the icy days of early spring lambing, she helps her does birth their lambs. She feeds and milks the herd year around. And she creates cheeses that are making international headlines in the world of cheese. Brenda's inspiring story has been told in the *New York Times Magazine* and the *Wall Street Journal*, on the BBC filming of Stephen Fry's *In America*, and in Aussie Will Studd's book *Cheese Slices*. A stay at Hidden Springs Farm is a chance to meet a modern-day Driftless pioneer.

Nancy Rhodes's green-thinking *Viroqua Heritage Inn* bed-and-breakfast is in a quiet neighborhood just a block from downtown Viroqua. Carefully restored historic buildings often beat conventional new construction in the sustainability department, and these two grand old Viroqua mansions—the Boyle House and the Eckhart House—definitely qualify. The historic houses, which face one another across Jefferson Street, have a total of nine rooms, including one with a tower. All but two have private baths and one has a Jacuzzi. The inn's décor is eclectic antique elegance with hardwood floors and oriental rugs—and a definite emphasis on comfort.

A committed recycler since her college days, Nancy loves recycling in all its forms—a castoff but ornamental table leg is refigured as a pretty fern stand with the addition of a top, for example. "It's a consciousness of being kind to our earth and not overusing—it's a lifestyle," she said. "I wash and reuse plastic bags until they wear out. We must do the right thing." Honoring her conviction that every guest has the right to the least toxic environment, she uses nontoxic cleaners and detergents.

Guests are served a full breakfast made with many organic and local ingredients, up to 85 percent during the growing season. Nancy shops at the local co-op and farmers' market and gets staples like eggs and maple syrup from individual farmers. She stores root vegetables in the cool cellar of her old house.

Nancy is a leader in local historic preservation and downtown revitalization. Along with a group of other citizens, she initiated a project to convert the abandoned railroad bed between Viroqua and Westby to a bike trail. When the folks at Bluedog Cycle came to town, they picked up the project, and in 2011, the trail will be complete.

In Westby, Mike and Marie Cimino's *Westby House* is a traditional bed-and-breakfast in a handsome big Victorian house with a wraparound porch. The main house has seven guest rooms, each with a private bath. An adjoining annex houses four suites. If you want to cook, choose one of the two suites that have full kitchens so you can take advantage of all the locally grown goodness.

The Westby House has a definite eco-orientation. All cleaning products and detergents are biodegradable, made by Shaklee. The Ciminos recycle and ask their guests to as well. They no longer sell bottled water to guests; instead they provide a large dispenser of tap water for filling durable water bottles, thus considerably reducing the inn's recycling load. They also use rain barrels. Cyclists will appreciate the B&B's extensive collection of bike route maps. The inn includes a restaurant, and local and organic foods comprise about 20 percent of their menu. This means buying local produce and fruits—the apples, a big part of their fruit usage, are grown only five miles away. Their dairy products are from Organic Valley and the Westby Creamery.

Wildcat Mountain State Park has a very nice campground on top of Wildcat Mountain with great views of the river valley all along the ridge. The sites have picnic tables and fire rings, and the campground has flush toilets and showers.

Where to Eat

In downtown Viroqua, Kay O'Brien's casual *Driftless Cafe* serves great coffee and espresso as well as delicious fresh local fare—homemade soups, salads, fresh-baked sourdough bread and pizza—about 80 percent of which is made with local ingredients. Daily specials are heavy on the veggies, but the staff is happy to add meat if you wish. Their organic fair trade coffee is from local microroaster Kickapoo Coffee, and they serve microbrews like New Glarus and Sand Creek as well as very nice fair trade wines. Half the town seems to pass through this cozy place sometime during the day—it's a community gathering spot as well as a tasty eatery. Live evening music about once a week draws even more.

Roseanne Boyett's Trillium Cottage Cranberry Cornbread

1 cup unbleached all-purpose flour
1 cup whole wheat flour
1 cup yellow cornmeal
1 teaspoon salt
1½ teaspoons baking powder
½ cup melted butter
½ cup granulated sugar
½ cup maple syrup
2 large eggs
1¼ cups buttermilk
½ teaspoon vanilla extract
½ cup chopped craisins (dried cranberries)
¾ cup chopped walnuts

In a large mixing bowl, sift together the all-purpose flour, whole wheat flour, cornmeal, salt, and baking powder. In a separate bowl, cream together the butter and granulated sugar. Mix in the maple syrup. Stir in the eggs, one at a time. Mix in the buttermilk (you may substitute 1 cup of milk mixed with 1 tablespoon lemon juice *or* 1 tablespoon vinegar) and add the vanilla extract. Mixture may appear curdled. Add the liquid mixture to the bowl of sifted dry ingredients and mix together. Stir in the craisins and chopped nuts.

Preheat oven to 350 degrees. Prepare a standard-size glass bread pan and a smaller loaf pan by buttering the baking surface and then lightly dusting with flour. Spoon the prepared batter into the pans and bake in the preheated oven for 70 to 75 minutes, until tests done when thin-bladed knife inserted into the center of the loaf is dry when removed. Remove from oven and cool for a few minutes in baking pans. Then turn out onto wire rack to finish cooling. Serve warm from the oven or at room temperature.

This recipe will require about an hour and a half total preparation/baking time. It will yield one standard size loaf and one smaller loaf.

This multigrain (corn and wheat) recipe offers additional nutrition from the dried cranberries and nuts. The dairy products and eggs provide calcium and protein. The grains provide essential minerals and fiber.

We are beginning a new family tradition this year at Thanksgiving by having this bread as part of our traditional feast. It is slightly sweet but not sweet enough to detract from the other foods when served as part of a meal. The eggs, butter, milk, and maple syrup are all produced on area farms. The cranberries are a regional product. Celebrate the bounty of the season and the Thanksgiving holiday by serving this tasty bread. ENJOY!!!

—Roseanne Boyett

The *Public Market at Main Street Station* is a remarkable spot—a collection of local businesses and additional entrepreneurial micromerchants located in one big historic brick building on Main Street—a sort of eco-shopping mall where customers hang out on the benches and chat. There's an event calendar as well. At *Sibby's Cafe Oz*, try the daily special—often made with ingredients from the Viroqua farmers' market—as well as yummy locally produced organic ice cream, coffee, and sweet treats. And if you ask to have your ice cream in a to-go cup, it'll be biodegradable.

If you stay at Trillium Cottage, you'll have a full kitchen and an outdoor grill for fixing local feasts. For sources of provisions, read on.

Local Foraging

Viroqua Food Co-op is a treasure. This beautiful green-built store, completed in 2005, has natural lighting, a polished concrete floor that needs no harsh chemicals to maintain, insulation made of scrap blue jeans, and high-efficiency refrigeration cases. It carries an inspiring variety of fresh, local, organic, and bulk foods, and the deli has hot soups, salad bar, and beverages. Bakery goods are made daily, using locally raised ingredients when possible.

At Hidden Springs Farm, a sustainable dairy east of Westby, Brenda Jensen produces sheep's milk cheese (and runs a B&B—see Where to Stay). This is not ordinary cheese—the fresh soft creamy cheese she calls Driftless won three awards at the 2007 American Cheese Society judging. At the 2008 American Cheese Society competition, she won six awards, including two first-place honors—the cranberry-flavored Driftless and her Ocooch Mountain cheese, a semifirm raw-sheep's-milk washed-rind cheese. All this after only two years of making cheese. Buy Brenda's amazing cheeses at the Viroqua Food Co-op.

The *Viroqua Farmers' Market* is held Saturday mornings from the end of May through October at 220 South Main Street.

There are so many organic and sustainable farms in the area that listing all of them would fill a book. Here's a sampling of those who welcome visitors by appointment. Some also have retail farm stores. Please call ahead for hours. *Driftless Organics* west of Soldiers Grove raises veggies, with potatoes as their largest crop; *Harmony Valley Farm* west of Viroqua raises veggies and beef; *Shining Hills Farm and Gardens* grows flowers near Avalanche; *One Sun Farm and Bakery* sells frozen pizzas homemade with organic ingredients at their retail store near Avalanche; and *Trout Palace* rainbow trout farm is northwest of La Farge. *Vernon Vineyards*, northwest of Viroqua, grows hardy Wisconsin grapes like Frontenac, and their free tasting room and retail store are open weekends from May to December.

What to Do

Set aside plenty of time for exploring the *Kickapoo Valley Reserve* just north of La Farge. Start with the handsome new visitor center, which features local building materials, passive solar and geothermal heat, and native plants landscaping. Inside you can learn the quite amazing story of the reserve's origins, an epic tale of landowners taking back control of their land from a huge government agency. There's also information on the flora and fauna of the reserve. Outside, you'll find three short hiking-only trails, one to two miles long. Hikers are also welcome on over fifty-five miles of mountain bike, equestrian, and multiuse trails. For bicyclists, the Kickapoo Valley Reserve has an extensive trail system with twenty-four miles of challenging mountain bike trails and twenty-five miles of road biking on lightly traveled paved roads in and around the reserve. The visitor center has maps.

The Kickapoo Valley Reserve offers an extensive schedule of interesting interpretive programs and hikes, including frequent Saturday and evening events. Its Summer Institute offers continuing education courses for credit to adults, a fun Middle School Adventure Camp, and innovative Summer Adventures for high school students. Want an example? In 2009, Adventures with GPS taught kids about the popular sport of geocaching while hiking, biking, and canoeing from one point on the reserve to another.

Tunnelville Cliffs *State Natural Area* along the banks of the Kickapoo on Tunnelville Road, southwest of La Farge, is a series of sandstone cliffs where you'll find seepages, waterfalls, and a wide variety of woodland ferns and wildflowers—and in winter, ice caves.

Ten miles southeast of Viroqua just off of County Road Y on Irish Ridge Road, Duck Egg County Forest is a good place to watch spring warblers, waterfowl, and herons. Hiking trails lead to an overlook.

An ever popular Driftless diversion is to paddle the gentle, winding Kickapoo River with its beautiful rock outcrops between Ontario and La Farge (twenty-one miles). If you have more time, you can continue on to the Wisconsin River (twenty-seven more miles), but the first stretch has the least deadfalls. Ontario is Canoe Central, with stacks of beached aluminum rental beasts lying around in the off season. *Titanic Canoe Rental* rents nonaluminum (read: quiet) Old Town Discovery canoes with comfortable molded seats—

and has a great name to boot. If you have your own canoe or kayak, Titanic will shuttle you. Mike Svob's *Paddling Southern Wisconsin* tells you all you need to know about one of his favorite rivers.

To the north of and contiguous with the reserve land, Wildcat Mountain State Park is located on a ridge rising steeply above the Kickapoo Valley. An observation point that overlooks the Kickapoo Valley provides spectacular views. The park's mostly wooded land is laced with a network of trails featuring scenic overlooks as well—25.8 miles of hiking trails, 17.5 miles of trails for snowshoeing, 7 miles of cross-country ski trails, and 1.3 miles of interpretive nature trail.

The Round Barn Tour takes cyclists past fifteen historic round barns, built from the late nineteenth century until the 1930s, primarily by Alga Shivers, son of a slave who escaped to the area via the Underground Railroad. Tour maps and historical information are available at the *Viroqua Tourism Office*.

Bluedog Cycles in Viroqua, owned by Pete and Alycann Taylor, has full sales and professional service for family, mountain, and road cyclists and workshop space available for rent. They lead several weekly group road and mountain bike rides year round (bring your snow tires). Pete is active in building sustainable trails in the area, and two ongoing shared-use trail projects are at Sidie Hollow (three miles west of Viroqua on County Road XX) and Jersey Valley (three miles north of Westby on County Road X) county parks. To help with trail projects, contact Pete at Bluedog.

At Westby's *Stabbur Information Center*, pick up a copy of "Venture into the Coulee Region," a brochure and map of five on-road bicycle tours ranging from seventeen to forty-three miles. All start and finish at the Stabbur. They're not easy. The Amish Tour is a thirty-mile route on twisting roads with 300- to 400-foot climbs. Your reward is amazing scenery—and rest stops at Amish farms where you can shop for crafts and other products.

The *Kickapoo Dam Challenge* in early October is one of the best-run amateur triathlons in the state. Paddle seven miles on the Kickapoo, bike fourteen miles through the hills, and run three miles on a trail over the same terrain. You can enter as an individual or as part of a team. It's a really fun day in the Driftless Area, with great volunteers and great participants.

The *Driftless Angler*, an environmentally friendly trout fishing guide service and full service fly shop, is headquartered in a nicely restored building on Viroqua's main street. Owner Mat Wagner explained that he moved here from the Rocky Mountains for the amazing local trout streams, "There's all these wonderful little streams—it makes you feel like a kid again. Trout

fishing is very accessible; it's not an art form. I just want everybody to fish."
Mat started a program to control invasive species; promotes leaving no trace
and recycling—including waders (www.recycledwaders.com); and, on guided
trips, serves lunches made with local and organic foods. He supports the River
Alliance, the Driftless Area Restoration Effort, Spring Creek Partner, and Wisconsin Trout Unlimited.

At *Full Circle Retreat* ten miles southwest of Viroqua, Kathleen Grittner
offers art, music, journaling, and writing workshops and retreats, complete
with dormitory-style lodging and a kitchen in which shared meal preparation
is possible. Retreats, scheduled from April through October, are designed to
inspire and energize your creative spirit in a beautiful remote setting.

The *Driftless Folk School* is a family-friendly school based in Viroqua. You'll
find classes in traditional arts and crafts, the natural world, and modern sustainable practices and skills. Half-day and full-day classes are held in various
locations around Viroqua—the homes and farms of the instructors or the
Landmark Center. Check out their extensive class schedule online.

Robert Clovis Siemon and Keiko Asaumi Siemon's *Little Country School*
offers family friendly food and farm tours for all ages that help people connect with rural culture, sustainable living, organic agriculture, and the natural environment. Robert is the son of Organic Valley CEO George Siemon,
and Keiko grew up in Japan. Tours often include participants from other
countries.

The La Farge headquarters building of *Organic Valley*, the nationwide cooperative that changed the way sustainable farms do business, was built with
locally sourced timber, insulated with blue jeans, and finished inside with low
VOC paint. Wood floors were recycled from the founder's farm kitchen, and
office furniture, from a Silicon Valley company. Waterless urinals save forty
thousand gallons per year. Heat from the computer server room helps heat
the building, which is designed with passive solar. There's much more, but
you'll have to visit to learn it all. To schedule a tour, complete their request
form online (allow at least two weeks). You'll have a chance to eat lunch in
their organic cafe with the Croppies (Organic Valley employees).

Local Arts

The *Temple Theatre* is a shining example of the power of volunteer effort. In
2002, an extensive restoration of the 1922 classic revival building was completed
and the theater reopened. The marquee is lit up and all kinds of live entertainment now fill the calendar.

An independent, locally owned and operated, full service bookstore, Susan Paull's *Bramble Bookstore*, also carries a good selection of regional and local titles. The large children's section features a cozy reading area.

Viroqua's downtown *VIVA Gallery Cooperative* displays and sells the work of local artists and artisans.

RESOURCES

Travel Green Wisconsin

Travel Green Wisconsin is a voluntary program that reviews, certifies, and recognizes tourism businesses and organizations that have made a commitment to reducing their environmental impact. Specifically, the program encourages participants to evaluate their operations, set goals, and take specific actions toward environmental, social, and economic sustainability. The public can read these evaluations on the program's Web site, www.travelgreenwisconsin.com.

Great Reading

Breckenridge, Suzanne, and Marjorie Snyder. *Wisconsin Herb Cookbook*. Madison: Prairie Oak Press, 1996.

Cates, Richard L., Jr. *Voices from the Heart of the Land*. Madison, WI: Terrace Books, 2008.

Diebel, Lynne Smith, and Jann Faust Kalscheur. *ABCs Naturally*. Black Earth, WI: Trails Books, 2003.

Dott, Robert H., Jr., and John W. Attig. *Roadside Geology of Wisconsin*. Missoula, MT: Mountain Press, 2004.

Feldman, Stephen. *Fabled Land, Timeless River: Life along the Mississippi*. Chicago: Quadrangle Books, 1970.

Hembd, Jerry, Jody Padgham, and Jan Joannides, eds. *Renewing the Countryside: Wisconsin*. Minneapolis: Renewing the Countryside, 2007.

Leopold, Aldo. *The River of the Mother of God and Other Essays by Aldo Leopold*. Madison: University of Wisconsin Press, 1991.

———. *A Sand County Almanac*. New York: Oxford University Press, 1949.

Logan, Ben. *The Land Remembers: The Story of a Farm and Its People*. New York: Viking Press, 1975.

McLimans, David. *Gone Wild*. New York: Walker Publishing Company, 2006.

———. *Gone Fishing*. New York: Walker Publishing Company, 2008.

Rogers, Elizabeth, and Thomas M. Kostigen. *The Green Book: The Everyday Guide to Saving the Planet One Simple Step at a Time*. New York: Three Rivers Press, 2007.

Schoff, Gretchen Holstein. *Reflections: The Story of Cranes.* Baraboo, WI: International Crane Foundation, 2007.

Sibley, David Allen. *The Sibley Guide to Birds.* New York: Alfred A. Knopf, Chanticleer Press, 2000.

Svob, Mike. *Paddling Southern Wisconsin.* Rev. ed. Black Earth, WI: Trails Books, 2006.

Trask, Crissy. *It's Easy Being Green: A Handbook for Earth-Friendly Living.* Layton, UT: Gibbs Smith, 2006.

Interesting Periodicals and Booklets

Ice Age Trail Companion Guide, www.iceagetrail.org

The Leopold Outlook, www.aldoleopold.org

The Places We Save: A Guide to the Nature Conservancy's Preserves in Wisconsin, www
.nature.org/wherewework/northamerica/states/wisconsin/preserves/art35.html

Stories of Stewardship: Tales from Wisconsin's Big Backyard, www.gatheringwaters.org

Sustainable Times, www.sustainabletimes.net

Wisconsin, Naturally: A Guide to 150 Great State Natural Areas, www.dnr.wi.gov/org/
land/er/forms/snaguide.htm

Other Useful Web Sites

Dane Buy Local, www.danebuylocal.com

Eat Local Wisconsin, www.eatlocalwisconsin.com

Home Grown Wisconsin, www.familyfarmed.org/homegrownwisconsin.html

International Crane Foundation, www.savingcranes.org

Land Stewardship Project, www.landstewardshipproject.org

Local Harvest, www.localharvest.org

Madison Area Community Supported Agriculture, www.macsac.org

Madison Environmental Group, www.madisonenvironmental.com

Mississippi Valley Conservancy, www.mississippivalleyconservancy.org

Natural Resources Foundation of Wisconsin, www.wisconservation.org

Reap Food Group, www.reapfoodgroup.com

Renewing the Countryside, www.renewingthecountryside.org

SHARE, www.sharewi.org

Slow Food Wisconsin Southeast, www.slowfoodwise.org

Sustain Dane, www.sustaindane.org

Valley Stewardship Network, www.kickapoovsn.org

Wisconsin Association of Lakes, www.wisconsinlakes.org

Wisconsin Dairy Artisan Network, www.wisconsindairyartisan.org

Wisconsin Department of Natural Resources, www.dnr.wi.gov

Wisconsin Environmental Initiative, www.wi-ei.org

Wisconsin's Farm Fresh Atlases, www.farmfreshatlas.org

Wisconsin State Natural Areas, www.dnr.wi.gov/org/land/er/sna

Wisconsin State Park System, www.dnr.state.wi.us/org/land/parks

DIRECTORY

Bicycling Green: Sugar River Area

Where to Stay

Earth Rider Hotel
929 West Exchange Street
Brodhead, WI 53520
(608) 897-8300 or (608) 214-3573
www.earthridercycling.com

Little Sugar River Farm
N5929 Schneeberger Road
Albany, WI 53502
(608) 862-2212 or (608) 214-3817
www.littlesugarriverfarm.com

Where to Eat

The Dining Room at 209 Main
209 North Main Street
Monticello, WI 53570
(608) 938-2200
www.209main.com

The Crossover
Monticello, WI 53570
(608) 214-3817

M & M Cafe
126 North Main Street
Monticello, WI 53570
(608) 938-4890
www.monticellowi.com/M&Mcafe

Puempel's Olde Tavern
18 Sixth Avenue

New Glarus, WI 53574
(608) 527-2045

Creamery Cafe
6858 Paoli Road
Belleville (Paoli), WI 53508
(608) 845-3388
www.artisangal.com/cafe.php

Paoli Local Foods
6895 Paoli Road
Belleville (Paoli), WI 53508
(608) 845-3663
www.paolilocalfoods.com

Real Coffee and Food
18 East Main Street
Evansville, WI 53536
(608) 882-0949

Local Foraging

Detweiler's Bulk Foods
N5055 Highway 104
Albany, WI 53502
(608) 897-8500

Detweiler's Bent and Dent
W363 Atkinson Road
Albany, WI 53502
(608) 897-2867

Detweiler and Kauffman
W509 Atkinson Road

Albany, WI 53502
(608) 897-8787

Sugar Maple Emu Farm
W805 Pedee Road
Brodhead, WI 53520
(608) 897-8224
www.sugarmapleemu.com

Silver Lewis Cheese Co-op
W3075 County Road EE
Monticello, WI 53570
(608) 938-4813

Decatur Dairy
W1668 County Road F
Brodhead, WI 53520
(608) 897-8661
www.decaturdairy.com

Blue Skies Berry Farm
10320 North Crocker Road
Brooklyn, WI 53521
(608) 455-2803
www.blueskiesfarm.com

Paoli Cheese Shop
6890 Paoli Road
Belleville (Paoli), WI 53508
(608) 845-7031
www.paolicheese.com

What to Do

Morningstar Farm
4737 County Road T
Brodhead, WI 53520
(608) 897-4653

Amish Country Lane Bakery
1602 Scotch Hill Road
Brodhead, WI 53520
(608) 897-3820

Scotch Hill Farm
910 Scotch Hill Road
Brodhead, WI 53520
(608) 897-4288
www.scotchhillfarm.com

Kinkoona Farm
Kinkoona Farm Day Camps
16734 West Dorner Road
Brodhead, WI 53520
(608) 897-3983
www.baabaashop.com

Sugar River State Trail
www.dnr.wi.gov/org/land/parks/
    specific/sugarriver

Badger State Trail
www.dnr.wi.gov/org/land/parks/
    specific/badger
www.badger-trail.com

Friends of Wisconsin State Parks
www.fwsp.org

New Glarus Brewing Company
County Road W and Highway 69
New Glarus, WI 53574
(608) 527-5850
www.newglarusbrewing.com

New Glarus Woods State Park
W5446 County Road NN
New Glarus WI 53574
(608) 527-2335
www.dnr.wi.gov/org/land/parks/
    specific/ngwoods

Dane County Recreation Map
danedocs.countyofdane.com/webdocs/
    PDF/lwrd/parks/brochure.pdf

Allen Creek Gallery
137 East Main Street
Evansville, WI 53536
(608) 882-2415
www.allencreekgallery.com
www.matthiasjames.com

Historic Walking Tour
City of Evansville
www.ci.evansville.wi.gov/visitors/
    walkingtour.htm

The Willow Tree
912 West Exchange Street
Brodhead, WI 53520
(608) 897-8390

Artisan Gallery
6858 Paoli Road
Belleville (Paoli), WI 53508
(608) 845-6600
www.artisangal.com

Paoli House Gallery
6891 Paoli Road
Belleville (Paoli), WI 53508
(608) 848-9606
www.paolihousegallery.com

Paoli Schoolhouse Shops
6857 Paoli Road
Belleville (Paoli), WI 53508
(608) 848-6261
www.paolischoolhouseshops.com

Tour the Farms Day
City of Brodhead
www.cityofbrodheadwi.us

14 South Artists
www.14southartists.com

Stoughton Opera House
381 East Main Street
Stoughton, WI 53589
(608) 877-4400
www.cityofstoughton.com

Yahara Grocery Co-op
229 East Main Street
Stoughton, WI 53589
(608) 877-0947
www.yaharagrocery.coop

Sugar River Bike Tour
www.brodheadoptimist.org

Clearview School Amish Auction
Highway 104 and Atkinson Road
Brodhead, WI 53520
(608) 897-8787

A Little Town with Heart: Elkhart Lake Area

Where to Stay

Osthoff Resort
101 Osthoff Avenue
Elkhart Lake, WI 53020
(800) 876-3399
www.osthoff.com

Where to Eat

Lola's on the Lake, Otto's Restaurant,
    L'ecole de la Maison
Elkhart Lake, WI 53020
(800) 876-3399
www.osthoff.com

Local Foraging

Feed Mill Shops
44 Gottfried Street
Elkhart Lake, WI 53020
(920) 876-3354
www.feedmillshops.com

Thyme Savours
44 Gottfried Street
Elkhart Lake, WI 53020
(920) 876-3655
www.feedmillshops.com/thymesavours
    .html

Feed Mill Market
44 Gottfried Street
Elkhart Lake, WI 53020
(920) 876-3354
http://www.feedmillshops.com/market
    .html

Brown Baer
181 Rhine Street
Elkhart Lake, WI 53020
(920) 876-3319

Grassway Organics Farm Store
N600 Plymouth Trail
New Holstein, WI 53061
(920) 894-4201
www.grasswayorganics.com

Farmer/Artisan Market
downtown Elkhart Lake
(877) 355-3554 or (920) 876-2922
www.elkhartlake.com

What to Do

Three Gables Consignment Shop
176 East Rhine Street
Elkhart Lake, WI 53020
(920) 876-2100

Mix and Mingle
111 East Rhine Street
Elkhart Lake, WI 53020
(920) 876-2299

Two Fish Gallery
244 East Rhine Street
Elkhart Lake, WI 53020
(920) 876-3192
www.twofishgallery.net

Ecology Outfitters
633 North Eighth Street
Sheboygan, WI 53081
(920) 452-9555
www.ecologyoutfitters.com

Greenbush Kettle
www.dnr.wi.gov/org/land/parks/
   specific/kmn/trails.html

Parnell Observation Tower
www.dnr.wi.gov/org/land/parks/
   specific/kmn/PDFs/KMNUmapc
   .pdf

Historic Race Circuits of Elkhart Lake
www.historicracecircuits.com

Sustain in Dane: Madison Area
Where to Stay

Arbor House
3402 Monroe Street
Madison, WI 53711
(608) 238-2981
www.arbor-house.com

Fountain Prairie Inn and Farms
W1901 Highway 16
Fall River, WI 53932
(920) 484-3618 or (866) 883-4775
www.fountainprairie.com

Speckled Hen Inn
5525 Portage Road
Madison, WI 53704
(608) 244-9368 or (877) 670-4844
www.speckledheninn.com

Where to Eat

L'Etoile Restaurant, Café Soleil
25 North Pinckney Street
Madison, WI 53703
(608) 251-0500
www.letoile-restaurant.com

Harvest
21 North Pinckney Street
Madison, WI 53703
(608) 255-6075
www.harvest-restaurant.com

Marigold Kitchen
118 South Pinckney Street
Madison, WI 53703
(608) 661-5559
www.marigoldkitchen.com

Bradbury's Coffee
127 North Hamilton Street
Madison, WI 53703
(608) 204-0474
www.bradburyscoffee.com

Restaurant Magnus
120 East Wilson Street
Madison, WI 53703
(608) 258-8787
www.restaurantmagnus.com

Weary Traveler Freehouse
1201 Williamson Street
Madison, WI 53703
(608) 442-6207

Lazy Jane's Cafe and Bakery
1358 Williamson Street
Madison, WI 53703
(608) 257-5263

Harmony Bar and Grill
2201 Atwood Avenue
Madison, WI 53704
(608) 249-4333

Monty's Blue Plate Diner
2089 Atwood Avenue
Madison, WI 53704
(608) 244-8505
www.montysblueplatediner.com

Cafe Zoma
2326 Atwood Avenue
Madison, WI 53704
(608) 243-1300

La Brioche True Food
2862 University Avenue
Madison, WI 53705
(608) 233-3388
http://truefoodrestaurant.com

Lombardino's
2500 University Avenue
Madison, WI 53705
(608) 238-1922
www.lombardinos.com

Pizza Brutta
1805 Monroe Street
Madison, WI 53711
(608) 257-2120
www.pizzabrutta.com

Barrique's Wine Cave
1831 Monroe Street
Madison, WI 53711
(608) 284-9463
www.barriquesmarket.com

Ancora
1859 Monroe Street
Madison, WI 53711
(608) 258-9881
www.ancoracoffee.com

Just Coffee
1129 East Wilson Street
Madison, WI 53703
(608) 204-9011
www.justcoffee.coop

RP's Pasta
1133 East Wilson Street
Madison, WI 53703
(608) 257-7216
www.rpspasta.com

Local Foraging

Community Pharmacy
341 State Street
Madison, WI 53703
(608) 251-3242
www.communitypharmacy.coop

Atomic Interiors
961 South Park Street
Madison, WI 53715
(608) 251-5255

Iconi Interiors
534 West Washington Avenue
Madison, WI 53703
(608) 441-0077
www.iconiinteriors.com

Hempen Goods
911 Williamson Street
Madison, WI 53703
(608) 287-0410
www.hempengoods.com

Willy Street Co-op
1221 Williamson Street
Madison, WI 53703
(608) 251-6776
www.willystreet.coop

Green Parasol
1370 Williamson Street
Madison, WI 53703
(608) 204-7434
blog.thegreenparasol.com

St. Vincent de Paul Thrift Store
1309 Williamson Street
Madison, WI 53703
(608) 257-0673
www.svdpmadison.org

Ace Hardware
1398 Williamson Street
Madison, WI 53703
(608) 257-1630
www.acehardware.com

Gayfeather Fabrics
1521 Williamson Street
Madison, WI 53703
(608) 294-7436
www.gayfeatherfabrics.com

Sugar Shack Records
2301 Atwood Avenue
Madison, WI 53704
(608) 256-7155
www.sugarshackrecords.net

Absolutely Art
2322 Atwood Avenue
Madison, WI 53704
(608) 249-9100
www.absolutelyartllc.com

Fair Indigo
Hilldale Shopping Center
570 North Midvale Boulevard
Madison, WI 53705
(608) 661-7662
www.fairindigo.com

Anaala Salon and Spa
Hilldale Shopping Center
562 North Midvale Boulevard
Madison, WI 53705
(608) 441-6918
www.anaala.com

A Room of One's Own Feminist
  Bookstore
307 West Johnson Street
Madison, WI 53703
(608) 257-7888
www.roomofonesown.com

Avol's Bookstore
315 West Gorham Street
Madison, WI 53703
(608) 255-4730
www.avolsbookstore.com

Paul's Book Store
670 State Street
Madison, WI 53703
(608) 257-2968
www.danebuylocal.com/member/50

JTaylor's Galleries
18½ North Carroll Street
Madison, WI 53703
(608) 255-6277
www.jtaylorsgalleries.net

Rainbow Bookstore Cooperative
426 West Gilman Street
Madison, WI 53703
(608) 257-6050
www.rainbowbookstore.org

Quintessence
334 West Lakeside Street
Madison, WI 53715
(608) 251-6915

Farmers' Markets
www.cityofmadison.com/residents/
  farmersMarket.cfm

What to Do

Tenney Park
1414 East Johnson Street
Madison, WI 53703
(608) 266-4364
www.cityofmadison.com/parks/
  boatpark.html

Wingra Boats
824 Knickerbocker Street
Madison, WI 53716
(608) 233-5332
www.wingraboats.com

Rutabaga, the Paddlesport Shop
220 West Broadway
Monona, WI 53716
(608) 223-9300
www.rutabaga.com

Budget Bicycle Center
1230 Regent Street
Madison, WI 53715
(608) 251-8413
www.budgetbicyclectr.com

Wheels for Winners
229 South Fair Oaks Avenue
Madison, WI 53704
(608) 249-2418
www.wheelsforwinners.org

Revolution Cycles
2330 Atwood Avenue
Madison, WI 53704
(608) 244-0009
www.revolutioncycles.net

Planet Bike
2402 Vondron Road
Madison, WI 53718
(866) 256-8510
www.planetbike.com

Trek Bicycle
8108 Mineral Point Road
Madison, WI 53719
(608) 833-8735
www.trekstoremadison.com

Williamson Bikes and Fitness
640 West Washington Avenue
Madison, WI 53703
(608) 255-5292
www.willybikes.com

Aldo Leopold Nature Center
300 Femrite Drive
Madison, WI 53716
(608) 221-0404
www.naturenet.com/alnc

University of Wisconsin Arboretum
1207 Seminole Highway
Madison, WI 53711
(608) 263-7888
www.uwarboretum.org

Friends of Lake Wingra
1000 Edgewood College Drive
Madison, WI 53711
(608) 663-2838
www.lakewingra.org

Vilas Park
702 South Randall Avenue
Madison, WI 53715
(608) 233-5332
www.cityofmadison.com/parks/major/
    vilasPark.html

University of Wisconsin Memorial
    Union Terrace
800 Langdon Street
Madison, WI 53706
(608) 265-3000
www.union.wisc.edu/terrace

Lakeshore Nature Preserve
lakeshorepreserve.wisc.edu/index.htm

Friends of the Lakeshore Nature
    Preserve
www.uwalumni.com/lakeshorepreserve

Wisconsin Union Theater
800 Langdon Street
Madison, WI 53706
(608) 265-3000
www.uniontheater.wisc.edu

Wisconsin Capitol
Tours and Information Office
2 East Main Street

Madison, WI 53702
(608) 266-0382
www.wisconsin.gov/state/core/
    wisconsin_state_capitol_tour.html

Dane County Farmers' Market
Capitol Square
www.dcfm.org/wandw.asp

Madison Environmental Group
25 North Pinckney Street, Suite 310
Madison, WI 53703
(608) 280-0800
www.madisonenvironmental.com

Madison Museum of Contemporary Art
227 State Street
Madison, WI 53703
(608) 257-0158
www.mmoca.org

Overture Center for the Arts
201 State Street
Madison, WI 53703
(608) 258-4177 or (608) 258-4141
www.overturecenter.com

State Street Gallery/Wine Shop
109 State Street
Madison, WI 53703
(608) 819-0304
www.statestreetgallery.com

Fanny Garver Gallery
230 State Street
Madison, WI 53703
(608) 256-6755
www.fannygarvergallery.com

Orpheum Theatre
Lobby Restaurant
216 State Street
Madison, WI 53703
(608) 255-6005
www.orpheumtheatre.net

CHEW (Culinary History Enthusiasts
    of Wisconsin)
www.chew.wisconsincooks.org

Barrymore Theatre
2090 Atwood Avenue
Madison, WI 53704
(608) 241-2345
www.barrymorelive.com

Ironworks Cafe, Goodman Community
    Center
149 Waubesa Street
Madison, WI 53704
(608) 241-1574
www.goodmancenter.org

Olbrich Botanical Gardens
3330 Atwood Avenue
Madison, WI 53704
(608) 246-4550
www.olbrich.org

Habitat for Humanity ReStore
208 Cottage Grove Road
Madison, WI 53716
(608) 661-2813
www.restoredane.org

Lakeside Fibers, Washington Island
    Hotel Coffee Room
402 West Lakeside Street
Madison, WI 53715
(608) 257-2999
www.lakesidefibers.com

First Unitarian Society
900 University Bay Drive
Madison, WI 53705
(608) 233-9774
www.fusmadison.org

Sundance Cinemas
Hilldale Shopping Center
430 North Midvale Boulevard
Madison, WI 53705
(608) 316-6900
www.sundancecinemas.com

Madison Area Open Arts Studios
www.maoas.com/OpenArtStudios

MMOCA Gallery Night, Art Fair on
the Square
www.mmoca.org

Concerts on the Square
www.wcoconcerts.org/new/cos/
concertsonthesquare.php

Jazz at Five
www.jazzat5.org

Madison Winter Festival
www.winter-fest.com

Food for Thought Festival
www.reapfoodgroup.org/
foodforthought

Wisconsin Book Festival
www.wisconsinbookfestival.com

Tales from Planet Earth
www.nelson.wisc.edu/tales

Wisconsin Film Festival
www.wifilmfest.org

Bike the Barns
www.macsac.org/bikethebarns

Underground Food Collective
www.undergroundfoodcollective.org

City of Madison Bicycle Map
www.cityofmadison.com/traffic
Engineering/bicyclingMaps.cfm

Mount Horeb Area Arts Association
Spring Art Tour
www.mhaaa.org

Kaleidoscope Marketplace
101 East Main Street
Mount Horeb, WI 53572
(608) 437-2787
www.kaleidoscopemarketplace.com

Trillium Natural Foods Community
Co-op
517 Springdale Street
Mount Horeb, WI 53572

(608) 437-5288
www.trilliumnaturalfoods.com

Holy Wisdom Monastery
4200 County Highway M
Middleton, WI 53562
(608) 836-1631
www.benedictinewomen.org

Bike It, Hike It, Like It: Milwaukee Area

Where to Stay

Hotel Metro
411 East Mason Street
Milwaukee, WI 53202
(414) 272-1937
www.hotelmetro.com

Where to Eat

Beans and Barley
1901 East North Avenue
Milwaukee, WI 53202
(414) 278-7878
www.beansandbarley.com

Roots Restaurant and Cellar
1818 North Hubbard Street
Milwaukee, WI 53212
(414) 374-8480
www.rootsmilwaukee.com

Lakefront Brewery
1872 North Commerce Street
Milwaukee, WI 53212
(414) 372-8800
www.lakefrontbrewery.com

Alterra Coffee
2999 North Humboldt Boulevard
Milwaukee, WI 53212
(414) 292-3320
www.alterracoffee.com

Alterra at the Lake
1701 North Lincoln Memorial Drive
Milwaukee, WI 53202
(414) 223-4551
www.alterracoffee.com

The Comet Café
1947 North Farwell Avenue
Milwaukee, WI 53202
(414) 273-7677
www.thecometcafe.com

Braise on the Go Traveling Culinary
    School
P.O. Box 070537
Milwaukee, WI 53207
(414) 241-9577
www.braiseculinaryschool.com

Meritage
5921 West Vliet Street
Milwaukee, WI 53208
(414) 479-0620
www.meritage.us

Le Rêve
7610 Harwood Avenue
Wauwatosa, WI 53213
(414) 778-3333
www.lerevecafe.com

Cafe Manna
3815 North Brookfield Road
Brookfield, WI 53045
(262) 790-2340
www.cafemanna.com

La Merenda
125 East National Avenue
Milwaukee, WI 53204
(414) 389-0125
www.lamerenda125.com

Local Foraging

Good Harvest Market
346 North Broadway
Milwaukee, WI 53202
(414) 727-3560
www.goodharvestmarket.com

East Town Farm Market
Cathedral Square Park at Kilbourn and
    Jefferson Streets
(414) 271-1416

www.easttown.com/categories/6-
    easttownmarket

East Side Open Market
Beans and Barley parking lot
1901 East North Avenue
Milwaukee, WI 53202
(414) 278-7878
www.theeastside.org/categories/10-
    green-market

Growing Power
5500 West Silver Spring Drive
Milwaukee, WI 53218
(414) 527-1546
www.growingpower.org

What to Do

Milwaukee Art Museum
700 North Art Museum Drive
Milwaukee, WI 53202
(414) 224-3200
www.mam.org

Discovery World
500 North Harbor Drive
Milwaukee, WI 53202
(414) 765-9966
www.discoveryworld.org

Oak Leaf Trail
Milwaukee County Parks
www.county.milwaukee.gov/
    OakLeafTrail8289.htm

Urban Ecology Center
1500 East Park Place
Milwaukee, WI 53211
(414) 964-8505
www.urbanecologycenter.org

Schlitz Audubon Nature Center
1111 East Brown Deer Road
Milwaukee, WI 53217
(414) 352-2880
www.schlitzauduboncenter.com

Menomonee Valley Community Park
Menomonee Valley Partners, Inc.
3500 West Canal Street
Milwaukee, WI
www.renewthevalley.org

Hank Aaron State Trail
Wisconsin Department of Natural
    Resources
www.dnr.state.wi.us/org/LAND/parks/
    specific/hank_aaron

Milwaukee RiverWalk
Department of City Development
www.mkedcd.org/Downtown
    Milwaukee/RiverWalk

Milwaukee Trolley Loop
Milwaukee County Transit System
www.ridemcts.com

Milwaukee Bike and Skate Rental
Veteran's Park
1750 North Lincoln Memorial Drive
Milwaukee, WI 53202
(414) 273-1343
www.milwbikeskaterental.com

Great Outdoors Weekend
www.greatoutdoorsweekendsewi.org

La Lune Collection
930 East Burleigh Street
Milwaukee, WI 53212
(414) 263-5300
www.lalunecollection.com

Cream City Ribbon
430 West Vliet Street
Milwaukee, WI 53212
(414) 277-1221
www.creamcityribbon.com

The Ice Age Trail's Youngest Legacy: Waukesha County Area

Where to Stay

Monches Mill House
W301 N9430 County Road E

Hartland, WI 53029
(262) 966-7546
www.lanierbb.com/inns/bb1479.html

Eagle Hostel
S91 W39381 Highway 59
Eagle, WI 53119
(262) 442-6360 or (262) 495-8794

Kettle Moraine State Forest–Southern
    Unit
S91 W39091 Highway 59
Eagle, WI 53119
(262) 594-6200
www.dnr.wi.gov/org/land/parks/
    specific/kms

Ice Age Trail Inn-to-Inn
www.iceagetrail.org/Inn-to-Inn.htm

Where to Eat

Good Harvest Market, Good Harvest
    Cafe
1850 Meadow Lane
Pewaukee, WI 53072
(262) 544-9380
www.goodharvestmarket.com

Wildflower Cafe
18 South Wisconsin Street
Elkhorn, WI 53121
(262) 723-4774

Local Foraging

The Robin's Nest
W324 S3555 County Road E
Dousman, WI 53118
(262) 305-4556 or (262) 392-5556

Prairie Hill Farms
W514 Hooper Road
Palmyra, WI 53156
(262) 495-2213
www.prairiehillfarms.info

Battle Creek Beef and Bison
38413 Delafield Road
Oconomowoc, WI 53066
(262) 468-4525
www.beefandbison.com

Rushing Waters Fisheries
N301 County Road H
Palmyra, WI 53156
(800) 378-7088
www.rushingwaters.net

Michael Fields Agricultural Institute
W2493 County Road ES
East Troy, WI 53120
(262) 642-3303
www.michaelfieldsaginst.org

Local Industry
W2463 County Road ES
East Troy, WI 53120
(262) 642-9665

Quednow's Heirloom Apple Orchard
Highway 12/67 and County Road ES
East Troy, WI 53120
(262) 642-9735
www.quednowappleorchard
  .bravehost.com

Delafield Farmers' Market
Fish Hatchery parking lot, just west of
  Genesee Street
514 West Main Street (County Road C)
Delafield, WI 53018
(262) 646-9305
www.delafieldfarmersmarket.com

Waukesha Farmers' Market
Downtown at Riverfront Plaza by
  the river
Waukesha, WI 53186
(262) 549-6154
www.localharvest.org/farmers-
  markets/M16741

East Troy Farmers' Market
East Troy Village Square
East Troy, WI 53120
www.easttroywi.org

What to Do

Monches Farm
5890 Monches Road
Colgate, WI 53017
(262) 966-2787
www.monchesfarm.com

Northwind Perennial Farm
7047 Hospital Road
Burlington, WI 53105
(262) 248-8229
www.northwindperennialfarm.com

Erin Hills
7169 County Road O
Hartford, WI 53027
(866) 724-8822
www.erinhills.com

Basilica of Holy Hill
1525 Carmel Road
Hubertus, WI 53033
(262) 628-1838
www.holyhill.com

Kettle Moraine State Forest–
  Southern Unit
S91 W39091 Highway 59
Eagle, WI 53119
(262) 594-6200
www.dnr.wi.gov/org/land/parks/
  specific/kms

Lapham Peak State Park
County Road C
Delafield, WI 53018
(262) 646-3025
www.dnr.wi.gov/org/land/parks/
  specific/lapham

Retzer Nature Center
S14 W28167 Madison Street
Waukesha, WI 53188
(262) 896-8007
http://www.waukeshacounty.gov/page
.aspx?SetupMetaId=10916&id=11078

Ice Age National Scenic Trail
www.iceagetrail.org

Backyard Bikes and Ski
La Grange General Store, Cafe,
and Deli
W6098 Highway 12
Whitewater, WI 53190
(262) 495-8600
www.backyardbikes.com

Wheel and Sprocket
528 Wells Street
Delafield, WI 53018
(262) 646-6300
www.wheelandsprocket.com

Lake Michigan's Harbor Towns: Port Washington and Sheboygan Area

Where to Stay

Port Washington Inn
308 West Washington Street
Port Washington, WI 53074
(262) 284-5583
www.port-washington-inn.com

Where to Eat

Java Dock Cafe
116 West Grand Avenue
Port Washington, WI 53074
(262) 284-1600

Field to Fork
511 South Eighth Street
Sheboygan, WI 53081
(920) 694-0322

Local Foraging

Beechwood Cheese Company
N1598W County Road A
Beechwood, WI 53001
(877) 224-3373
www.beechwoodcheese.com

Log Cabin Orchard
N4797 County Road E
Plymouth, WI 53073
(920) 893-6073

Port Washington Farmers' Market
North Franklin and East Main Streets
Port Washington, WI
(262) 305-4220
www.localharvest.org/farmers-
markets/M4502

What to Do

Light Station Museum
311 Johnson Street
Port Washington, WI 53074
(262) 284-7240
www.terrypepper.com/Lights/
michigan/portwashold/
portwashold.htm

Lottie Cooper shipwreck exhibit
821 Broughton Drive
Sheboygan, WI 53081
(920) 458-6665

Ozaukee Interurban Trail
www.interurbantrail.us

Ozaukee Trailside Birding Guide
www.interurbantrail.us/
BirdingGuide

Sheboygan Urban Rec Trail
www.ci.sheboygan.wi.us/
Development/UrbanRec
Trail.html

Old Plank Road Trail
www.co.sheboygan.wi.us/html/d_
planning_plankrdtrail.htm

Expedition Outdoor Supply
668 South Pier Drive
Sheboygan, WI 53081
(920) 208-7873
www.eosoutdoor.com

Ecology Outfitters
633 North Eighth Street
Sheboygan, WI 53081
(920) 452-9555
www.ecologyoutfitters.com

Henry S. Reuss Ice Age Visitor Center
(920) 533-8322
www.dnr.wi.gov/org/land/parks/
    specific/kmn/iac.html

Kettle Moraine State Forest–
    Northern Unit
Forest Headquarters
N1765 Highway G
Campbellsport, WI 53010
(262) 626-2116
www.dnr.state.wi.us/org/land/parks/
    specific/kmn

Kohler-Andrae State Park
1020 Beach Park Lane
Sheboygan, WI 53081
(920) 451-4080
www.dnr.wi.gov/org/land/parks/
    specific/ka

Ellwood H. May Environmental Park
3615 Mueller Road
Sheboygan, WI 53083
(920) 459-3906
http://216.56.5.7/

Bahr Creek Llamas and Fiber Studio
N1021 Sauk Trail Road
Cedar Grove, WI 53013
(920) 668-6417
www.bahrcreek.com

Dear Old Books
404 East Mill Street
Plymouth, WI 53073

(920) 892-4447
www.dearoldbooks.com

Exchange Bank Coffeehouse
301 East Mill Street
Plymouth, WI 53703
(920) 893-2326
www.exchangebankcoffeehouse.com

John Michael Kohler Arts Center
608 New York Avenue
Sheboygan, WI 53081
(920) 458-6144
www.jmkac.org

James Tellen Woodland Sculpture
    Garden
5634 Evergreen Drive
Wilson, WI 53081
(920) 458-6144
www.jmkac.org/JamesTellen
    WoodlandSculptureGarden

The Baraboo Hills, a True American Relic: Wisconsin Dells Area

Where to Stay

Sundara Inn and Spa
920 Canyon Road
Wisconsin Dells, WI 53965
(888) 735-8181 or (608) 253-9200
www.sundaraspa.com

Birchcliff Resort
4149 River Road
Wisconsin Dells, WI 53965
(608) 254-7515
www.birchcliff.com

Seth Peterson Cottage
Seth Peterson Cottage Conservancy, Inc.
Reedsburg, WI 53959
(877) 466-2358
www.sethpeterson.org

Where to Eat

Del-Bar
800 Wisconsin Dells Parkway
Lake Delton, WI 53940
(608) 253-1861
www.del-bar.com

The Cheese Factory
521 Wisconsin Dells Parkway S
Wisconsin Dells, WI 53965
(608) 253-6065
www.cookingvegetarian.com

Local Foraging

Carr Valley Cheese
807 Phillips Boulevard
Sauk City, WI 53583
(608) 643-3441
www.carrvalleycheese.com

Cedar Grove Cheese
E5904 Mill Road
Plain, WI 53577
(800) 200-6020 or (608) 546-5284
www.cedargrovecheese.com

Sauk County Farm Connect Guide
www.uwex.edu/ces/cty/sauk

What to Do

International Crane Foundation
E11376 Shady Lane Road
Baraboo, WI 53913
(608) 356-9462
www.savingcranes.org

Devil's Lake State Park
S5975 Park Road
Baraboo WI 53913
(608) 356-8301
www.devilslakewisconsin.com

Aldo Leopold Legacy Center
P.O. Box 77
E13701 Levee Road
Baraboo, WI 53913
(608) 355-0279
www.aldoleopold.org

Nature's Acres Farm, Four Elements
  Herbals
E8984 Weinke Road
North Freedom, WI 53951
(608) 522-4492
www.fourelementsherbals.com

Necedah National Wildlife Refuge
W7996 Twentieth Street W
Necedah, WI 54646
(608) 565-2551
www.fws.gov/midwest/necedah

Wormfarm Institute
E7904 Briar Bluff Road
Reedsburg, WI 53959
(608) 524-8672
www.wormfarminstitute.org

Woolen Mill Gallery
26 East Main Street
Reedsburg, WI 53959
(608) 524-8672
www.wormfarminstitute.org/gallery
  .html

Vertical Illusions
933 Highway 12
Wisconsin Dells, WI 53965
(608) 253-2500
www.verticalillusions.com

Delaney's Surplus Sales
S7703 Highway 12
North Freedom, WI 53951
(608) 643-8009
www.delaneyssurplus.com

Badger Army Ammunitions Plant
Highway 12
Baraboo, WI 53913

Sauk Prairie Conservation Alliance
www.saukprairievision.org

National Resources Foundation of
  Wisconsin
www.wisconservation.org

Back to the Land: Boscobel Area
Where to Stay

Life O'Riley Farm and Guesthouses
15706 Riley Road
Boscobel, WI 53805
(608) 375-5798
www.bbonline.com/wi/lifeoriley

Inn at Lonesome Hollow
15415 Vance Road
Soldiers Grove, WI 54655
(608) 624-3429
www.lonesomehollow.com

Where to Eat

Our Little Restaurant and Bakery
940 Lincoln Avenue
Fennimore, WI 53809
(608) 822-6331

Local Foraging

Carr Valley Cheese Store
1675 Lincoln Avenue
Fennimore, WI 53809
(608) 822-3777
www.carrvalleycheese.com

Sugar and Spice Bulk Food
12115 Highway 61
Fennimore, WI 53809
(608) 822-7733

Fennimore Produce Auction
14800 County Road T
Fennimore, WI 53809
(608) 988-6464 or (608) 822-3854

What to Do

Fly Fisherman's Lair
(608) 763-2802 or (608) 822-3575

Wisconsin River Outings
715 Wisconsin Avenue
Boscobel, WI 53805
(608) 375-5300 or (866) 41 CANOE
  (22663)
www.86641canoe.com

Wisconsin Natural Areas
www.dnr.wi.gov/org/land/er/sna

Great Wisconsin Birding and Nature
  Trail
www.wisconsinbirds.org/trail
dnr.wi.gov/org/land/er/birds/trail.htm
www.travelwisconsin.com

Solar Town
www.soldiersgrove.com
www.solartownusa.com

Orthodox Byzantine Icons
25266 Pilgrims Way
Boscobel, WI 53805
(800) 814-2667
www.skete.com

Driftless Area Art Festival
Beauford T. Anderson Park
Soldiers Grove, WI 54655
www.crawfordcountywi.com/art_
  festival/index.htm

Art by the Stream
Boscobel, WI 53805
www.artbythestream.com

True Green: Monroe Area
Where to Stay

Inn Serendipity
7843 County Road P
Browntown, WI 53522
(608) 329-7056
www.innserendipity.com

Where to Eat

Baumgartners Cheese Store and
  Tavern
1023 Sixteenth Avenue
Monroe, WI 53566
(608) 325-6157
www.baumgartnercheese.com

Chocolate Temptation
1004 Seventeenth Avenue
Monroe, WI 53566
(608) 328-2462

Garden Deli
1602 Eleventh Street
Monroe, WI 53566
(608) 325-3526

Kookaburra's
1609 Tenth Street
Monroe, WI 53566
(608) 325-3955
www.kookaburrasclosetgourmet.com

Turner Hall Ratskeller
1217 Seventeenth Avenue
Monroe, WI 53566
(608) 325-3461
www.turnerhallofmonroe.org

Local Foraging

Monroe Market on the Square
Courthouse Square
(608) 328-4023

Christensen's Farm
N2780 County Road M
Browntown, WI 53522
(608) 966-3886

Jordandal Farm
W7977 Sunset Road
Argyle, WI 53504
(608) 328-1052
www.jordandalfarm.com

Grass Is Greener Gardens
W8473 Smock Valley Road
Monroe, WI 53566
(608) 966-1128
www.grassisgreenergardens.com

Goose Chaser Farm
N8855 Badger Road
Blanchardville, WI 53516
(608) 293-3925
www.thegoosechaserfarm.com

Roth Käse/Alp and Dell Cheese Store
657 Second Street
Monroe, WI 53566
(608) 328-2122 or (608) 328-3355
www.rothkase.com

Historic Cheesemaking Center
2108 Sixth Avenue
Monroe, WI 53566
(608) 325-4636

Chalet Cheese Cooperative
N4858 County Road N
Monroe, WI 53566
(608) 325-4343

Edelweiss Graziers Co-op
www.edelweissgraziers.com

Edelweiss Creamery
W6117 County Road C
Monticello, WI 53570
(608) 938-4094
www.edelweisscreamery.com

Maple Leaf Cheese Factory Outlet
W2646 Highways 11/81
Juda, WI 53550
(608) 934-1237

What to Do

Badger State Trail
http://dnr.wi.gov/org/land/parks/
    specific/badger

Argyle Fiber Mill
200 East Milwaukee Street
Argyle, WI 53504
(608) 543-3933
www.argylefibermill.com

Homestead Wool and Gift Farm
W8298 County Road Y
Monroe, WI 53566
(608) 966-3943
www.homesteadwoolandgiftfarm.com

Monroe Arts Center
1315 Eleventh Street
Monroe, WI 53566
(608) 325-5700
www.monroeartscenter.com

Sky-Vu Outdoor Theater
1936 Highway 69 North
Monroe, WI 53566
(608) 325-4545

Mississippi River Adventure:
Cassville and Potosi Area

Where to Stay

Upper Miss Lodging
105 West Amelia Street
Cassville, WI 53806
(608) 732-6184
www.uppermisstours.com/lodging.htm

Nelson Dewey State Park
County Highway VV
Cassville, WI 53806
(608) 725-5374
www.dnr.wi.gov/org/land/parks/
    specific/nelsondewey

Wyalusing State Park
13081 State Park Lane
Bagley, WI 53801
(608) 996-2261
www.dnr.wi.gov/org/land/parks/
    specific/wyalusing

Where to Eat

Potosi Brewing Company
209 South Main Street
Potosi, WI 53820
(608) 763-4002 ext. 106
www.potosibrewery.com

Cafe Manna Java
269 Main Street
Dubuque, IA 52001
(563) 588-3105

Local Foraging

Cassville Farmers' Market
Riverside Park
(608) 725-5400

Driftless Market
95 West Main Street
Platteville, WI 53818
(608) 348-2696
www.driftlessmarket.com

Platteville Farmers' Market
Platteville City Park
www.platteville.org

What to Do

Upper Mississippi River Adventures
105 West Amelia Street
Cassville, WI 53806
(608) 732-6184
www.uppermisstours.com

National Brewery Museum
209 South Main Street
Potosi, WI 53820
www.nationalbrewerymuseum.org

St. John Mine and Canoe Rentals
P.O. Box 93
129 North Main Street
Potosi, WI 53820
(608) 763-2121

Cassville Tourism
P.O. Box 576
Cassville, WI 53806
(608) 725-5855
www.cassville.org/HistoricWalking
    Tour.htm

Unique Creations
112 East Amelia Street
Cassville, WI 53806
(608) 725-5336
www.cassville.org/unique%20
    creations.htm

State Natural Areas
www.dnr.wi.gov/org/land/er/sna

Bald Eagle Days
P.O. Box 576
Cassville, WI 53806
(608) 725-5855
www.cassville.org

Grant River Canoe Rental
9761 County Road U West
Beetown, WI 53802
(608) 794-2342

Stonefield Village
12195 County Road VV
Cassville, WI 53806
(608) 987-2122
www.wisconsinhistory.org/stonefield

Cycle Southwest Wisconsin
www.cyclesouthwestwisconsin.com

Great River Road online cycling maps
www.dot.wisconsin.gov/travel/
    bike-foot/grrmap.htm

National Mississippi River Museum
    and Aquarium
Port of Dubuque
350 East Third Street
Dubuque, IA 52001
(563) 557-9545 or (800) 226-3369
www.mississippirivermuseum.com

Dominican Sisters of Sinsinawa
585 County Road Z
Sinsinawa, WI 53824
(608) 748-4411
www.sinsinawa.org

Dickeyville Grotto
305 West Main Street
Dickeyville, WI 53808
(608) 568-3119
www.dickeyvillegrotto.com

Helen Anderson Gallery
11045 Borah Road
Lancaster, WI 53813
(608) 723-2795
www.helenanderson.net

Switchback
Five Points Road
Lancaster, WI 53813
www.wingsoverwisconsin.org

Coulee Hideaway: La Crosse Area
Where to Stay
Paulsen Cabin at Norskedalen
N455 O. Ophus Road
Coon Valley, WI 54623
(608) 452-3424
www.norskedalen.org

Where to Eat
Root Note
115 Fourth Street South
La Crosse, WI 54601
(608) 782-7668
www.therootnote.com

Hackberry's Bistro
315 Fifth Avenue South
La Crosse, WI 54601
(608) 784-5798, ext. 243
www.pfc.coop/hackberrys.asp

Local Foraging
People's Food Co-op
315 Fifth Avenue South
La Crosse, WI 54601
(608) 784-5798
www.pfc.coop

Cameron Park Farmers Market
King Street between 4th Street and
    5th Avenue
La Crosse, WI 54601
www.cameronparkmarket.org

What to Do

Norskedalen Nature and Heritage
  Center
N455 O. Ophus Road
Coon Valley, WI 54623
(608) 452-3424
www.norskedalen.org

Myrick Hixon EcoPark
789 Myrick Park Drive
La Crosse, WI 54601
(608) 784-0303
www.myrickecopark.com

Human Powered Trails
www.humanpoweredtrails.com

Three Rivers Outdoors
400 Main Street
La Crosse, WI 54601
(608) 793-1470
www.threeriversoutdoors.com

National Resources Foundation of
  Wisconsin
www.wisconservation.org

Driftless Farm
Whole Trees Architecture and
  Construction
E2890 Lorenz Road
Stoddard, WI 54658
(608) 452-3894
www.wholetreesarchitecture.com

Wisconsin Solar Tour
Midwest Renewable Energy Association
www.the-mrea.org

Sylvan Workshop:
Mineral Point Area

Where to Stay

Maple Wood Lodge
2950 Highway 39
Mineral Point, WI 53565
(608) 987-2324
www.maplewoodlodge.com

Bluebird Hill Country Cottage
557 Ferndale Road
Mineral Point, WI 53565
(608) 987-4528
www.bluebirdhillcountrycottage.com

Mineral Point Hotel
121 Commerce Street
Mineral Point, WI 53565
(608) 987-3889
www.mineralpointhotel.com

Where to Eat

Cafe Four at the Chesterfield
20 Commerce Street
Mineral Point, WI 53565
(608) 987-2030
www.fourcafe.com

Walker House
1 Water Street
Mineral Point, WI 53565
(608) 987-1660
www.walkerhousemineralpoint.com

Local Foraging

Mineral Point Market
Water Tower Park
Mineral Point, WI 53565
www.mineralpointmarket.com

Shooting Star Farm
6970 McNeill Road
Mineral Point, WI 53565
(608) 967-2319

Hook's Cheese Company
320 Commerce Street
Mineral Point, WI 53564
(608) 987-3259
www.hookscheese.com

What to Do

Mineral Point Chamber of Commerce
225 High Street
Mineral Point, WI 53565
(608) 987-3201 or (888) 764-6894
www.mineralpoint.com

Bleu Mont Dairy
Blue Mounds, WI
(608) 767-2875
www.cheeseforager.com/bleumont

Learn Great Foods
www.learngreatfoods.com

King's Hill Farm
19370 Highway G
Mineral Point, WI 53565
(608) 776-8413
www.kingshillfarm.com

Cycle Southwest Wisconsin
www.cyclesouthwestwisconsin.com

Military Ridge State Trail
www.dnr.wi.gov/org/LAND/parks/
    specific/militaryridge

Governor Dodge State Park
4175 Highway 23 North
Dodgeville, WI 53533
(608) 935-2315
www.dnr.wi.gov/org/LAND/parks/
    specific/govdodge

Blue Mound State Park
4350 Mounds Park Road
Blue Mounds, WI 53517
(608) 437-5711
www.dnr.wi.gov/org/land/parks/
    specific/bluemound

State Natural Areas
www.dnr.wi.gov/org/land/er/sna

Gallery Nights
www.mineralpoint.com/art/gallery_
    night.html

High Street Gallery
33 High Street
Mineral Point, WI 53565
(608) 987-3701
www.highstreetartists.com

Green Lantern Studios
261 High Street
Mineral Point, WI 53565
(608) 987-2880
www.greenlanternstudios.com

Longbranch Gallery
203 Commerce Street
Mineral Point, WI 53565
(608) 987-4499
www.longbranchgallery.com

Fall Art Tour
www.fallarttour.com

La Bella Vita
210 Commerce Street
Mineral Point, WI 53565
(608) 987-1123
www.labellavitamp.com

Foundry Books
105 Commerce Street
Mineral Point, WI 53565
(608) 987-4363
www.foundrybooks.com

Mineral Point Opera House
139 High Street
Mineral Point, WI 53565
(608) 987-2516
www.mineralpoint.com/mineral_
    point_opera_house.html

Mineral Point Film Society
www.emstudio.com/mpfs.html

Shake Rag Alley Center for Arts and
    Crafts
Alley Stage
18 Shake Rag Street
Mineral Point, WI 53565
(608) 987-3292
www.shakeragalley.com
www.alleystage.com

Woodlanders Gathering
www.danielmack.com

Folklore Village
3210 County Road BB
Dodgeville, WI 53533
(608) 924-4000
www.folklorevillage.org

Art and Ancient Heritage: Muscoda Area

Where to Stay

Valley Ridge Art Studio and Retreat
    Center
1825 Witek Road
Muscoda, WI 53573
(608) 943-6212
www.valleyridgeartstudio.com

Where to Eat

Milkweed
www.milkweedclub.com

Local Foraging

Morel Mushroom Festival
Village of Muscoda
(608) 739-3182
www.muscoda.com

What to Do

Natural Resources Foundation of
    Wisconsin
www.wisconservation.org

Blooming Valley Perennial Nursery
2868 County Road I
Avoca, WI 53506
(608) 583-2427
www.bloomingvalley.com

Lower Wisconsin State Riverway Board
202 North Wisconsin Avenue
Muscoda, WI 53573
(608) 739-3188
www.lwr.state.wi.us

Cultural Landscape Legacies
www.clli.org

Bison Prairie I Ranch
33502 Sand Lane
Muscoda, WI 53573
(608) 739-3360
www.muscodabison.com

Head for the Hills: Sparta Area

Where to Stay

Justin Trails Resort
7452 Kathryn Avenue
Sparta, WI 54656
(608) 269-4522 or (800) 488-4521
www.justintrails.com

Where to Eat

Northwood Country Market
1003 West Wisconsin
Sparta, WI 54656
(608) 269-9005

Ginny's Cupboard
127 North Water Street
Sparta, WI 54656
(608) 269-6669
www.ginnyscupboard.com

Angelini's Pizzeria and Ristorante
142 North Water Street
Sparta, WI 54656
(608) 269-6393
www.angelinis.com

What to Do

Down a Country Road
12651 Highway 33
Cashton, WI 54619
(608) 654-5318
www.downacountryroad.com

Sparta Depot
Sparta Chamber of Commerce
111 Milwaukee Street
Sparta, WI 54656
(608) 269-4123 or (800) 354-2453
www.bikesparta.com

Elroy-Sparta State Trail
www.dnr.wi.gov/org/land/parks/
    specific/elroysparta

La Crosse River State Trail
www.dnr.wi.gov/org/land/parks/
    specific/lacrosseriv

Speed's Bicycle Shop
1126 John Street
Sparta, WI 54656
(608) 269-2315
www.speedsbike.com

La Crosse River Trail Prairie
www.dnr.wi.gov/org/land/er/sna/
    sna184.htm

Along the Lower Wisconsin: Spring Green Area

Where to Stay

Hill Street Bed and Breakfast
353 West Hill Street
Spring Green, WI 53588
(608) 588-7751
www.hillstreetbb.com

Tower Hill State Park
5808 County Road C
Spring Green, WI 53588
(608) 588-2116
www.dnr.wi.gov/org/land/parks/
    specific/findapark.html#tower

Where to Eat

Bank Restaurant and Wine Bar
134 West Jefferson Street
Spring Green, WI 53588
(608) 588-7600
www.thebankrestaurantandwinebar
    .com

Spring Green General Store
137 South Albany Street
Spring Green, WI 53588
(608) 588-7070
www.springgreengeneralstore.com

Riverview Terrace Cafe
5607 County Road C
Spring Green, WI 53588
(608) 588-7900
www.taliesinpreservation.org/
    visitorsguide/dining.htm

Old Feed Mill
114 Cramer Street
Mazomanie, WI 53560
(608) 795-4909
www.oldfeedmill.com

Wall Street Gallery and Bistro
14 Brodhead Street
Mazomanie, WI 53560
(608) 576-6694
www.wallstreetgallery.com

Local Foraging

Black Earth Meat Market
1345 Mills Street
Black Earth, WI 53515
(608) 767-3940
www.blackearthmeats.com

What to Do

American Players Theatre
5950 Golf Course Road
Spring Green, WI 53588
(608) 588-2361
www.playinthewoods.org

Taliesin
5607 County Road C
Spring Green, WI 53588
(608) 588-7900 or (877) 588-7900
www.taliesinpreservation.org

Architectural Driving Tour
www.springgreen.com/things-to-
    do/architectural-driving-tour

Cedar Grove Cheese
E5904 Mill Road
Plain, WI 53577
(800) 200-6020
www.cedargrovecheese.com

Wisconsin Riverside Resort
S13220 Shifflet Road
Spring Green, WI 53588
(608) 588-2826
www.wiriverside.com

State Natural Areas
www.dnr.wi.gov/org/land/er/sna

Hemlock Draw
The Nature Conservancy
www.nature.org/wherewework/
    northamerica/states/wisconsin/
    preserves/art27.html

Jura Silverman Gallery
143 South Washington Street
Spring Green, WI 53588
(608) 588-7049
http://www.springgreen.com/jsgallery

Spring Green Literary Festival
www.springgreenlitfest.org

BobFest
www.springgreengeneralstore.com

Cates Family Farm
5992 County Road T
Spring Green, WI 53588
(608) 588-2836
www.catesfamilyfarm.com

Lake Louie Brewery
7556 Pine Road
Arena, WI 53503
(608) 753-2675
www.lakelouie.com

Mazomanie Historic Art Center
103 Crescent Street
Mazomanie, WI 53560
www.mazoart.com

Hembrough Gallery
33 Brodhead Street
Mazomanie, WI 53560
(608) 575-7750
hembroughgallery.com

Woven Palette Weaving Studio
29 Brodhead Street
Mazomanie, WI 53560

Creative Edge Gallery
25 Brodhead Street
Mazomanie, WI 53560
(608) 795-0162

Halle's Vintage Shoppe
15 Brodhead Street
Mazomanie, WI 53560
(608) 795-0150
www.mazomaniemills.com/halles/
    index.htm

Crossroads Coffee House
2020 Main Street
Cross Plains, WI 53528
(608) 798-2080
www.crossroadscoffeehouse.net

River Alliance of Wisconsin
www.wisconsinrivers.org

New Ideas in the Old Hills: Viroqua Area

Where to Stay

Trillium Cottage
E10596 East Salem Ridge Road
La Farge, WI 54639
(608) 625-4492
www.trilliumcottage.com

Hidden Springs Bed and Breakfast
S1597 Hanson Road
Westby, WI 54667
(608) 634-2521
www.hiddenspringscreamery.com

Viroqua Heritage Inn
220 East Jefferson Street
Viroqua, WI 54665
(608) 637-3306 or (888) 443-7466
www.herinn.com

Westby House
200 West State Street
Westby, WI 54667
(800) 434-7439 or (608) 634-4112
www.westbyhouse.com

Wildcat Mountain State Park
P.O. Box 99
E13660 State Highway 33
Ontario, WI 54651
(608) 337-4775
www.dnr.wi.gov/org/land/parks/
   specific/wildcat

Where to Eat

Driftless Cafe
118 West Court Street
Viroqua, WI 54665
(608) 637-7778

Public Market at Main Street Station
215 South Main Street
Viroqua, WI 54665
(608) 637-1912
www.viroquamainststation.com

Sibby's Cafe Oz
213 South Main Street
Viroqua, WI 54665
(608) 637-3202
www.sibbysozone.com

Local Foraging

Viroqua Food Co-op
609 North Main Street
Viroqua, WI 54665
(608) 637-7511
www.viroquafood.com

Viroqua Farmers' Market
viroqua-wisconsin.com/quality/
   downtown.asp

Driftless Organics
50561 County Road B
Soldiers Grove, WI 54655
(608) 624-3735
www.driftlessorganics.com

Harmony Valley Farm
S3442 Wire Hollow Road
Viroqua, WI 54665
(608) 483-2143
www.harmonyvalleyfarm.com

Shining Hills Farm and Gardens
E9569 Smart Hollow Road
La Farge, WI 54639
(608) 634-2745
www.shininghills.com

One Sun Farm and Bakery
S4374 Haugrud Hollow
La Farge, WI 54639
(608) 637-6895

Trout Palace
E14214 County D
La Farge, WI 54639
(608) 625-2084

Vernon Vineyards
S3457A Dahl Road
Viroqua, WI 54665
(608) 634-6734
www.vernonvineyards.com

What to Do

Kickapoo Valley Reserve
S3661 Highway 131
La Farge, WI 54639
(608) 625-2960
http://kvr.state.wi.us

State Natural Areas
www.dnr.wi.gov/org/land/er/sna

Titanic Canoe Rental
300 Highway 131 N
Ontario, WI 54651
(877) GET-SUNK (438-7865)
www.titaniccanoerental.com

Viroqua Tourism Office
220 South Main Street
Viroqua, WI 54665
(608) 637-2575
www.viroquatourism.com

Bluedog Cycles
325 South Main Street
Viroqua, WI 54665
(608) 637-6993
www.bluedogcycles.com

Stabbur Information Center
P.O. Box 94
Westby, WI 54667
(608) 634-4011 or (866) 493-7829
http://www.westbywi.com/stabbur
.html

Kickapoo Dam Challenge
http://kvr.state.wi.us/category.asp?link
catid=2197&linkid=949&locid=115

Driftless Angler
106 South Main Street
Viroqua, WI 54665
(608) 637-8779
www.driftlessangler.com

Full Circle Retreat
P.O. Box 463
Viroqua, WI 54665
(608) 675-3828 or (952) 920-2384
www.fullcircleretreat.com

Driftless Folk School
P.O. Box 405
Viroqua, WI 54665
(888) 587-6540
www.driftlessfolkschool.org

Little Country School
E2932 Newton Road
Viroqua, WI 54665
(608) 386-8161
www.thelittlecountryschool.com

Organic Valley
One Organic Way
La Farge, WI 54639
(888) 444-6455
www.organicvalley.coop

Temple Theatre
116 South Main Street
Viroqua, WI 54665
(608) 637-8190
www.temple-theatre.com

Bramble Bookstore
117 South Main Street
Viroqua, WI 54665
(608) 637-8717 or (800) 383-1064
www.bramblebookstore.com

VIVA Gallery Cooperative
217 South Main Street
Viroqua, WI 54665
(608) 637-6918
www.vivagallery.net

INDEX

Numbers in italics refer to photos. All locations are in Wisconsin unless otherwise noted.